Davy Crockett

THE MAN, THE LEGEND, THE LEGACY, 1786–1986

Davy Crockett

THE MAN, THE LEGEND,

THE LEGACY

1786–1986

EDITED BY

Michael A. Lofaro

The University of Tennessee Press

Knoxville

Frontispiece.
"Frank Mayo as 'Davy Crockett,'" in the stage melodrama
Davy Crockett; Or, Be Sure You're Right, Then Go Ahead.
(From the collection of John Seelye.
Reproduction courtesy of Clinton Lindley, Ltd., Hillsborough, North Carolina.)

Library of Congress Cataloging in Publication Data
Main entry under title:

Davy Crockett: the man, the legend, the
legacy, 1786–1986.

Bibliography: p.
Includes index.
1. Crockett, Davy, 1786–1836–Legends–
History and criticism–Addresses, essays, lectures.
2. Crockett, Davy, 1786–1836–Addresses, essays,
lectures. 3. Pioneers–Tennessee–Biography–
Addresses, essays, lectures. 4. Tennessee–
Biography–Addresses, essays, lectures.
I. Lofaro, Michael A., 1948- .
GR105.37.D3D38 1985   976.8'04'0924   84-25737
ISBN 0-87049-459-7

"Born on a mountain top in Tennessee,
   Greenest state in the Land of the Free,
Raised in the woods so's he knew ev'ry tree,
   kilt him a b'ar when he was only three.

   Davy, Davy Crockett,
   King of the wild frontier."

—"The Ballad of Davy Crockett," lyrics by
Tom Blackburn, music by George Bruns
(© 1954 Wonderland Music Co., Inc.)

"Where's the mountain top?"—The question
disappointed visitors ask most frequently
at the Davy Crockett Birthplace State
Historic Area in Greene County, Tennessee. They actually expected to see a
mountain top.

—Robert Fulcher, Tennessee State Park Service

This book
is dedicated to the
Lofaro and Durish families.

Contents

SPECIAL FEATURES

Illustrations

Preface

On Monday morning, July 28, 1834, a newly founded newspaper, the New York *Transcript*, stole a march on many of the future interpreters of Crockett's career by pronouncing him a sure candidate for immortality nearly two years before his death at the Alamo.

> When the name of any person is accounted of sufficient importance to be conferred on negroes, dogs, horses, steamboats, omnibuses, and locomotive engines, he may be considered as pretty certainly on the road to immortality. This is now the case with Colonel David Crockett, whose go-a-head name, with great propriety, has been, or is about to be, conferred on one of the locomotive engines on the Boston and Lowell Rail Road. This will doubtless be imitated by other locomotives, by steamboats, and by race horses, as indicative of their go-a-head qualities; and will do more to secure the immortality of the redoubtable Colonel, than forty Lives, written by himself or by any of his friends and admirers. (Reprinted in the Boston *Daily Evening Transcript*, August 1, 1834).

The informed writer who penned this piece made his judgment based on the legend already gathering around the historical David Crockett. He had no idea of how much fame and confusion the fictional *Davy* Crockett, or, to be precise, Crocketts, would contribute to this portrait.

This book addresses that issue. The essays explore various avenues of Crockett's growth from an obscure backwoods hunter turned politician with a knack for storytelling to the representative symbol of the American frontier in both its noble and savage aspects. We see the development of Crockett's legend, his ability to manipulate it during his lifetime for political ends, and, after his death, its boundless expansion in the popular media of his day and ours. He grows

John Gadsby Chapman's portrait of David Crockett painted in 1834. (The Alamo, San Antonio, Texas.)

A fictional woodcut of Davy Crockett pointing to his battle scars as his regimental "decorations" to deflate the egos of the dandyish Mexican generals. From the *Crockett Almanac 1855* (Philadelphia, New York, Boston, and Baltimore: Fisher and Brother), p. [25]. (St. Louis Mercantile Library Association, St. Louis, Missouri.)

to gigantic proportions, as the United States likewise expands, in the tall tales which dominate the Crockett almanacs (1835–1856), wins the hearts of Americans of two centuries through the romantic melodramas of stage and silver screen, both stirs us with a military march and surprises us with a minstrel ballad tradition, and, in Walt Disney's hands, creates a "Crockett craze." In all this he reflects the range and diversity of the country whose hero he became and documents as well the ever-changing mental image we have of ourselves as a nation and as individuals. Remember as you read, however, that Davy is not the kindest of mirrors; he shows both our halos and our warts off to full advantage.

Much of the material in this volume has never been presented before. The tall tale Crockett "hidden" in the Nashville almanacs, his historical kinship with the wild man of ancient tradition, rare Crockett songs and music, a previously unknown silent film in which he is the leading man, the extent of the Crockett craze of the 1950s, and over forty illustrations, are all here examined and placed in a larger critical framework to highlight the inseparability of the historic and fictional components of the legend and to reveal how great an effect this composite Crockett has come to have on American popular thought and culture.

A NOTE ON EDITORIAL METHOD

This edition follows the standard convention of referring to the historical Crockett as David and the fictional Crockett as Davy. It also retains the often inconsistent original spelling and punctuation of the primary texts. The best selected bibliography of primary and secondary sources of information on David Crockett is contained in James A. Shackford's *David Crockett: The Man and the Legend* (Chapel Hill: University of North Carolina Press, 1956), pp. 317–24. It is updated and expanded with more information on Davy Crockett in Richard Boyd Hauck's *Crockett: A Bio-Bibliography* (Westport, Connecticut: Greenwood Press, 1982), pp. 150–58. The present volume, in turn, brings this bibliography up to August 1984 in its notes.

I wish to thank the National Humanities Center for the fellowship funded by the National Endowment for the Humanities which allowed me to begin my study of Crockett and the Department of English of the University of Tennessee for providing the release time and additional funds necessary to accept that fellowship. Without the insightful help and understanding of my wife, Nancy Durish Lofaro, this volume could not have been completed.

University of Tennessee   Michael A. Lofaro

Two Hundred Years

A CROCKETT CHRONOLOGY

Michael A. Lofaro

·

1786   On August 17, David is born to John and Rebecca Hawkins Crockett in Greene County, Tennessee.

1796   Tennessee joins the Union. The Crocketts open a tavern on the road from Knoxville to Abingdon, Virginia.

1798   John Crockett hires his son out to Jacob Siler to help to drive a herd of cattle to Rockbridge County, Virginia. Siler tries to detain David by force after the contract is completed, but the boy escapes and eventually arrives home in late 1798 or early 1799.

1799   David starts school, prefers playing hookey, and runs away from home to escape his father's punishment. He works as a wagoner and a day laborer and at odd jobs for two and one-half years.

1802   David returns home and is welcomed by all his family.

1803   David willingly works and discharges his father's debts of seventy-six dollars.

1805   He takes out a license to marry Margaret Elder of Dandridge, Tennessee, on October 21, but she decides to marry another.

1806   Crockett courts and marries Mary (Polly) Finley on August 14 in Jefferson County, Tennessee.

1811   David, Polly, and their two sons, John Wesley and William, leave East Tennessee after September 11 and settle on the Mulberry fork of Elk River in Lincoln County, Tennessee.

1813   Crockett leaves Lincoln County to settle on the Rattlesnake Spring Branch of Bean's Creek in Franklin County, Tennessee, near the present Alabama border. He names his homestead "Kentuck." In September, Crockett enlists in the militia in Winchester, Tennessee, to avenge the Indian attack on

Fort Mims, Alabama, and serves as a scout under Major Gibson. Under Andrew Jackson, he participates in the retributive massacre of the Indian town of Tallussahatchee on November 3. David's ninety-day enlistment expires on the day before Christmas and he returns home.

1814   Jackson defeats the Creeks at the Battle of Horse-shoe Bend on March 28. Crockett reenlists on September 28 as 3rd sergeant in Captain John Cowan's company and serves until March 27, 1815. He arrives the day after Jackson's taking of Pensacola on November 7, 1814. Crockett attempts to ferret out the British-trained and supplied Indians from the Florida swamps.

1815   Discharged as a 4th sergeant, David returns home to find himself again a father. His wife, Polly, dies the summer after Margaret's birth, although David found her in good health on his return.

1816   Crockett is elected a lieutenant in the 32nd Militia Regiment of Franklin County on May 22 and marries Elizabeth Patton, a widow with two children (George and Margaret Ann), before summer's end. In the fall, he explores Alabama with an eye towards settlement, catches malaria, and nearly dies. He is reported dead and astonishes his family with his "resurrection."

1817   By about September, the Crocketts have settled in the territory soon to become Lawrence County, Tennessee, at the head of Shoal Creek. David becomes a justice of the peace on November 17.

1818   He becomes town commissioner of Lawrenceburg before April 1. Crockett is also elected colonel of the 57th Militia Regiment in the county.

1819   Crockett resigns his position as justice of the peace.

1821   On January 1, he resigns as commissioner, having decided to run for a seat in the state legislature as the representative of Lawrence and Hickman counties. After two months of campaigning, Crockett wins the August election. From the very first of his political career, he takes an active interest in public land policy regarding the West. The House adjourns on November 17, and David, his son John Wesley, and Abram Henry, explore the Obion River country.

1822   The Crocketts move west and settle near the Obion River after the second legislative session ends.

1823   David defeats Dr. William E. Butler and is reelected to the state legislature.

1824   Crockett ends his state political career on October 22, when the House adjourns.

1825   In August, Crockett is defeated in his first bid for a seat in Congress.

1826   Nearly dying as his boats carrying barrel staves wreck in the Mississippi River, David is brought to Memphis and is encouraged to run for Congress again by M. B. Winchester.

1827   Crockett defeats General William Arnold and Colonel Adam Alexander for a seat in the United States House of Representatives.

1828   Andrew Jackson is elected president.

1829   Crockett is reelected. He splits with Jackson and with the Tennessee delegation on several issues during this term in office.

1830   David attacks the Indian removal bill.

1831   James Kirke Paulding's play, *The Lion of the West*, with James Hackett playing the leading character of Nimrod Wildfire, opens in New York City at the Park Theater on April 25. In his campaign for a third congressional term, David speaks openly against Jackson's policies. He is defeated by William Fitzgerald in a close election.

1833   Mathew St. Clair Clarke's *Life and Adventures of Colonel David Crockett of West Tennessee* is deposited for copyright on January 5. The volume is soon reprinted under the title *Sketches and Eccentricities of Colonel David Crockett of West Tennessee*. Crockett defeats the incumbent Fitzgerald and again wins a seat in Congress.

1834   Crockett publishes his autobiography, *A Narrative of the Life of David Crockett of the State of Tennessee*, written with the help of Thomas Chilton. On April 25, he begins his three-week tour through the eastern states in an anti-Jacksonian alliance with the Whigs.

1835   Two Whig books are published under Crockett's name: *Col. Crockett's Tour to the North and Down East* in late March and *Life of Martin Van Buren* less than three months later. The earliest known copy of "The Crockett Victory March" ("*Go Ahead*" *a march dedicated to Colonel Crockett*) and the first Crockett almanac are published. (The almanac was very likely published in 1834 for 1835.) Adam Huntsman defeats Crockett in the election for Congress, and Crockett, together with William Patton, Abner Burgin, and Lindsey K. Tinkle, set out for Texas on November 1.

1836   In January, Crockett and Patton sign the oath of allegiance to the "Provisional Government of Texas or any future republican Government that may be hereafter declared. . . ." In early February, Crockett arrived in San Antonio De Bexar. On March 6, he is captured and executed after Santa Anna's army captures the Alamo. Early in the summer *Col. Crockett's Exploits and Adventures in Texas* is compiled and fabricated by Richard Penn Smith. That fall, Jackson's handpicked successor, Martin Van Buren, is elected president.

1837   *Crockett's Free-and-Easy Songbook* is published.

1839   "Colonel Crockett: A Virginia Reel" is published.

1846   The first known publication of "Pompey Smash: The Everlastin and Unkonkerable Skreamer" occurs in *The Negro Singer's Own Book; Containing Every Negro Song That Has Ever Been Sung or Printed.*

1856   The last Crockett almanac is issued for this year.

1872   The play *Davy Crockett; Or, Be Sure You're Right, Then Go Ahead,* by Frank Murdock and Frank Mayo, begins a twenty-four year run in this country and in England that terminates only with the death of Frank Mayo, who played Davy, in 1896.

1909   The New York Motion Picture Company brings out a silent film entitled *Davy Crockett—in Hearts United.* Charles K. French plays the lead.

1910   The film *Davy Crockett* is released by Selig Polyscope Company.

1911   Davy is a minor character in the film *The Immortal Alamo* (Melies).

1915   Davy, played by A. D. Sears, again has a small part in *The Martyrs of the Alamo,* released by Fine Arts-Triangle, but his is the title role in *Davy Crockett Up-to-Date,* a slapstick farce released by United Film Service.

1916   The Oliver Morosco Photoplay Co. produces *Davy Crockett* starring Dustin Farnum. It is released by Pallas (Paramount).

1926   The last Crockett silent film (not extant), *Davy Crockett at the Fall of the Alamo,* is released by Sunset with Cullen Landis playing Crockett.

1934   Constance Rourke publishes *Davy Crockett.*

1937   Lane Chandler stars in the first "Crockett talkie," *Heroes of the Alamo,* which is produced by Sunset and released by Columbia.

1939   Richard Dorson extracts 108 tales from the Crockett almanacs to produce *Davy Crockett: American Comic Legend.* Robert Barrat portrays Crockett in *Man of Conquest,* a film released by Republic.

1940   Walter Blair delineates "Six Davy Crocketts," in *Southwest Review,* 25 (1940), 443–62.

1950   The film *Davy Crockett, Indian Scout* is released by Reliance. George Montgomery plays Davy Crockett, "cousin" of the hero.

1953   Trevor Bardette plays Crockett in the film *Man from the Alamo* (Universal).

1954   Walt Disney broadcasts "Davy Crockett, Indian Fighter" in his *Frontierland* series on December 15. Fess Parker stars. "The Ballad of Davy Crockett," written by George Bruns and Tom Blackburn, also makes its debut.

1955   The year of the Crockett craze. Two more episodes, "Davy Crockett Goes to Congress" (January 26) and "Davy Crockett at the Alamo" (February 23), were shown and then combined with the first episode to form the Disney movie *Davy Crockett, King of the Wild Frontier.* Two more episodes, "Davy Crockett's Keelboat Race" (November 16) and "Davy Crockett and the River Pirates" (December 14), were also shown. Franklin J. Meine's *The Crockett Almanacks: Nashville Series, 1835–1838* is published. Arthur Hunnicutt portrays Crockett in the film *The Last Command* (Republic).

1956   The last two Disney television shows are combined into a movie, *Davy Crockett and the River Pirates,* that is released in July. James Shackford publishes *David Crockett: The Man and the Legend,* the definitive biography of the historical Crockett. The film *The First Texan* is released by Allied Artists with James Griffith playing Crockett.

1959   Fess Parker portrays Crockett in a walk-on part in the film *Alias Jesse James* (United Artists).

1960   John Wayne produces, directs, and stars as Crockett in *The Alamo* (United Artists).

1975   José Enrique de la Peña's *With Santa Anna in Texas: A Personal Narrative of the Revolution* is translated and edited by Carmen Perry.

1978   *How Did Davy Die?* is published by Dan Kilgore.

1982   Richard Boyd Hauck publishes *Crockett: A Bio-Bibliography*.

1985   *Davy Crockett: The Man, The Legend, The Legacy* is published.

1986   Bicentennial of the birth of David Crockett. Sesquicentennial of his death, the battle of the Alamo, and the founding of the Republic of Texas.

Davy Crockett

THE MAN, THE LEGEND, THE LEGACY, 1786-1986

1. The Man in the Buckskin Hunting Shirt

FACT AND FICTION
IN THE CROCKETT STORY

Richard Boyd Hauck

.

His favorite costume was a coonskin cap and a buckskin
jacket. It is assumed that he wore trousers of some sort, although they are never mentioned.
—Richard Armour
It All Started with Columbus (1953)

EARLY IN 1823, David Crockett was hard at work carving out a
new homestead in the Obion River country of West Tennessee. Just
before moving there, he had completed his first term in the state
legislature, as the representative from Hickman and Lawrence counties. In February, he went into Jackson to sell a load of skins, and
there he met with some of his fellow soldiers from the Creek Indian
wars. While taking a few drinks together, they were joined by three
candidates for the state legislature. One of these was a Jackson town
commissioner, Dr. William Butler, Andrew Jackson's nephew-in-law.
During the conversation, Crockett's old comrades—half kidding, half
serious—told him he ought to join the campaigners and run again,
so that he could represent the new district in the next general assembly. Crockett dismissed the notion, responding that he lived too
far out in the woods. The following week he was surprised when
a visitor to his cabin showed him a newspaper clipping announcing
that Crockett was now a candidate. He told his wife, Elizabeth, that
this was a burlesque aimed at him, and he resolved to get revenge
by running—and winning. "I hadn't been out long," Crockett writes
in his autobiography, "before I found the people began to talk very
much about the bear hunter, the man from the cane." In March,
the three candidates Crockett had seen in Jackson met to plot a
strategy for countering his threat. Two of them withdrew, and the
third—Dr. Butler—came out against Crockett.[1]

At a campaign meeting held by Colonel Adam Alexander, who was running for the United States Congress, Crockett met Butler again, and the two engaged in a round of good-natured insults. Then, as Crockett tells it, he revealed to Butler his surefire plan for winning the election.

> I told him that when I set out electioneering, I would go prepared to put every man on as good footing when I left him as I found him on. I would therefore have me a large buckskin hunting-shirt made, with a couple of pockets holding about a peck each; and that in one I would carry a great big twist of tobacco, and in the other my bottle of liquor; for I knowed when I met a man and offered him a dram, he would throw out his quid of tobacco to take one, and after he had taken his horn, I would out with my twist and give him another chaw. And in this way he would not be worse off than when I found him; and I would be sure to leave him in a first-rate good humour. He said I could beat him electioneering all hollow. I told him I would give him better evidence of that before August, notwithstanding he had many advantages over me, and particularly in the way of money; but I told him that I would go on the products of the country; that I had industrious children, and the best of coon dogs, and they would hunt every night till midnight to support my election; and when the coon fur wa'n't good, I would myself go a wolfing, and shoot down a wolf, and skin his head, and his scalp would be good to me for three dollars, in our state treasury money; and in this way I would get along on the big string. He stood like he was both amused and astonished, and the whole crowd was in a roar of laughter.[2]

Crockett's campaign against Butler was hilarious. He ridiculed his opponent's wealth by telling the voters that the man walked on rugs made of better stuff than their wives ever wore. He memorized Butler's basic oration and once got up and gave it before Butler did, leaving the doctor literally speechless (Butler was no slouch as a campaigner, and he extemporized a satisfactory response).[3] One of Crockett's favorite tricks was to take the last turn as a speaker in a debate, let his opponent talk the audience to death, then get up and tell a single joke and offer to treat the voters at the bar. They loved it, and Crockett was elected.

I see in the anecdote of the deerskin hunting shirt an early and exemplary instance of how Crockett participated in – or even initiated – the process of fabrication that produced his legend. The process would soon pass from his hands into the public domain, eventually to produce an image so wildly expanded and diversified that even he was astonished when at last he met his legendary self coming back. The image Crockett was promoting in 1823 had been publicly confirmed the preceding year by an incident that occurred in the state legislature. A representative from East Tennessee—a man who liked to dress in fine clothes—had ridiculed Crockett, sarcastically referring to him as "the gentleman from the cane." Crockett joshed the man in return by pinning a cambric ruffle to his woodsman's shirt, puffing out his chest, and displaying the mockery to the whole legislature. Flustered, the East Tennessean tried to back out by saying he had meant simply that Crockett really was a gentleman who happened to hail from canebrake country.[4] From then on, Crockett earnestly cultivated his image as one of nature's gentlemen—commonsensible, honest, equal in native intelligence to any man. He played up his reputation as a bear hunter, which to the people of West Tennessee was a mark of his independence. He said he was proud of being an unschooled backwoodsman. This unselfconscious display of wholesome naiveté defined him as a self-made man squarely opposed to the rich, educated politicians perceived by the settlers to be their primary enemies in the Tennessee legislature. The voters loved his humor, his offhand approach to the issues, his irreverent attitude toward the entrenched elite. His ability with a rifle provided a metaphor for his political stance: to his constituency, he was a straight shooter. Clearly they believed the folk wisdom of a good-hearted local boy outweighed the hypocritical high-mindedness of wealthy East Tennessee landowners.

Almost certainly, Crockett's deerskin hunting shirt was purely a symbol, worn for electioneering but never for hunting. It is even possible that he never owned such a shirt at all, since he might have made the whole story up ten years later, for the benefit of potential voters who would read his book, *A Narrative of the Life of David Crockett of the State of Tennessee*. Published early in 1834, it was designed as a campaign autobiography, to support his bid if he should be nominated for the presidency, and to further promote his career as a congressman if he should not. An important portrait painted by John Gadsby Chapman in 1834 depicts Crockett in garb that he said was his standard hunting outfit: a long linsey-woolsey jacket and leggings with flaps pulled down over his moccasins to keep his feet dry when it rained. He holds a long rifle, and at his belt is a knife inscribed "Crocket"—he thought the extra "t" entirely unnec-

John Gadsby Chapman's oil portrait of Congressman Crockett in 1834. (From the collections of the Harry Ransom Humanities Research Center, The University of Texas at Austin.)

essary. Three mongrels rounded up from the alleys of Washington sit at his feet—dogs more like his own than the noble breeds usually found in formal portraits. Also notable in this picture is the fact that Crockett wears no animal's skin. His hat appears to be manufactured of felt, with a wide brim and rounded crown.[5] Crockett's modern biographer, James A. Shackford, found considerable evidence, including observations recorded by people who knew him personally, that Crockett never wore a coonskin cap.[6] The common conception of Crockett's hat probably arose originally from Ambrose Andrews's portrait of the actor James Hackett in the role of Nimrod Wildfire in James Kirke Paulding's play *The Lion of the West*. In this picture, Colonel Wildfire wears a wildcat skin that might be mistaken for a raccoon cap. Copies of an engraving made from this portrait were widely circulated in the popular periodicals of the 1830s and 1840s, and a woodcut imitation of it was published as a picture of Crockett on the cover of an 1837 Crockett almanac.[7] (See pages 106-107, Chapter 5). This is exactly the kind of fabrication that went into the promotion of Crockett's political career and the expansion of his image as a folk hero.

Crockett was in many ways what he appeared to be—tough, cantankerous, humorous, independent, and commonsensible. But the historian who insists that the "true" Crockett can be defined only by the facts of his life is inevitably thwarted, and dismayed, by the sheer density of the labyrinthine legend. Paradoxically, the facts of Crockett's life, by themselves, would hardly justify an exhaustive historical investigation. He was a perfectly ordinary pioneer who had a brief flirtation with greatness. He was a minor hero and a colorful campaigner, but it is no secret that he was ineffective as a state legislator and national congressman. His one chance for the presidency turns out to have been a political setup in which the Whigs advertised him as a Democrat who had crossed over to their party in reaction to Andrew Jackson's betrayal of backwoods ideals. The stories of Crockett's valiant stand at the Alamo have been diluted by the discovery that he was captured and executed rather than cut down fighting.[8] He did die heroically, but not in a way that satisfies a whole nation's hunger for mythic exaggeration. The researcher who tries to retrieve the factual historical details about the man from beneath the enormous overlay of invention should keep in mind that he would not be searching for the "real" Crockett at all if it were not for the magnitude of the legend. The Crockett sought by the historian is, of course, not the only real Crockett: the fictional Crockett is also a complicated set of facts, sprawling and rich, and constitutes by far the more important "reality." The set of facts constituting the legend reveals a few things about the man, largely because he made concrete contributions to it, but its primary value is that it tells us a great deal about the sensibilities, both noble and detestable, of the Americans who have expanded the Crockett story by investing it with their own mythos.

Professor James Shackford deserves great credit for delineating the reliable details about David Crockett's life. To him, the legend was an unfortunate obstacle, and perhaps this attitude was essential to the act of unearthing long-buried information. His formal biography "aims at correcting the time-honored fictional versions of his life." The word *fictional* here is pejorative. "So shrouded in fiction and myth and error has Crockett become that only the most careful and painstaking research into all the available sources can hope to recapture the man himself."[9] Certainly Shackford did honor to the goal of discovering the Crockett who actually lived, but an ironic result of his findings is that he is forced to fabricate an exaggerated case for Crockett's stature that is in direct contradiction to those findings. The truth is that our hero's deeds, while usually admirable, were only rarely exciting, and he was subject to petty jealousies and unrealistic ambitions. His faults and failures are embarrassing when contrasted to the claims of the legend. Shackford's concluding argument is that Crockett symbolizes the mastery of a new frontier, "the spiritual frontier of universal brotherhood where all men are their brothers' keepers."[10] It is difficult to find anything in the biography or the legend to support this conclusion; like all Crockett scholars, serious or casual, Shackford ended by seeing in the hero's image some reflection of what he regarded as our own collective hopes.

James Shackford died in 1953, before the biography was published (it was edited by his brother John) and before he could finish his work on an edition of Crockett's autobiography. The edition was completed (and published in 1973) by Stanley J. Folmsbee. I have found Folmsbee's extensions of Shackford's groundbreaking investigation useful, but his attitude toward the legend is puzzling. He seems to think that the historical Crockett is "an authentic folk hero," while the legendary Crockett is nothing but a patchwork image made up of distracting and useless lies. "The myth of David Crockett was long evolving, and it is dying hard even yet," he writes.[11] But it is the myth, not the biographical record, that depicts the "authentic folk hero." Why would anyone want to kill it?

In this century, the scholars who helped build the legend of Davy Crockett (as distinguished from the biography of David Crockett) include Walter Blair, Constance Rourke, and Irwin Shapiro.[12] They found in the Crockett story a history of America's humor, mythology, and frontier spirit. Folmsbee charges that they dismissed the "authentic" Crockett as "unknowable."[13] Actually, people like Rourke, Blair, and Shapiro, along with Franklin J. Meine, Richard M. Dorson, V. L. O. Chittick, Benjamin A. Botkin, and Bernard DeVoto, simply recognized early in their pursuit that the legend of Davy was richer diggings than a pile of mere facts about David. Shapiro admitted "with shame" that now and then he had to fall back on history. Mainly, he wrote about the Crockett who stood "in the grand American tradition of Paul Bunyan, John Henry, Old Stormalong, and Pecos Bill," for this was, of all possible Crocketts, "obviously the most credible, authentic, significant, and true."[14]

That "authentic" Crockett has his life in a formidable body of literary fabrications, including scores of comic almanacs, several plays and movies, and innumerable fictional narratives from tall tales to dime novels. The historian who insists that the "true" Crockett is to be discovered only in the bare facts of his life rejects all these, but reserves a special contempt for the promoters who published four "biographical" or "autobiographical" books in his name during the years 1833 to 1836. These books are in fact spurious. They are deliberately contrived "media productions" designed to further the dubious ends of hack writers and political lackeys. But they are part of the original foundation of the legend, and they all have something of the historical Crockett in them, not the least of which is the very spirit of that great American tradition, the hoax, itself. The first of these is Mathew St. Clair Clarke's *Sketches and Eccentricities of Colonel David Crockett of West Tennessee*, published in 1833.[15] Clarke was a writer for the Whig party and a clerk in the House of Representatives. It is not clear whether he was trying to advance his own standing with the Whigs by satirizing Crockett or was genuinely promoting Crockett's next bid for Congress. He may have been given the task of preparing the way for the publicizing of Crockett's supposed intent to cross party lines and run for president.[16] The problem is that the book's tone is hopelessly mixed: sometimes Clarke seems to praise Crockett; sometimes he makes the congressman look like a fool. Clarke's pompous style is part of the trouble. Apparently he had heard some of his anecdotes from Crockett himself, but his attempt to tell Davy's stories in a pseudoliterary voice is simply mawkish. Nonetheless, the book was wildly successful, and the periodicals immediately began reprinting yarns and character sketches out of it. Much of Crockett's reputation as a practical joker, crack shot, man of common sense, frontier egalitarian, and belligerent braggart can be traced to Clarke's book.

An even more important historical function of *Sketches and Eccentricities* is that it motivated Crockett to write his own autobiography. Unlike the four spurious books that appeared from 1833 through 1836, the *Narrative* is authentic in the strictly historical sense, even though it contains plenty of promotional rhetoric. Crockett presents himself as a man who remained true to Jacksonian principles after Jackson himself had given them up. He tells the story of his life in a straightforward, mock-modest style. The book displays a high level of comic art. Crockett has good timing, firm control of the literary devices that suggest the backwoods idiom, and a way of letting realistically presented details speak for themselves. His accounts of his bear hunting stand as prime examples of the tradition we call the humor of the Old Southwest.

> At the crack of my gun here he came tumbling down; and the moment he touched the ground, I heard one of my best dogs cry out. I took my tomahawk in one hand, and my big butcher-knife in the other, and run up within four or five paces of him, at which he let my dog go, and fixed his eyes on me. I got back in all sorts of a hurry, for I know'd if he got hold of me, he would hug me altogether too close for comfort. I went to my gun and hastily loaded her again, and shot him the third time, which killed him good.[17]

The picture of Crockett in close combat with a bear persisted through the almanacs, the dime novels, and the movies. The image is a fiction based on the facts of Crockett's life, exaggerated by himself just a little, and expanded enormously by the inheritors of his legend. By 1835, the Whigs were vigorously and shamelessly exploiting

Crockett's fame, and in that year party hacks published the second and third of the spurious books that name Davy as author. One is a satirical biography of Martin Van Buren, who was obviously being groomed to succeed Jackson.[18] If the campaign biography was a useful tool for promoting a politician, its counterpart (the anti-campaign biography?) was useful for smearing one's opponent, and that is all this book accomplishes. The other, *An Account of Colonel Crockett's Tour to the North and Down East,* has been thoroughly assimilated into the legend. Much of it is factual, but not autobiographical — its first-person narration is a sham. Here can be found the stories of Crockett's reception in the big cities, told in a style that is a Whig ghostwriter's imitation of Crockett's. The congressman's legend had preceded him, and Crockett played the role he believed was appropriate to his public image.

> It struck me with astonishment to hear a strange people huzzaing for me, and made me feel sort of queer. It took me so uncommon unexpected, as I had no idea of attracting attention. But I had to meet it, and so I stepped on to the wharf, where the folks came crowding round saying "Give me the hand of an honest man." I did not know what all this meant; but some gentlemen took hold of me, and pressing through the crowd, put me up into an elegant barouche, drawn by four fine horses; they then told me to bow to the people: I did so, and with much difficulty we moved off. The streets were crowded to a great distance, and the windows full of people, looking out, I supposed, to see the wild man. I thought I had rather be in the wilderness with my gun and dogs, than to be attracting all that fuss.[19]

Historians generally agree that Crockett neglected his congressional duties while he was touring the northern cities. The man's legendary identity had absorbed much of his authentic self.

The fourth book, and the most notorious of the Crockett fictions, was published in the summer following his death. This was *Col. Crockett's Exploits and Adventures in Texas . . . Written by Himself,* a raw mixture of news reports, contrived anecdotes, plagiarized snatches from randomly selected humorous books, and two Crockett letters (actually "Written by Himself"!) that constituted the first two chapters. The fabricator was Richard Penn Smith, who put the whole mess together — tradition says overnight — for the firm of Carey and Hart in Philadelphia. Smith's book has never been accepted as genuine by historians, yet it remains a fundamental part of the Crockett legend because it is the source of most of the stories about his journey into Texas. The part of the text that actually was written by Crockett includes the famous recounting of his farewell to his Tennessee neighbors. "I concluded my speech by telling them that I was done with politics for the present, and that they might all go to hell, and I would go to Texas."[20] In spite of the spurious character of Smith's book as a whole, this story, like almost everything else in the two Crockett letters, is very likely true.

Ironically, among the other randomly purloined bits and pieces of *Col. Crockett's Exploits and Adventures in Texas*, there is a historical account that turns out to be true, after having been dismissed by serious historians for one hundred and forty years. The book's odd version of Crockett's death at the Alamo comes from a report that had circulated among the newspapers in the spring. It said Crockett survived the seige, surrendered, and was executed.[21] The story was soon obliterated by the fierce processes of mythmaking, and tradition has always held that Crockett died in hand-to-hand combat, fighting on even after his trusty rifle had been smashed, using its barrel as a club. The translation and publication in 1975 of a careful and accurate diary kept by Mexican Army Lieutenant José Enrique de la Peña and Dan Kilgore's 1978 monograph *How Did Davy Die?* have established that Crockett, along with five or six other Americans, were, in fact, alive when the battle was over. Crockett did not surrender voluntarily but was captured by force. Several battle-weary Mexican officers recognized him and urged General Santa Anna, who had ordered that no prisoners be taken, to spare the lives of the famous frontiersman and his comrades. Enraged, Santa Anna demanded that they be executed immediately, and his order was carried out by aides who had not fought in the battle. Lieutenant de la Peña reports that Crockett and the others died bravely, "without complaining and without humiliating themselves before their torturers."[22]

Taken literally, these events alone establish Crockett's reputation as a minor hero. But in 1836 the burgeoning legend of Davy left the facts far behind. Indeed, it was not long before the fictional Davy enjoyed a media-sponsored resurrection. Reliable reports said he had been captured and sentenced to forced labor in a Mexican mine. His rescue was expected any day. For many years after his death, trustworthy correspondents regularly informed newspapers that they had seen him, and the ultimate proof was a drawing made of him on his ninety-ninth birthday.[23]

Such revelations about the media and audiences that built Crockett's legend are surprising and funny, but sometimes what we learn about the perceptions of the legend makers is embarrassing and even repulsive. The Crockett almanacs of the 1830s, 1840s, and 1850s are remembered for their folksy humor, but the fact is they are also riddled with nastiness. They contain racist tirades against slaves and Indians, blindly chauvinistic proclamations of expansionism, and a cynical, deeply bigoted vision that represents the backwoodsman as a stereotype of violence and stupidity. Some of the Crockett yarns, a few of which may have derived from authentic folktales, are entertaining, but a great many others are marked by coarse physical buffoonery. A number of them can be traced to the Crockett "biographies" of 1833–1836, but their inherent roughness is amplified in the almanacs, where they become grossly violent and scatological. Furthermore, the almanacs are probably not even authentic in the sense that they are actually folk or western in their origins. As John Seelye has demonstrated (see Chapter 2), they were begun as a hoax by a hack writer in Boston, and were substantially expanded by a publishing firm in New York.[24]

Original Crockett almanacs are rare, but a number of tall tales and comic yarns from them are accessible in the collections published by Richard M. Dorson and Franklin J. Meine. Two important Crockett books that were based on the material in the almanacs are Walter Blair's and Constance Rourke's.[25] In these, Davy is portrayed as a comic god, riding the lightning, wringing the tail off Halley's comet, drinking up the Gulf of Mexico, steering an alligator up Niagara Falls, kicking the earth loose from its frozen axis and lighting his pipe on the sun. The almanac folktales, along with some hack inventions that mimic folktales, show us Crockett wrestling with bears, talking to animals, delivering thundering boasts and bombastic speeches.

At the other end of the almanac spectrum is the Davy who gives expression to the most sordid impulses of the human race. In an 1837 almanac, we find our hero bragging that he can "swallow a nigger whole without choking if you butter his head and pin his ears back."[26] Seelye observes that after 1843, when they were taken over

by Turner and Fisher in New York, this strain of hateful bigotry
evolved into the almanacs' dominant tone, "overblown exaggeration
in harmony with the expansionist mood expressed throughout, a
jingoism with a crudely racist, even genocidal, bite." Mexicans and
Cubans were portrayed as "degenerate outlaws," Indians as "red niggers," and Negroes as "ape-like caricatures of humanity."[27] The hacks
who assembled the almanacs had just as vicious an attitude toward
backwoods westerners. Their stereotyped Davy spits tobacco juice
on a fine carpet and doesn't recognize a spittoon when it's offered;
he rarely drinks water and then only as a change from whiskey; he
boils an Indian to make medicine for curing his pet bear's indiges-
tion; he is promiscuous, and his women—backwoods women, of
course—are invariably gross. In one yarn Davy punishes a squatter
who tried to trick him into telling a lie by forcing the man—at
gunpoint—to eat a cow pie with a spoon.[28]

As a student of American humor, I have had the dubious plea-
sure of reading thousands of raw stories. With them, of course, are
to be found the rare treasures that make up the foundation of the
frontier tradition of tall yarn spinning. But the crude specimens
in the Crockett almanacs win my vote as the ugliest in the whole
genre. If there is an absolute low point in the history of American
humor, the yarn about the squatter and the cow pie is surely it.
Some scholars give the Crockett almanacs great credit for their role
in building the Crockett legend; I have often wondered how the legend managed to survive the almanacs. But it did survive, and the
processes that perpetuated the legend absorbed, and eventually diluted, the worst characteristics of this most disreputable of Davy's
many images.

If the almanacs reflect the darker streak in American humor, the
Crockett dramas have exploited instead the popular American sympathy for the nobler qualities in the stock character of the backwoodsman, who may rightly be regarded as having become a comic
and heroic stereotype by Crockett's time. The type had been solidi-
fied by the fame of Daniel Boone and widely popularized by ballads
and theatrical skits celebrating the role of the "Kentuckians" in the
battle of New Orleans.[29] Four Crockett dramatizations especially command our attention because they have most influenced the image
we all hold in our minds as the picture of the "real" Davy Crockett.
To many audiences today, the real Davy looks like Fess Parker in

Walt Disney Productions' television series. I personally like to picture Davy as John Wayne in United Artists' *The Alamo*. Our grand-
parents and great-grandparents may have seen him "live" in a very
popular, long-running melodrama, Frank Murdock and Frank Mayo's
Davy Crockett; Or, Be Sure You're Right, Then Go Ahead. (See Chapter 5 in this volume, where I discuss the important Crockett dramas
at greater length.) It makes sense to think about these portrayals in
reverse chronological order here, partly because the modern ones
are familiar to us, but primarily because the first, Hackett's, was one
that Crockett himself met, in an astonishing confrontation between
the living legend and the living legend's theatrical counterpart. Saving Paulding's *Lion of the West* for last allows us to see that believing
in only one "real" Davy Crockett—the historical one—is simply a
failure to recognize that artistic images are more important to the
building of a legend than biographical facts.

The Davy most of us know best, Fess Parker's, comes to us in
five *Disneyland* installments made for the 1954–55 television season
and regularly shown since then in reruns. The series generated an
astonishing popular response in the form of a full-fledged, media-
hyped, mass-marketed children's fad.[30] Parker's performance was tail-
ored to the Disney Studio's ample knowledge of its market: this Davy
Crockett was a role model for children. Parents in 1955 may have
been grateful that the model was thoughtful, upright, and clean-
minded, but millions of them went slowly crazy as their children
endlessly sang the refrain "Davy, Davy Crockett" and repeatedly insisted on wearing their coonskin caps to bed. But one remarkable
effect of the fad is never mentioned by the historians, for it left no
tangible record. For a year or two, the story of Davy Crockett came
alive as a veritable folk drama, reinvented and acted out every day
by children playing in the alleys and woodlots of neighborhoods
across America.

John Wayne's portrayal of Crockett in *The Alamo* (1960) is, as
Crockett would say, a beauty. Wayne himself produced and directed
the film for United Artists. Here two legends fuse perfectly: to play
Crockett in all his legendary glory, Wayne had only to play Wayne
in his. Both images contain everything essential to a portrait of
the mythic American frontier hero. Curiously, John Wayne was
probably a head taller than the historical David Crockett. The legendary phrase puts Davy at six foot four in his stocking feet; Chap-

man's portrait shows that he was, not thin, but stocky, and contemporary descriptions suggest he was much less than six feet tall.
Thus, John Wayne's height, build, and bearing reflected and rein-
forced what the legend has made of Crockett. We would expect a
big late-fifties Hollywood movie about a big historical event to have
as its star a very big man. Some day, no doubt, a more "realistic"
or "revisionist" Crockett movie will be made: its chunky antihero
will be five foot nine with his boots on.

Be Sure You're Right is a melodrama of the genre exemplified by
Ellen Wood's East Lynne (1861).[31] The original script, by Frank Murdock, was revised and brought into production in 1872 by the popular character actor Frank Mayo. This Davy is one of nature's noblemen
—awkward and illiterate, but wholesome, brave, and wise. He is a
bachelor living with his mother way back in the Tennessee mountains. The humorous, sentimental action departs from the genre in
a delightful way when the heroic resolution is shared by the female
lead. While it is Davy—in the classic stance, rifle pointed at the
man's breast—who drives the villain away, it is the heroine, Eleanor,
whose generosity saves her uncle from the law and her family name
from disgrace. Hamlin Garland saw the play when he was a student, and many years later, in the preface of a life of Crockett he
edited, he wrote, "The soft-voiced, bashful, handsome young hunter
in his fringed buckskin jacket and coonskin cap quite won the hearts
of the audience, and we were all grateful when the girl of his adora-
tion offered to teach him his alphabet."[32] This fusion of the melodramatic form and the legendary image of Crockett was absolutely
successful—everybody loved it. The play ran continuously in the
United States and Europe for twenty-four years and was closed only
by the death of Frank Mayo, in 1896.

If there is any single literary characterization that has more to
do with boosting Crockett's image as a backwoods type than any
other, it is Paulding's Colonel Nimrod Wildfire. Paulding wrote The
Lion of the West in response to an announcement by the actor James
Hackett that he would award a prize for a new play depicting a
uniquely American character. Hackett saw in Wildfire exactly what
he was looking for, and he and Paulding worked together on the
production until it was first presented in New York in April 1831.
A few months earlier, the newspapers had published Paulding's de-
nial that he intended any resemblance between Wildfire and Crock-

ett, but in fact he and Hackett had developed the likeness well before the play opened.[33] The audiences and the press certainly had no reservations about making the comparison: Wildfire was instantly received as a sympathetic caricature of Colonel Crockett in his public role as the exemplar of the backwoods type.

The rhetoric of Paulding and Hackett's production is deliberately ambivalent. It satirizes the backwoodsman but confirms the nobility of his straight-shooting, egalitarian common sense. Although Crockett once objected to Hackett's portrayal, the day would come that he himself would affirm it. In December 1833, Hackett brought a benefit performance to the Washington Theater, and Crockett requested that he play some scenes from *The Lion of the West*. A special box down front was reserved for the congressman and his friends. When Crockett entered the theater, the band struck up *Crockett's March* and the audience cheered. A hush fell as the curtain rose. Nimrod Wildfire stepped to the footlights and bowed to David Crockett. Crockett rose and bowed in return. The theater exploded—they loved it, and Crockett loved it too. For one stellar moment, the distinctions between fact and fiction were utterly banished.[34]

In the next couple of years, Crockett's political career fell apart, and he left West Tennessee to search for a homestead in Texas. He was given the opportunity to become land agent for the Red River Valley but decided to pursue history instead.[35] He read the signs of war with Mexico and deliberately chose to go to San Antonio. He stayed in the Alamo knowing there was little chance to survive the siege. The fiction he had begun and others had expanded had never left his imagination. He died at the Alamo because he was determined to live up to his legend. In this one gesture, he outdid all the artists and journalists and promoters and politicians who had built him up. The final and most decisive act of legend making was entirely his own.

NOTES

1. *A Narrative of the Life of David Crockett of the State of Tennessee*, ed. James A. Shackford and Stanley J. Folmsbee (Knoxville: Univ. of Tennessee Press, 1973), 167; hereafter cited as *Narrative*. This is a facsimile edition, with introduction and notes,

of the only authentic Crockett autobiography, published by E.L. Carey & A. Hart, Philadelphia, 1834. For scholarly extension (and occasional revision) of Crockett's claims, see James A. Shackford's definitive biography *David Crockett: The Man and the Legend*, ed. John B. Shackford (Chapel Hill: Univ. of North Carolina Press, 1956), 63–66.

2. *Narrative*, 169–70.

3. Shackford, *David Crockett*, 64.

4. Ibid., 52–53; *Narrative*, 167 n. 4.

5. This important portrait, a small oil about two feet high, is in the Iconography Collection of the Humanities Research Center of the University of Texas. During the sitting, Chapman wrote down his impressions of Crockett and some of their conversations; see Curtis Carroll Davis, "A Legend at Full-Length: Mr. Chapman Paints Colonel Crockett—and Tells about It," *Proceedings of the American Antiquarian Society*, 69 (1960), 155–74. Davis mistakenly thought this portrait to have been lost in the Texas state capitol fire of 1881; Shackford (*David Crockett*, 288–89) had earlier shown that to have been another portrait. For further details on Chapman's full-length portrait, a bust portrait (now hanging in the Alamo) he did at the same time, and the importance of his remarks, see Richard Boyd Hauck, *Crockett: A Bio-Bibliography* (Westport, Conn.: Greenwood Press, 1982), 60–67, 107–8, 140–41; hereafter cited as *Crockett*.

6. Shackford, *David Crockett*, 281–91.

7. For a side-by-side comparison of the two pictures, see pages 106–107, Chapter 5; for discussions, see *Crockett*, 45–47, 67–79; Shackford, *David Crockett*, 253–55; James N. Tidwell, ed., *The Lion of the West*, by James Kirke Paulding (Stanford: Stanford Univ. Press, 1954), 7–14; and Joseph John Arpad, "John Wesley Jarvis, James Kirke Paulding, and Colonel Nimrod Wildfire," *New York Folklore Quarterly*, 21 (1965), 92–106.

8. Dan Kilgore, *How Did Davy Die?* (College Station: Texas A & M Univ. Press, 1978); *Crockett*, 47–54.

9. Shackford, *David Crockett*, vii.

10. Ibid., 251.

11. *Narrative*, x.

12. Walter Blair, *Davy Crockett—Frontier Hero: The Truth as He Told It—the Legend as His Friends Built It* (New York: Coward-McCann, 1955); Constance Rourke, *Davy Crockett* (New York: Harcourt, 1934); Irwin Shapiro, *Yankee Thunder: The Legendary Life of Davy Crockett* (New York: Julian Messner, 1944). An important article basic to any discussion of Crockett's many images is Walter Blair's "Six Davy Crocketts," *Southwest Review*, 25 (1940), 443–62, which is also incorporated into chapter 2 of his book *Horse Sense in American Humor* (Chicago: Univ. of Chicago Press, 1942).

13. *Narrative*, x–xii.

14. Shapiro, *Yankee Thunder*, 6–8.

15. Reprinted in New York by J. & J. Harper, this is the title by which the book is most generally known; its original title was *Life and Adventures of Colonel David Crockett of West Tennessee* (Cincinnati: "For the Proprietor," 1833).

16. Shackford, David Crockett, 258–64; Crockett, 45–46, 65–77.

17. Narrative, 163–64.

18. Probable author, Augustin Smith Clayton, The Life of Martin Van Buren (Philadelphia: Robert White, 1835).

19. The original publisher of the Tour was E.L. Carey & A. Hart of Philadelphia (1835), and this quotation is in ch. 1, pp. 17–18. The reader will find it more convenient to refer to ch. 18 of Life of David Crockett, The Original Humorist and Irrepressible Backwoodsman (Philadelphia: Porter & Coates, 1865), 174–75. This is a one-volume compilation of the Narrative, the Tour, and Col. Crockett's Exploits and Adventures in Texas . . . (see the paragraph that follows in text). There is no definitive edition of any of the Crockett books, and this compilation is one of a great many similar volumes—by far the most accessible "Life" of Crockett and the main source of the legend's details as they are popularly known. The original edition of Crockett's Exploits and some of the later one-volume compilations have a fake preface signed by an "Alex J. Dumas" who never existed; see Shackford, David Crockett, 273–81.

20. Carey & Hart edition of Col. Crockett's Exploits, 31 (ch. 2); or Porter & Coates compilation, 252 (ch. 24).

21. Tour, Carey & Hart edition, 203–5 (ch. 14); or Porter & Coates compilation, 395–97 (ch. 36). See Kilgore, How Did Davy Die? 19–20.

22. José Enrique de la Peña, With Santa Anna in Texas: A Personal Narrative of the Revolution, trans. and ed. Carmen Perry (College Station: Texas A. & M. Univ. Press, 1975), 53. Kilgore, How Did Davy Die?

23. John Seelye, "A Well-Wrought Crockett: Or, How the Fakelorists Passed through the Credibility Gap and Discovered Kentucky," in the present volume, 27–28; Shackford, David Crockett, 239. The drawing can be seen in Richard M. Dorson, America in Legend: Folklore from the Colonial Period to the Present (New York: Random House, 1973), 80.

24. Seelye, 21–45.

25. Richard M. Dorson, ed., Davy Crockett: American Comic Legend (New York: Spiral Press for Rockland Editions, 1939); Franklin J. Meine, ed., The Crockett Almanacks: Nashville Series, 1835–1838 (Chicago: Caxton Club, 1955); Blair, Davy Crockett, and Rourke, Davy Crockett. Rourke's book contains a descriptive bibliography of forty-four Crockett almanacs. See also Dorson, "The Sources of Davy Crockett, American Comic Legend," Midwest Folklore, 8 (1958), 143–49.

26. Meine, The Crockett Almanacs, 106–7.

27. Seelye, 28.

28. Dorson, Davy Crockett, 89–90, 145–52.

29. Constance Rourke, American Humor: A Study of the National Character (New York: Harcourt, 1931), 33–76; Michael A. Lofaro, "From Boone to Crockett: The Beginnings of Frontier Humor," Mississippi Folklore Register, 14 (1980), 57–74.

30. Fine studies of this phenomenon are Margaret King's article that appears as Chapter 7 in the present volume and her dissertation, "The Davy Crockett Craze: A Case Study in Popular Culture," Univ. of Hawaii, 1976.

31. Be Sure You're Right appears on pp. 115–48 of America's Lost Plays, vol.

4, ed. Isaac Goldberg and Hubert Heffner (Bloomington: Indiana Univ. Press, 1963).

32. Hamlin Garland, Preface to his edition of *The Autobiography of David Crockett* (New York: Scribners, 1923), 3.

33. Shackford, *David Crockett,* 254; see also Tidwell's introduction and Arpad's article (note 7, above).

34. *Crockett,* 47.

35. Shackford, *David Crockett,* 212–22; *Crockett,* 47–50.

2. A Well-Wrought Crockett

OR, HOW THE FAKELORISTS PASSED THROUGH THE CREDIBILITY GAP AND DISCOVERED KENTUCKY

John Seelye

.

"Half-horse, half-alligator," Davy Crockett is an amphibian likewise where studies in American folk literature are concerned: his upper half is identifiable as a historical figure, a colorful politician from the Tennessee backwoods, while his hinder parts are obscured by mythic waters, the Mississippi River. And as with the great river, the effect is to enlarge, and by enlarging, to distort. A politicized version of Daniel Boone, Crockett in his own day represented a distinct stage in the development of subliterary types: where Boone was shaped into an epic hero, a champion of national expansion into the Ohio Valley, Crockett emerged as a much more complex expression of the American spirit, a braggart buffoon who was martyred at the Alamo. Half hero, half horse's ass, Crockett even as a practical politician found himself torn between local and national interests, and the literature he inspired is divided into authentic and spurious anecdotes, with a great deal of questionable material in between.

Walter Blair early on enumerated six separate identities for this Krishna of the American folk pantheon, and threw up his hands over the task of distinguishing between the "real" and the "legendary" parts.[1] Blair opted for celebrating the legend, letting the other half slide, and his decision, coming at the end of the thirties, pretty much sums up the attitude of scholars who dealt with Davy Crockett during that decade, like Blair's co-workers, Franklin J. Meine, Constance Rourke, and Richard M. Dorson. This uncritical period begins with Rourke's *American Humor* (1931), and ends with Ben A.

Botkin's *Treasury of American Folklore* and Blair's *Tall Tale America*, both published in 1944 and given an added degree of chauvinism thereby. Blair's book, subtitled *A Legendary History of Our Humorous Heroes*, in effect enlisted Crockett—along with the likes of Mike Fink, Pecos Bill, John Henry, Paul Bunyan, and Joe Magarac—in the war effort, "native American" supermen set in motion to smash the Nazi menace. Like World War II itself, this act of massive cultural naiveté would not be repeated.

As early as 1930, professional students of folklore had discovered the extent to which, as in the case of the ballad of John Henry, commercialization had polluted traditional wellsprings. And by 1950, a number of so-called folk figures celebrated by Walter Blair were turning out to be artificial creations, hokum heroes invented by journalists and publicists with not even a remote connection to any popular oral tradition. In 1939, in *Davy Crockett: American Comic Legend*, Richard Dorson enthusiastically lumped his champion in with Pecos Bill and Paul Bunyan as native American versions of European mythic types, but by the end of the next decade Dorson made a distinction between folk- and what he called "fake" lore, which last was associated with Botkin's popular *Treasury*. The most egregious example of fakelore hero was Paul Bunyan, whose very size symbolized the giantism of the hoax, for as Daniel Hoffman demonstrated in *Paul Bunyan: The Last of the Demigods* (1952), the legend had more to do with the ledgers of a lumber company than with loggers' tales told around the campfire.

In 1956 there appeared James Atkins Shackford's *David Crockett: The Man and the Legend*, which in very strong terms dismissed "the mythological Crockett" celebrated by Blair and Dorson. Moreover, in a lengthy series of appendixes, Shackford turned a merciless gaze on the printed material from which Rourke and the rest derived their "folk" hero. Only *A Narrative of the Life of David Crockett* (1834) was dependable, Shackford opined, for the other books were either doubtful in origin or posthumous attempts to capitalize on the hero's notoriety. And as for the comic Crockett almanacs, from which Rourke drew much of her most colorful material and which Dorson anthologized as his *Legend*, Shackford dismissed them as a "gargantuan hoax . . . part of the exploitation of his renown which yet goes on . . . that point, I think, at which a low type of literary exploitation joined hands with the economic need of inferior literary ability."[2] That is, though there was a very real and genuinely heroic historic David Crockett, the Davy of the almanacs (and Rourke) was a hokey hero sprung from the printer's font.

Shackford's sentiments remained a matter of opinion, however, until 1973, when Joseph Arpad's "The Fight Story: Quotation and Originality in Native American Humor" appeared in *The Journal of the Folklore Institute*. For Arpad demonstrates the extent to which the earliest of the Crockett almanacs were inspired by a popular play, *The Lion of the West*, the hero of which, Nimrod Wildfire, was conceived by James K. Paulding and modeled loosely after the Davy Crockett of burgeoning public notoriety. Concentrating on Wildfire's "fight story," a monologue that was widely circulated in newspapers of the day, Arpad traces it back, not to an oral source, but to Paulding's own *Letters From the South* (1817). Arpad assumes that Paulding got the original story (about a fight between a boatman and a waggoneer) from some "local storyteller," but the earlier analogues that he cites come also from printed, not oral, sources, all of which are presented as eyewitness accounts by literate (and literary) travelers. Behind this tradition there may lie an oral or even a folk tradition, but the evidence gathered by Arpad necessarily promotes a strictly literary metamorphosis, a sequence in which the popular and mass-produced Crockett of the almanacs represents a final stage. A significant icon in this evolution is the picture of Crockett on the cover of the *Davy Crockett Almanac* for 1837, a woodcut copy of a widely circulated picture of Nimrod Wildfire as played by James H. Hackett, twin images printed side by side (or back to back) in Arpad's article. (See pages 106 and 107, Chapter 5).

Richard Dorson included this iconographic metamorphosis in his discussion of Crockett's place in *America in Legend* (1973), where he concedes that the almanac stories represent a move from folk anecdote to "popular literature": "Hack writers in Eastern cities hammered out fanciful escapades for the annual almanac issues . . . yarns [that] constitute a subliterature rather than a folklore."[3] Dorson maintains however that the almanac-makers' Crockett represents "a transition not a sharp break" in the evolution of folk to popular hero, and shows how a number of the almanac stories derive from European folktales and myths. But so, one might respond, does the story of Rip Van Winkle, yet Irving's "Hudson-River tale" does not appear in *America in Legend*. Still, Dorson's revised view of the Crockett almanacs must be regarded as a major development in folklorist scholarship, for it was the "grandiose" phase of the Crockett almanacs on which Dorson, along with Blair and Rourke, had chiefly relied for the tallest of the Tennessean's tales, stories which now must be regarded as largely fakelore.

A point has been reached, apparently, in which the difference between Shackford's opinion and Dorson's concerning the authenticity of the Crockett almanacs is negligible. No longer regarded as directly derived from folk tales, the Crockett almanacs are seen as an early version of popular literature: relying on oral conventions, the comic "legends" were the invention of literary hacks who consciously introduced mythic (archetypal) elements. Though Dorson does not make the point, we can see that from superheroes like Davy Crockett to supersleuths like Nick Carter and on to Superman himself, there is a continuity that has its origins in the ur-hero, Hercules. In America, this is the Kentucky connection, but the men who made it, whatever the nature of their sources, were, like Paulding and Irving, well aware of the Old World analogues. Fakelorists of considerable acumen, they discovered long before Paul Bunyan hove into view the literary potential of the American forest, whether as scenery or as the stuff of crudely cut engravings and the paper they were printed upon.

Henry Nash Smith in *Virgin Land* (1950) and Richard Slotkin in *Regeneration through Violence* (1973) have variously charted the literary metamorphosis of Daniel Boone, the prototype of subsequent "myths," whose heroic advent was the work of John Filson, who in 1784 celebrated the feats of the Long Hunter by way of promoting Kentucky real estate. With some help perhaps from Daniel Bryan's Miltonic *Mountain Muse* (1813), Boone found his way into an apostrophe in Byron's *Don Juan,* from whence he was elevated by the talents of Fenimore Cooper to literary apotheosis as Leatherstocking. Cooper's creation undoubtedly encouraged a long line of popular biographies of Boone, such as the one written by Timothy Flint in 1833, so that by the end of the nineteenth century the Long Hunter and a host of fictional counterparts had become familiar figures in the Beadle dime novels. Much as Davy Crockett became a woodcut ventriloquist's dummy for Whig interests, so Leatherstocking served as a spokesman for Cooper's conservative Jeffersonianism, and Walt Disney's resurrected Crockett may be seen as a wilderness prophet heralding John F. Kennedy's New Frontier. This ulterior dimension has a sinister slant, for in America the wilder versions of pastoral have a radically reactionary bias. Designed for popular consumption, these literary sharpshooters are the invention chiefly of a mon-eyed elite, and the "legendary" Davy Crockett like the literary "Jack Downing" may, like the wit and wisdom of Abraham Lincoln and Mark Twain, be traced to Whiggish origins.

This is particularly true of An Account of Col. Crockett's Tour to the North and Down East (1835), an attack on the Democrats with which Crockett himself had little connection, and the spurious Col. Crockett's Exploits and Adventures in Texas (1836) is at once fiercely chauvinistic and anti-Jacksonian, a curious compound of expansionism and conservatism that matches the paradoxicalness of Whig politics in the southwest. But even the two books either authorized or in part authored by Crockett, the Sketches and Eccentricities of Colonel David Crockett (1833) and A Narrative of the Life (1834), sometimes (as in 1923) printed as Crockett's Autobiography, seem to have been designed to further his political career. Though Crockett disclaimed any connection with the Sketches in his introduction to the autobiography, which he said was written to correct the many errors in the other book, Shackford is convinced that the first-published account of Crockett's exploits was compiled with his connivance. The Tennessee Congressman most certainly acted ambivalently where Paulding's play was concerned, for though he graciously accepted the author's statement that no conscious caricature was intended, there is a tradition that he once publicly returned from his theatre box Hackett's congé of acknowledgment. If Shackford is right, and Crockett did authorize the Sketches and Eccentricities, then the link Arpad has established between the book and the play suggests that the congressman was willing to benefit from notoriety, which—as he later discovered to his dismay—he seems to have confused with fame.

Though copyrighted by "Davy Crockett," and after 1835 in the name of his heirs, not even the earliest Crockett almanacs have been traced to Crockett himself. The initial number was printed in 1834 (for the year 1835), and given his repudiation that year of the comic version of his life and adventures, we may be sure Crockett would have regarded any such continuation of the Eccentricities version with displeasure. The first four issues of the Crockett almanacs, all bearing a Nashville imprint, most certainly derive from the 1833 collection of anecdotes and, like that book, seem to have been inspired by the popularity of Paulding's play. Nimrod Wildfire has no Whiggish coloration, but is distinguished by a native American chauvinism that is, if anything, Jacksonian in its hues, and so also with the bulk of the *Sketches and Eccentricities*, which are hunting stories for the most part, and lack the anti-Democratic bias revealed in the last pages of the book. The almanacs, as the penultimate stage in this evolution, preserve the sugar and throw away the pill. Totally lacking in definable party politics, the Nashville almanacs continue to portray the wilderness sporting life, and differ from the *Sketches and Eccentricities* in a general coarsening of tone and broadening of humor, with Crockett serving as often as a butt of jokes as their perpetrator. Thus the fight story stressed as the genetic literary link by Arpad appears with a significant variation in the first number of the Nashville series: not discussed by Arpad, this version involves Crockett's amorous adventures with the mistress of a stagecoach driver. Though caught at the worst possible moment by the driver, Crockett is victorious in the fight that follows, but acknowledges he never told *this* story to "Mrs. Crockett," nor did Dorson include it in his *Legend*.

The only episode in the Nashville almanacs having the faintest political implication is the appearance, in the second number, for 1836, of "Ben Harding, Member of Congress from Kentucky," who relates his "Early Days, Love and Courtship." But what follows has nothing to do with politics and even less with the historical Ben Hardin (*sic*), a colorful Whig politician from Bardstown. "Ben Harding's" autobiograpy is a compressed reprise of Crockett's almanac adventures, and includes an enlistment under Jackson at New Orleans and a rough-and-tumble courtship with "one Betsey Blizzard." Hardin in fact never served in the army and was, unlike Crockett, a member of the relatively refined middle-class gentry of southwestern society. His nineteenth-century biographer, Lucius P. Little, places Hardin between Crockett and John Randolph as being halfway between the backwoods screamers and the Tidewater aristocracy. Randolph himself fastened the epithet "Old Kitchen Knife" on Hardin, claiming that his speaking style was both rough-honed and deep-cutting, and the chosen instrument is symbolic, being, not the bowie knife associated with the wilder parts of the west, but a domestic implement.[4]

Though lacking a college education, Hardin was a learned man and a witty raconteur, whose biography is pieced out by Little with the kinds of anecdotes that made him a local celebrity if not a national one. He belonged to that middling class of professional men who were more apt to be the authors of southwestern humor than the central figures in it, circuit-riding men of the law who maintained an uneasy peace with the predominantly Jacksonian population of the southwestern states. As Little acknowledges, "the comic almanac maker of his day made Mr. Hardin the unwilling vehicle for communicating jokes rather broader than he ever indulged in the most unreserved moments."[5] This considerably understates the situation. By 1839, "Ben Harding" had become the "editor" and "publisher" of the Nashville almanacs, and continued in that capacity long after the Crockett almanacs dropped the Tennessee association, figuring in many stories as the boon companion of the rambunctious colonel. However, it is not as a Kentucky congressman that he figures in 1839 and afterwards, but as a stereotyped American version of Jack Tar, a sailor who first meets "Kurnel Krockett" while "cruising down the Massippy [sic] on a raft." Hearing of the Colonel's "disease" in Texas, and having in the meantime suffered a "game leg and a short hip" that made him "unseaworthy," Harding "went on a cruise down into Kentuck, and there . . . cum across the Kurnel's papers." Out of respect for the "old Kurnel," Ben announced in the almanac for 1839 that he will continue his good work, that he will "cruize about among the gravers and printers in person," seeing to it that "everything [is] done ship-shape and Bristol fashion."

By 1841, in the last of the almanacs bearing the Nashville imprint, Harding had grown a wooden leg and established contact once again with Davy Crockett, who was alive and as well as could be expected while working in the Mexican mines. Instead of dying at the Alamo, Crockett had been taken prisoner, and he writes his old friend Harding in the hope of obtaining the funds necessary to effect his escape. In 1843, by which time the Crockett almanacs were being published by Turner and Fisher in New York (as well as other eastcoast cities), "Harding" had been corrected to "Hardin," and the sailor-editor is still trying to raise the money "for getting Crockett out of the mines."

But there he remains, increasingly a hostage to political fortunes, for under the Turner and Fisher imprint the almanacs took on a definably expansionist note. In the 1843 number, there appears a letter from Crockett expressing chauvinistic anxiety on the Oregon question, and in 1845 he declares himself as being "like my salt-water friend, Ben Hardin, of the rale American grit, and like him I go for Texas and Oregon, clar up to the very gravel stone, for they both belong to Uncle Sam's plantation." It is these Turner and Fisher almanacs that are chiefly responsible for the "grandiose" stage of the Crockett "legend," overblown exaggeration in harmony with the expansionist mood expressed throughout, a jingoism with a crudely racist, even genocidal, bite. Mexicans and Cubans are depicted as degenerate outlaws, Indians are "red niggers," and Negroes are tacitly accepted as handy victims of wrath, being apelike caricatures of humanity. In sum, under the "editorship" of Ben Harding/Hardin the Crockett almanacs begin to express a spirit that is closer to the dark side of Jacksonianism than to the Whig élan.

Commentators have noted the strategic differences between the earliest and later Crockett almanacs, and though the genuineness of the Nashville imprint has been questioned, as a grouping the first four Nashville "Crocketts" have a definitive uniformity of design, attested to by Franklin J. Meine in his 1955 edition of them. An important register of the distinction to be made between early and later almanacs is found in the woodcuts that were a constant feature. Where the Nashville imprints contain anonymous illustrations notable for charm and naiveté, bold even primitive designs whose archaic qualities evoke native American folk art, under the aegis of Turner and Fisher the pictures are executed (and signed) by professional craftsmen, and evince the same tendency toward grandioseness that characterizes the anecdotes they were designed to accompany.[6] Though less crude than the pictures in the Nashville almanacs, the Turner and Fisher illustrations are far more ugly, an increase in grotesqueness matching the violence and bigotry of the tales.

As Shackford observes, the chief motivation seems to have been economic opportunism, a willingness to pander to the American propensity for mayhem that would thenceforth remain a constant factor in the popular or mass marketplace. Though the expansionist ideology expressed by the Turner and Fisher almanacs did not accord well with the Whig platform during the 1840s, the commercial spirit was thoroughly Whiggish, and it is notable that Turner and Fisher were the publishers during this same period of such obvious Whig documents as *Gen. Zachary Taylor's Old Rough & Ready Almanac for 1848*. In fact, as Milton Drake's bibliography suggests, almanacs were, when openly political, generally in support of Whig candidates. But though printers and publishers were loyal to the Whig cause, they were willing to pander to the prejudices of Jacksonian democracy, expressing hostilities of a sectional and racial sort which, as a legendary mix, is much closer to the American monomyth isolated by Richard Slotkin in *Regeneration through Violence* than to the earliest anecdotes associated with Davy Crockett. Since this element is introduced by Ben Harding/Hardin's appearance as sailor/editor, that advent perhaps deserves more study than it has hitherto received.

Several Ben Harding stories are included in Dorson's anthologized *Legend*, and Constance Rourke gives him passing mention, but the congressman turned sailor as either a folk or fake figure has generally been neglected. Moreover, the Crockett "legend" in its telling by Rourke or in descriptions by Blair and Dorson does not include the Colonel's survival in the Mexican mines. Though obviously a fictional convenience, a device allowing for further Crockett stories even after the "Kurnel's papers" gave out, the Mexican mines business is no less "legendary" than the stories that the situation permitted. It is, however, less heroic than having Crockett die at the Alamo, and one suspects that modern scholars of folklore have yielded to the same chauvinistic impulse governing much of the production of the original Crockett stories. So also with Ben Harding/Hardin, who is if anything more "legendary" than Crockett—because almost entirely fictitious—and who figures in more tall tales than Mike Fink. Yet Walter Blair and Franklin Meine pay him little attention, and he is not included in Blair's roundup of "folk" heroes in *Tall Tale America*, though one would think that such a belligerent tar would have been of great service against his old adversaries—people of any color but white. Perhaps because he is a sailor, Ben Harding/Hardin was exempted from consideration by folklore scholars of the 1930s, who were chiefly concerned with legends generated by the frontier, the mythic matter that occupied the popular mind after the Civil War to the exclusion of all others. Having generated a considerable maritime literature, on both elite and popular levels,

American writers after the war gave in to the frontier necessity, a phenomenon matched and in part accounted for by the decline of the United States as a major sea power during those years. Even the rediscovery of Melville's novels in the 1920s was accompanied by no equivalent interest in maritime folklore.

Moreover, Ben Harding/Hardin is chiefly of interest here because of his Kentucky connection: his appearance as "editor" of the Crockett almanacs occurs at just that point variously described by Shackford and Dorson when the anecdotes left the sphere of "oral" or "folk" creation and became early manifestations of "popular" literature. The authenticity of even the earliest Crockett stories as "folk" literature is still open to question, but there is no denying that under the aegis of Ben Harding/Hardin the "legend" became consciously manipulated for profit. Though taking his name from an historical figure, moreover, Ben Harding/Hardin is a stereotyped literary creation, a sailor sprung from the decks of Cooper's seagoing romances. As a "folk" figure, then, he is ascertainably "fake," and is therefore an important addition to that growing pantheon of phony heroes, being a giant's step toward Paul Bunyan. To understand the full implication of this fact, however, we need to consider two important questions: 1. Why was Ben Harding transformed from a Kentucky congressman to a tar? and, 2. What is a sailor doing on the Mississippi River?

The first question can be relatively easily, though conjecturally, answered. Ben Harding/Hardin was first introduced to the almanac audience in the year after Crockett's death—in the second "Nashville" imprint—and though Crockett is the medium, Harding's first words are suggestive: "As the public seems to be very anxious to hear all about my friend Colonel Crockett, I don't see no reason why I should not make some stir in the world too, as we are both members of Congress. I have long had an intention to write my life, and tell about the wild varmints that I have killed, and how I got to be elected member of Congress, and all that." What follows, again, bears no relation to the historical Hardin but is imitative of Crockett's adventures. It seems reasonable to assume that the editor of the "Nashville" almanacs felt it was necessary to find a replacement for the martyred Tennesseean, and hit upon the happy idea of introducing the Kentucky Whig as a convenient substitute. As the misspelling of the Kentuckian's name and the fictitiousness of his adventures suggest, the editor had no real knowledge about Ben Hardin, but then Crockett in the almanacs is increasingly identified as a Kentuckian, suggesting that the pervasive influence of Paulding's fictional character was more powerful than any geopolitical reality.

Whatever the reasons for the editor's creation of a Crockett replacement, the idea died in the same issue in which it was born. Perhaps Hardin did not wish to undergo the painful process of becoming a folk hero, which had meant for Davy Crockett first the loss of his office and then of his life. Being a lawyer, Hardin had the means at his disposal for objecting in an effective manner, and being a Kentuckian he had other resources to draw upon also. Whatever the reason, when Ben Harding next appeared it was as a sailor, and as a sailor he remained, editing the almanacs and having adventures of his own and with Crockett on the Mississippi and in foreign climes. This second appearance was in the "Nashville" almanac for 1839, and later in that same number (see page 32) the opening account of the initial meeting between the backwoodsman and the sailor is considerably expanded upon, once again in the words of Crockett:

I was laying asleep on the Mississippi one day, with a piece of river scum for a pillow, and floating down stream in rail free and easy style, when all at once I was waked up by something that cum agin my ribs like it was trying to feel for an opening into my bowels. So I just raised my head to see what kind of a varmint was sharpening his teeth agin my ribs, and seed it was something that lookt so much like a human cretur that I was half a mind to speek to it. But it had a tail to its head about as big around as my arm and as long as a hoss pistle. The cretur was floating on three kegs fastened to a log, and held a pole in his hand that he had punched me with in the ribs, when I fust woke up. His trowsers was made of white sail cloth, and they was so wide about the legs that I knowed he had stold 'em from some big fat feller, for they didn't fit him no more than my wife's raccoon skin shift would fit the fine ladies in Washington. He had on light thin shoes with big ribbons in 'em and a painted hat with another big ribbon in that. So then I concluded rite off he had ben robbing a Yankee pedlar and got away all his flashy trumpery. Says I, 'Stranger, I take it you are a human by the looks of your face, but you are one of the greatest curosities I've seen in these parts. I don't wonder you wake me up to look at ye.' 'By the devil!' says he, 'the thing has got the use of lingo like a Christian. I thought I had

31

"Ben Harding falling in with Col. Crockett" from *The Crockett Almanac, 1839* (Nashville, Tennessee: Published by Ben Harding), p. 32. (University of Tennessee Library.)

spoke a catfish. Where are you cruising, old rusty bottom? You are the queerest rigged sea craft that I ever saw on soundings or off.' 'You infarnal heathen,' says I, 'I don't understand all your stuff, and I spose you are fresh down this way. But I'll have you understand that I'm a snorter by birth and eddycation, and if you don't go floating along, and leave me to finish my nap I'll give you a taste of my breed. I'll begin with the snapping turtle, and after I've chawed you up with that, I'll rub you down with a spice of the alligator.' With that he looked as mad as a shovel full of hot coals, and he took a long string of tobakkur out of his pocket, and arter he had bit off a piece long enough to hang a buffalo, he roared out, 'I'll shiver your mizen in less time than you can say Jack Robinson, you fresh water lubber! You rock crab! You deck sweeper! swab!' Says I then, for my steam begun to get rather obstropolous, 'I'll double you up like a spare shirt. My name is Crockett and I'll put my mark on your infarnal wolfhide before you've gone the length of a panther's tail further.' With that he roared right out a laffing, and I was so astonished, I held my breath to see the cretur laff on the eve of a battle, but I soon seed the reeson of it, for he stooped down and reached out his hand, and says, 'tell me for God's sake, old fogy, are you the feller that makes them all-mynacks about cruising after panthers and snakes and swimming over the Mississippi?' Says I, 'I'm a roarer at that bizness that you've mentioned, stranger. Going to Congress and making allmynacks is my trade.' 'Give us your flipper then, old chap,' says he, 'I woodn't hurt a hare of your head for the world. Isn't there a grog shop here on the coast, for by G——— I'll treat you if I sell my jacket. I'd give two weeks allowance if our boson was here—Hurra! three cheers for old Crockett! He used to read your allmynack to us on the forecastle, for d'ye see, I can't read. I got my larning under the lee of the long boat, and swear my prayers at a lee earing in a gale o' wind. But I can read pikturs to a d———n, and I could spell out your crocodile's tails from their heads when I see 'em drawed out in your book.'

The anecdote continues, with Crockett taking Harding home with him for dinner and the old sailor drinking whiskey and telling "such stories about what he had seed as made the gals dream o' nights for a fortnite arter he was gone; and as I spose the reader would like to hear some of 'em, I think I shall put 'em in print." Crockett even gives the readers a woodcut of Ben Harding's voice because it "was so ruff, I can't rite it doun." (See page 34.) But the main point of the story is contained in the quoted portion above, which is rendered at length because it is a significant variation of the fight story which Professor Arpad views as the central link between *The Lion of the West*, the *Sketches and Eccentricities*, and the Crockett almanacs.

For this hostile meeting between the backwoodsman and the sailor, unlike the violent encounters between Davy Crockett and riverboatmen on the Mississippi, does not end in a bloody fight. Instead, the two antagonists become friends because of Harding's flattering overtures, a reversion of the conventions that is a meliorating device: the fight story is being consciously manipulated so as to emphasize the friendly mingling of salt water and fresh, signaling the entrance of Ben into Davy's world. Unlike Crockett's other antagonists, who end by acknowledging his superior strength but go their separate ways, Ben will remain. He will become not only Davy's companion but his equal, in effect a maritime equivalent and counterpart to the "Kentuckian." The symbolic implication of this union is clarified by the cover of a Crockett (Turner and Fisher) almanac for 1845 (the issue that contains Davy's imperialistic sentiments concerning Oregon and Texas), for the picture is a monumentally chauvinistic

"Picture of Ben Harding's Voice" from *The Crockett Almanac, 1839* (Nashville, Tennessee: Published by Ben Harding), p. 24. (University of Tennessee Library.)

composition, including a spread eagle and a pediment featuring a melee between white men and red, as jingoistic and Jacksonian a composition as one could possibly conceive. (See page 35). Yet there is a Websterish and Whiggish cast to this emblem also, for the back-to-back bond of sailor and frontiersman expresses the mystic idea of Union, the kind of politics of compromise that did not admit to the physical impediment of the Alleghanies.

By 1845, the publication of the almanacs was openly associated with northeastern cities, and Ben-the-Sailor is likewise an east coast (seaport) figure. His appearance in the "Nashville" almanacs, in 1839 and afterwards, therefore suggests an eastern influence, even an eastern place of publication. Further evidence corroborating this possibility is found in the first almanac "edited" by Harding, a gruesome full-page woodcut entitled "The Pirates Head, As drawn by Ben Harding," illustrating the sailor's account of one of his seagoing (anti-Hispano-American) adventures. An identical woodcut may be found

Ben Harding and Davy Crockett back-to-back. Cover page of the 1845 *Almanac*. (American Antiquarian Society.)

The Pirates Head,
As drawn by Ben Harding.   See Page 24.

Benevides does double duty. *The Crockett Almanac, 1839* (Nashville, Tennessee: Published by Ben Harding), p. 21 and *The Pirates Own Book* (1837), p. 189. (American Antiquarian Society.)

in *The Pirates Own Book*, where it is entitled "the head of Benevides stuck on a pole" (see page 36). First published in Boston in 1837 by Samuel N. Dickinson, this compilation of maritime mayhem was reprinted up and down the eastern seaboard frequently thereafter, and has been credited to Charles Ellms, an illustrator-editor residing in Boston in the 1830s and 1840s. The *Pirates Own* was produced anonymously, but Ellms's name appears on later collections of similarly nautical material, including *Robinson Crusoe's Own Book* (1842) and *The Tragedy of the Seas* (1841), sensational nonfiction embellished with crude woodcuts similar to those that make up much of the Nashville almanacs' rough-hewn appeal.

Moreover, in *Crusoe's Own Book* there appears verbatim a story about "Mike Shuck[well], the Beaver Trapper" that was printed in the first Nashville almanac, and though we cannot put too much weight on this particular link—given the propensity of anthologists to gather material from various sources—the use of the "Pirates Head" picture does suggest a certain printshop propinquity. Equally suggestive is the claim of Ellms's publisher, Dickinson, that his firm originated the Crockett almanacs. The statement, according to Clarence Brigham of the American Antiquarian Society in a letter to Franklin Meine in 1950, appears "on the back page of a pink cover which Dickinson issued, wrapped around his two publications of the *Old American Comic* and the *People's Almanac*, in that way issuing them as a pair with a general title of *Almanacs for 1844*":

> About ten years since, the first Comic Almanac that was ever published, was the American Comic. The idea was a novel one, and not more than two seasons had passed before a covetous spirit brought into the field other Comic Almanacs. A few years later and the Crockett Almanac was started, by us, and we thought the idea quite as novel as that of the Comic. But one season passed before Crockett Almanacs sprang up spontaneously, almost, in different parts of the Union.[7]

Addressed to "The Editorial Fraternity," the publisher's statement goes on to complain about the cheapening of price—and quality—of his competitors' almanacs, but the pertinent part of the statement is contained above. "Ten years since" is not quite accurate, for the *American Comic Almanac* was first published, in Boston, in 1831 (for 1832). Moreover, the statement may have been merely a publisher's self-praising blurb. But the Crockett connection becomes somewhat stronger when one realizes that both the *American Comic Almanac* and the *People's Almanac* first appeared over Charles Ellms's name, and were published by him until 1839, when they were taken over by Dickinson. Given this genesis, Dickinson certainly had the right to claim priority for these two almanacs, and given that right, we may give some credence to his claim of having originated the idea for the first Crockett almanac. Most important, such a possibility puts the "Nashville" imprint square in the heart of the northeast, suggesting that Charles Ellms not only originated "Ben Harding" but the "Davy Crockett" celebrated by folklorists of the 1930s.

A quick comparison between the *American Comic Almanac* and the Nashville imprints would seem to disprove any such assumption, for the title of Ellms's first comic almanac appears to be a contradiction in terms: as "American," it is distinctly British in derivation, with an emphasis on puns, witticisms, and exaggerated, nonsensical illustrations, that are quite sophisticated in execution for the most part. True, this is characteristic of much "American" humor of the day, as much "American" literature in the 1830s bore the impress of Scott and Goldsmith, a derivativeness that makes the sudden appearance of native humor all the more fresh and startling. But if we turn to Ellms's other almanac, the *People's* (first published in 1833), we pick up a very strong trace of American pungency. Like Ellms's maritime collections, the *People's* (as its very title suggests) is designed for a low level of literacy, and contains largely sensational and not comic material. But so do the earliest of the Nashville imprints, which give equal space to stories of hunting and adventure as to backwoods humor, interspacing these narratives with encyclopedic accounts of American wildlife. *The People's Almanac* follows a similar practice, and though the fauna, like the settings for the anecdotes, are exotic and not native, the layout of the publication, the style of the woodcuts, and the obviously popular appeal may be compared to the first four Crockett almanacs in the Meine edition bearing the Nashville imprint.

Moreover, there appears in the first number of *The People's Almanac* a woodcut that provides the most conclusive link between Ellms's acknowledged publications and the "Nashville" almanacs. Illustrating "the ferocity of alligators," it is a picture of an encounter between an alligator and a very large snake. This same woodcut, with strategic alterations, was used in the Crockett almanac for 1836, the first Nashville imprint in which Ben Harding appears, illustrating Ben's "method" for killing alligators (see page 40). This is Harding the Kentucky congressman, not the sailor, but the association of man and beast does put additional meaning on Ben's declaration in 1839 that though he cannot read, he understands pictures, "and could spell out your crocodile's tails from their heads when I see 'em drawed out in your [Crockett's] book." Like the other evidence linking Ellms to the Nashville imprints, this is circumstantial, but until similar correspondences between the first Crockett almanacs and other popular productions are detected, the iconographic evidence points directly to Charles Ellms as the originator of the Crockett "legend" in one of its most influential avatars, an early stage in its "folkloric" history. We can only lament that Ellms's letter book in the collections of the American Antiquarian Society covers the period 1833-34 only, giving out during the critical year in which he, in my opinion, undertook the publication of an American almanac comparable to *Poor Richard's* as a contribution to our popular literature.

There is in that regard one letter sent by Ellms that is particularly suggestive.[8] Written to a bookseller on October 4, 1833, it announces the publication of "The Hickory Almanac," which would be "a political work and advocate Mr Van Burens [*sic*] election to the Presidency," but which would also "contain a number of fine engravings and be perfectly respectable":

> The engravings will be many of them Historical such as the view of the battles of Bunker Hill & New Orleans, Portraits of Jefferson and other distinguished men of the democratic Party. It will be edited by a man who was in favour of Jackson when he was first nominated for the Presidency, in opposition to John Quincy Adams and Cra[w]-ford—But there will be some views of scenery and nautical history so as to instruct and amuse all readers—I think you might sell a great many if you had your name in the imprint. It will be continued annually with new Engravings executed expressly for the work.

As with a number of his other proposals, Ellms was overly optimistic concerning the future of the "Hickory Almanac," which was never published. Instead, perhaps, he hit upon the idea of a comic almanac that would profit from the rage for the eccentricities of another

Alligator from *The People's Almanac, 1834*, p. [33]. (American Antiquarian Society.)

Alligator from *Davy Crockett's Almanack, of Wild Sports in the West, And Life in the Backwoods. 1836* (Nashville, Tenn.: Published for the Author), p. [17]. (American Antiquarian Society.)

man "who was in favour of Jackson when he was first nominated for the Presidency" but who later reneged, and by that act lost his congressional seat and gained a permanent place in our pantheon of popular heroes.

Though hardly "perfectly respectable," the Crockett almanacs most certainly were designed "so as to instruct and amuse all readers" of whatever party. As in Ellms's first almanac, the short-lived *United States Working Man's* (1831), his democratic sympathies were completely in keeping with Whig rhetoric as voiced by Webster and Everett in their speeches to organizations of "working men," being designed to encourage greater productivity and programs of self-help. Thoroughly apolitical, the earliest Crockett almanacs were the products of commercial considerations, and seem to have been created in New England, as the introduction of the spurious "Ben Harding" certifies. Divorced from any direct contact with the trans-Alleghany zone, Ellms and his co-workers relied on Paulding's play and the *Sketches and Eccentricities* for their initial inspiration, then allowed their imaginations freer play as the "legend" gained momentum. Ellms's most distinctive contribution to American humor seems to be the wonderful woodcuts that give the Nashville almanacs their "folk" flavor, but in this graphic dimension there is evidence of metamorphosis also. Thus the cover for the first Nashville imprint differs little from the *American Comic Almanac* designed and published by Ellms the year before (see pages 42 and 43). It is with the second and subsequent covers that the "myth" begins to shape the matter, but as with the Crockett trimmed in wildcat fur for the almanac of 1837, the Kentucky connection remains both a derived and a literary one.

Whether Charles Ellms or some anonymous hack was responsible for creating the "legendary" Ben Harding we will probably never know, but as a Boston-bred attempt to manufacture a maritime, East Coast equivalent to the Southwest's Davy Crockett, the colorful sailor attests even further to the literary origins of our "popular" myths. Moreover, as an agent important to the transition from the comic tradition derived from Paulding's play to the increasingly violent mode developed by Turner and Fisher, Ben Harding bears witness that the movement had more to do with creating and then holding a popular audience than with the recording of authentic folk stories. As in pornography, an appetite having been created must be fed increasingly bizarre variations upon a basic situation, and as in an

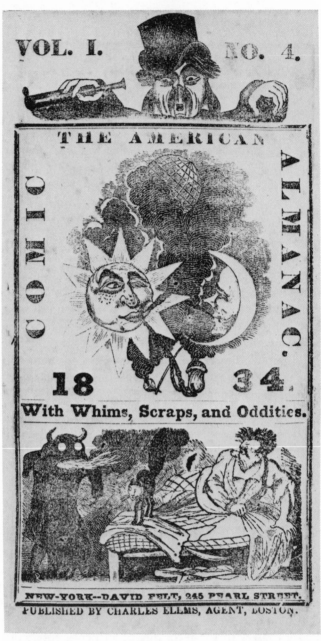

Cover page of *The American Comic Almanac, 1834*. (American Antiquarian Society.)

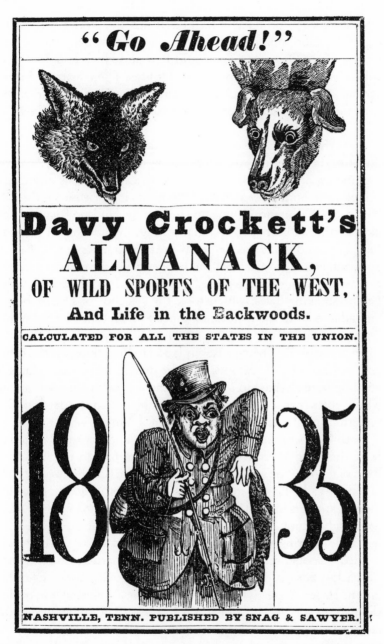

Cover page of the first Nashville *Crockett Almanack, 1835.* (American Antiquarian Society.)

adventure series on television, the settings and stories become increasingly exotic and unlikely. So *Wagontrain* sows Samurai warriors on the Great Plains and Davy and Ben and Huck and Tom have wild adventures amongst pirates and Injuns. These matters deserve further study, but any such investigation should at the start divest itself from the unquestioning acceptance of the Crockett almanacs as "folk" material.

As early as Joel Barlow's *Vision of Columbus*, the rise of a national literature in America was informed by a self-consciously "native" mythology, an eclectic mingling of American materials and classical, biblical, and, more latterly, folk motifs imported from the Old World. So Washington Irving, in shaping his Hudson River stories, gave mythic substance to regional settings by drawing on German *Volksagen*, and what was going on in the almanacs of the 1840s is an ephemeral version of what was happening in novels now regarded as classic examples of the genre.[9] At the one end we have Cooper's Leatherstocking Tales, which took the "legend" of Daniel Boone and adapted it to the historic romance as established by Sir Walter Scott—in effect developing an American literary counterpart to the legendary Rob Roy, being a Robin Hood in buckskins. At the other end we have *Moby-Dick*, in which the dreary, monotonous facts of whaling were elevated to a Gothic romance starring a mad captain whose epical heroics bear a closer resemblance to the deeds of Perseus than to the real-life adventures of a Yankee whaler.

Both Cooper and Melville were aware of and borrowed materials from the marginal zones of American literature, in the hope perhaps of gaining the widest possible readership. Of the two authors, Cooper was by far the more successful in capturing a popular audience, and it is interesting to note that when, in 1840, he returned to the adventures of Leatherstocking after the hiatus of more than a decade—during which time the "legend" of Davy Crockett was created—Cooper mixed his maritime and wilderness genres, giving his backwoods Pathfinder an old salt, Charles Cap, for companion, and in Jasper Western, the freshwater sailor, he created a hybrid of the two stereotypes. If Cooper was inspired to do so because of the advent in 1839 of Ben Harding as Crockett's seagoing friend, the match was paradoxical, for it was Cooper who, in *The Prairie*, gave Leatherstocking a partner called Paul Hover, a Kentuckian bee hunter who embodies many of Davy Crockett's "legendary" characteristics.

Since the congressman from Kentucky first appeared on the national scene in the year that Cooper's novel was published, we may doubt any direct connection—even though the bee hunter becomes a successful candidate for Congress. But when Richard Penn Smith set about, in 1836, to arrange for Crockett's apotheosis at the Alamo, he seems to have kept this coincidence in mind, for on the way to his tragic appointment with destiny, the Tennessee hero was given a bee hunter as guide. Such arrangements suggest that our premier mythic terrain, the trans-Mississippi West, was from the beginning a creation of the East, being almost entirely a territory of the literary imagination.

NOTES

1. Walter Blair, "Six Davy Crocketts," *Southwest Review*, XXV (July 1940), 443-62.

2. James A. Shackford, *David Crockett: The Man and the Legend* (Chapel Hill: Univ. of North Carolina Press, 1956), 248-49.

3. Richard M. Dorson, *Davy Crockett: American Comic Legend* (New York: Spiral Press for Rockland Editions, 1939), 76.

4. Lucius Powhattan Little, *Ben Hardin: His Times and Contemporaries, With Selections from his Speeches* (Louisville: Courier-Journal Job Printing Co., 1887), 63.

5. *Ibid.*, 288.

6. See also, Joshua C. Taylor, *America as Art* (Washington, D.C.: Published for the National Collection of Fine Arts by the Smithsonian Institution Press, 1976), 88-94, for a discussion (with reproductions) of the "Nashville" woodcuts aesthetically considered.

7. I should like to thank Mr. Marcus A. McCorison, director of the American Antiquarian Society, for providing me with a copy of this letter, which is quoted by Franklin J. Meine in his edition of the first four "Nashville" almanacs.

8. Quoted here with the permission of the American Antiquarian Society, Marcus A. McCorison, Director.

9. In "Root and Branch: Washington Irving and American Humor," *Nineteenth-Century Fiction*, 38 (1984), 415-26, I discuss this subject further.

3. The Hidden "Hero" of the Nashville Crockett Almanacs

Michael A. Lofaro

·

Few traces of a political bias appear in these small paper-bound volumes.

—Constance Rourke

The fictional Crockett—resembling the historical one who had died at the Alamo in 1836—was preeminently a political man, a congressman and an ardent advocate of the expansionist politics of the era of Manifest Destiny in the 1840s and 1850s.

—Catherine L. Albanese

The uniquely American figure that emerged from *The Sketches and Eccentricities of Col. David Crockett* in 1833 and the *Narrative of the Life of David Crockett* in 1834 grows to bizarre proportions in the series of Crockett Almanacs; from the cumulative myth is shaped the outlines of America's first superman, grinning with the silent humor of the day.

—Richard M. Dorson

Prometheus chained to the rock is not only myth but reality, while the image of Davy Crockett striding over the mountains, exempt from sacrifice for the piece of sunlight in his pocket, is our nation's self-defeating dream.

—Daniel G. Hoffman

The Davey [*sic*] Crockett myths flourished during the same years that fear of youthful masturbation reached its apex—the 1830s through the 1850s. . . . The Crockett myth offered the young men of Jacksonian America a fabled frontier, . . . , an outlet for hostility and frustration in the violence of Jingoism and racism, which it defined as the natural characteristic of the young white American male.

—Carroll Smith-Rosenberg

One of the primary reasons that assures the continuance of Davy Crockett as a quintessential American hero is his ability to be nearly all things to all people. So great a quantity of primary material from the popular press and media exists that when eager readers or critics delve into the various "autobiographies," tall tales in newspapers and especially almanacs, dime novels, plays, movies, and television shows, they invariably manage to discover a good deal of evidence to support the virtues or vices, the significance or lack of it, that they think or hope they might find in his character. Those who wish to extract a theme or thesis from the works are as blessed by the multiplicity of available interpretations as those who seek a synthesis are plagued by it. Fortunately or unfortunately, Davy is a true shape-shifter, a character who parallels the trickster-transformers of folklore in his ability to speak to the needs or desires of each person that seeks him in one or another of his avatars. His almost universal malleability for over a century and a half in the public eye simultaneously insures his heroic status and frustrates any attempt to posit either the relative importance of his overlapping factual and fictional lives or the meaning of his place in the American mind at any given time.

The extent of the problem is highlighted by the divergent critical commentaries that serve as an extended epigraph to this article.[1] They focus specifically upon the Crockett almanacs rather than upon the entire range of accessible materials and, in so doing, deal with only one of the six Davy Crocketts whom Walter Blair attempted to delineate in 1940.[2] The present exposition of yet another Davy Crockett, one hidden in the Nashville almanacs, however, hinges more upon fact than interpretation. There is no question that most scholars correctly view the comic Crockett almanacs of 1835 to 1856 as the single most influential genre in the creation and propagation of Davy's legendary life, but the full recognition of the problems that result from the ephemeral, naturally superannuated, and eminently disposable nature of these items is, for the most part, a series of unturned pages in Crockett scholarship. The then current popularity of the almanac tales has not translated into modern availability of the original texts.

The investigation of this dilemma begins with the early publishing history of the almanacs, and as such follows a complex trail that is constructed from the few printers' records that survive, together

with whatever internal evidence the works provide.[3] A few general-
izations are possible. The places of publication, which are cited on
the title page, are usually major cities such as Boston, Albany, Buffalo, New York, Philadelphia, Baltimore, Richmond, Louisville, Nashville, and New Orleans. Although the actual printing of all of the
almanacs but one takes place in Boston, New York, or Philadelphia,[4]
the stated origins of the original and variant imprints argue persuasively for a wide distribution east of the Mississippi. The intended
range of the almanacs is wider yet, if one judges by the intended
audience for the astronomical calculations. The publishers' hopes
of increasing sales by increasing the practical applicability of their
volumes are noted in the first two Nashville almanacs in which the
data is "Calculated for all the States in the Union" and the last two,
which take in "The Canadas" as well.[5] In general, the calculations
grow progressively more specific and expansive along with the growth
of the United States, so that by the last issue of 1856, the reader
of that Crockett almanac can survey data for the roughly rectangu-
lar area bounded by Massachusetts, Georgia, California, and Oregon.[6] In addition, if the number of surviving almanacs and variant
imprints can serve as a tentative index for distribution, then those
issued in the 1840s under the imprint of the publishing firm of
Turner & Fisher reached the widest audience. Perhaps not coinci-
dentally, this era also saw the flowering of the majority of the extremely audacious and sometimes vicious tall tales told by or about
Davy Crockett. Subsequent issues printed in the 1850s, however,
revealed a general displacement of Crockett from "his" almanacs as
the publisher reverted in part to the "amazing but true" type of factual frontier adventure and hunting tales that focused upon no particular figure and, in the main, emphasized stories about Kit Car-
son and by Mike Fink. After over twenty years of intense public
scrutiny, the Davy of fact and fiction was old news to the popular
press, and perhaps sensing this, Fisher and Brother(s), the sole publisher of the 1850 to 1856 almanacs, ended the series, but did so on
a superlative note. They presented an almanac completely domi-
nated by Crockett that contained some of the finest and most memorable tall tales ever printed under Davy's name.[7]

It was truly a fitting send-off for the comic hero, but a bit pre-
mature. The Davy of the almanacs never died; he hibernated until
his rediscovery by Constance Rourke and Richard M. Dorson in

the 1930s.[8] Their work with the then rare and now virtually unobtainable almanacs marked the beginning of modern scholarship's relationship to the Crockett tall tales.[9] This scarcity unintentionally placed Dorson's estimable selection of certain tales for inclusion in *Davy Crockett: American Comic Legend* in the unfortunate role of a sacred text. Writers, particularly those involved in producing juvenile and children's books and other popular works, often took Dorson's choices as the entire legend. Indeed, unless they wished to travel across the country, or at a minimum, to the Library of Congress and the American Antiquarian Society, his was likely the only large group of the fantastic stories available to them. There was no fault involved on either side in the matter, but it resulted in progressive projections from a limited base defined by a small portion of the entire canon of the tales. Dorson sought to present the reader with stories that he found attractive and, guided as well by the limitations of space, included those that he thought were "the best" rather than a representative selection of the entire panorama of the available adventures. The same factors operated in his selections from the woodcuts that originally accompanied nearly all the tales.[10] A final barrier to the use of Dorson's *Davy Crockett* by modern scholars was the result of the silent editorial method he employed to aid a general readership: "The present text by no means purports to be a faithful transcript of the almanacs. Liberties taken in wrestling with the text—and a good many are necessary—have been designed to produce clarity rather than consistency."[11]

For four decades the image of Crockett's tall tale adventures remained essentially one that was filtered through Richard M. Dorson's sense of humor and editorial principles. His was and is, through the reprinting of his book, the only available selection of any significant number of these stories.[12] In the past few years, however, a second generation of scholars has investigated more of the phenomenon that is the almanacs' Davy Crockett. They have expanded and altered Dorson's creation to a degree by revealing glimpses of a harsher, cruder, more sexual, and more racist protagonist who, in turn, provides the support for diverse reinterpretations of the values and views of his nineteenth-century publishers and readers.[13] The link which ties these critical perspectives together is that Davy, as the hero of the almanacs, is still elusive, malleable, and universal, a fun house-like mirror of his times and those of his interpreters.

While the present study provides another new perspective on Davy by examining the stories from the Nashville almanacs that Richard M. Dorson excluded from his collection, it also avoids some of the theses-oriented eclecticism of other investigations. This intentional focus upon a significant body of material rather than upon an argument allows the presentation of many more of the different facets of Davy's legendary life and, as a test case, underscores the obvious need for a complete scholarly edition of the tall tales for critical evaluation.[14]

The almanacs bearing the Nashville imprint and copyright were almost assuredly produced in Boston.[15] The seven issues were presented in two series, the first containing four numbers which treated the years 1835 through 1838 and the second containing three numbers for 1839 through 1841. They were chosen as a sample for this investigation for several reasons: the 1835 issue was the first Crockett almanac produced and proved the existence of a market to other publishers; the series possesses a certain unity of format and design not discernible in other of the early imprints over a reasonable span of years and has received the most critical attention; and finally, all seven items were available to the late Professor Dorson when he was selecting the stories for *Davy Crockett: American Comic Legend* at the American Antiquarian Society.

Although the thrust of this survey is illustrative rather than statistical, a simple tally and classification does demonstrate the extent of the hidden material. Of the one hundred and fifty-five tales in the Nashville almanacs, Dorson chooses to print only twenty-five. After the stories are divided, however, into four categories — those told by Crockett about himself, those told by Crockett about someone else, those told by someone else about Crockett, and those that do not involve Crockett in any way[16] — it becomes apparent that while Dorson appropriately chooses seventeen of his tales from the first category, he excludes forty-two others of the same type. Of the sixteen tales told by Davy about someone else, he records but one. Therefore, of these two types of tales, which constitute the "surefire" Crockett stories of the Nashville almanacs, the reader of Dorson's book sees just less than one-quarter in print.

Numbers, however, reveal nothing about merit or humor. Perhaps one-third of the omitted forty-two stories, for example, are not as tall as the majority of those included by Dorson, but some, if shorter on exaggeration and dialect, are longer on humor, albeit in a less aggressive fashion. Several attempts at having different groups rate the stories as to appeal lead to the conclusion that the question of which stories are "the best," to use Dorson's term, is deeply mired in the subjectivity of personal opinions and verges upon the unanswerable. Given the present confines of space, it is also impossible to replicate that experiment by reprinting the forty-two hidden stories that Davy told about himself, much less the eighty-eight additional omissions in the other categories. What is possible, through a roughly chronological approach to the Nashville almanacs and with some indulgence of sustained quotation, is the tracing of certain patterns in the exclusions to produce a sketch that places a significantly different face upon Dorson's portrait of the legendary Crockett.

The first Nashville almanac does little to reveal Crockett as a "ring-tailed roarer." Although the cover (see page 43, Chapter 2) and the double-page woodcut of Davy's house (see page 52) promise much, the issue itself yields little legend. The "'Go Ahead' Reader" introduction, which Dorson includes, gives only a hint of the Crockett soon to be created, when Davy states the now familiar boast that he "can run faster,—jump higher,—squat lower,—dive deeper,—stay under longer,—and come out drier, than any man in the whole country" (1835, p. 2). These claims are modest in comparison with those of subsequent introductions. There are also no truly unbelievable adventures and very little of the backwoods dialect marked by outrageous coinages and bastardizations of words that one expects when delving into Crockett's legendary life. Instead, those stories devoted to Crockett center upon biographical and pseudobiographical details usually taken from Crockett's *Narrative* and his *Sketches and Eccentricities*.[17] Many of the other stories are descriptions of wildlife and of other interesting or unusual occurrences in the backwoods.

It is in the 1836 Nashville almanac that "The Legend Full-Blown," as Dorson terms it, first emerges.[18] A quick glance at the cover which depicts Crockett's unique "Method of Wading the Mississippi" (see page 53) provides an image of Davy that mirrors the new set of tales. Both have grown a good deal taller. The use of the long crutches and stilts that allow Davy to keep his feet dry and whiskey undiluted parallel the growth in exaggeration and dialect in the stories. In the "'Go Ahead' Reader" introduction to the almanac, the Colonel's language takes on the familiar backwoods diction and twang

"View of Col. Crockett's Residence in West Tennessee," from *Davy Crockett's Almanack, of Wild Sports of the West, And Life in the Backwoods. 1835* (Nashville, Tenn.: Snag & Sawyer), pp. [24–25]). (University of Tennessee Library.)

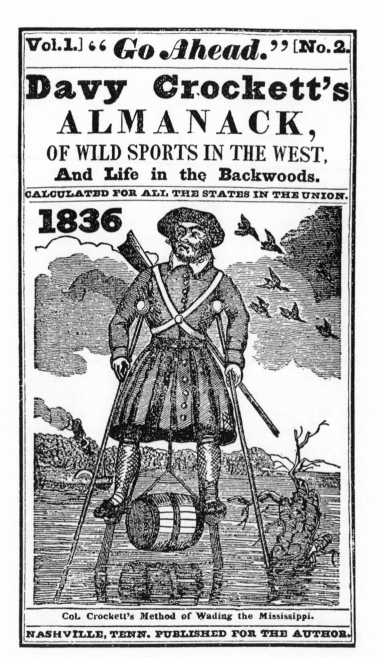

"Col. Crockett's Method of Wading the Mississippi." Cover page of the 1836 *Almanack*. (Caxton Club, Chicago.)

(as conceived by Boston literary hacks) when he discusses the success of his previous almanac which "has gone ahead like a steamboat": "I don't doubt I shall not only be able to tree a little change, but also a little fame into the bargain. It isn't every member of Congress that knows how to *authorise* as well as to speechify. And it remains to be larnt whether I shall go down to posteriors with the most credit as a Congressman, or a writer." On the more practical side, the publishers have Davy recognize his limitations and also show his concern for the accuracy of the data in the almanac's calculations by allowing him to hire "a very great *Gastronomer*" to do the work for him (1836, p. 2).

Although this almanac continues the tradition of non-Crockett hunting stories and descriptions of animals, it contains three noteworthy tall tales told by Davy about himself that Dorson chooses to ignore in favor of a long story by Ben Harding, one about Judy Coon, and two short fillers not related to Crockett. In "The Boat Race," Davy defeats a bragging Yankee "who was at least seven foot high, and as broad between the two eyes as a New-Orleans cat-fish" by half the length of the course by surreptitiously tying his canoe to a huge wildcat that he trapped specifically for that purpose. The Yankee refused to pay the five dollar bet until, as Crockett said, "when he seed me sharpening my thumbnail on a whetstone, and twisting my forefinger into the right turn for playing with his hair, he thought best to hand over, and own himself served up by a Kentuckian" (1836, p. 3).[19]

The omission of the other two tall tales perhaps reveals one of Dorson's unconscious criteria for selection—an aversion to retelling those tales that presented Davy in his birthday suit. The first, "Crockett's Fight with a Cat-Fish," centers upon his epic underwater battle with the twelve-foot long "monstratious great Cat-Fish, better known by the name of a Mississippi Lawyer." At the height of the combat, the knife-wielding Davy grabbed the huge fish "right around his body, and rammed one arm down his throat, while I tried to stab him with the other hand—then I tell you the fire flew." Crockett triumphs, but has his breeches torn "clear off" him by the fish at the beginning of the struggle (1836, pp. 6–7). In the other story, "A Love Adventure and uproarious fight with a Stage Driver," Crockett learns the location of his stage driver's love nest, doubles back to it, but is unexpectedly interrupted by him in the midst of a two-day affair with his mistress in the loft of her house. Davy tells it best himself:

> Zounds! here was a pretty predikyment. I must either play possum by jumping out of the window and running off, or jump down and fight. I found I must do the latter, as the window was so small I could'nt get out of it. As quick as the critter saw me, he flew into such a rage that he crooked up his neck and neighed like a stud horse, and dared me down. Says I, stranger! I'm the boy that can double up a dozen of you. I'm a whole team just from the roaring river.— I've rode through a crab apple orchard on a streak of lightning. I've squatted lower than a toad; and jumped higher than a maple tree; I'm all brimstone but my head, and that's aquafortis. At this he fell a cursing and stamping, and vowed he'd make a gridiron of my ribs to roast my heart on. I kicked the trap door aside, and got sight at the varmint; he was madder than a buffalo, and swore he'd set the house on fire. Says I take care how I lite on you; upon that I jumped right down upon the driver, and he tore my trowsers right off of me. I got hold of his whiskers and gave them such a twitch that his eyes stuck out like a lobster's. He fetched me a kick in the bowels that knocked all compassion out of them. I was driv almost distracted, and should have been used up, but luckily there was a poker in the fire which I thrust down his throat, and by that means mastered him. Says he, stranger you are the yellow flower of the forest. If ever you are up for Congress again, I'll come all the way to Duck river to vote for you. Upon this I bade them good morning, and proceeded on my journey. This adventure I never told to Mrs. Crockett. (1836, pp. 43–44)

Despite many parallels to combat in classical heroic narrative,[20] in this story Davy would have preferred to run rather than to fight, but the small window made flight impossible. The view of a Crockett who believes discretion is the better part of valor is as rare in the almanacs as is the naked Crockett in Dorson's edition of the tales. Both add more of a human dimension to Davy's legendary characterizations.

The picture of Crockett displayed on the cover of the 1837 Nashville almanac is apparently copied from an engraving of Ambrose Andrews's portrait of the actor James Hackett when he played the lead in James Kirke Paulding's popular play *The Lion of the West* (see page 107, Chapter 5). The character, Nimrod Wildfire, was conceived

as a Crockettesque frontier figure and soon lost his identity to become an inseparable part of the Crockett legend.[21] The growth of the legend is visually underscored by the many faces Davy is given on just the covers of the first three Nashville almanacs. He is Hackett as Nimrod Wildfire in 1837, a full-bearded figure in a broad hat crossing the Mississippi in 1836, and perhaps even the comic fisherman in a top hat with a fish dangling from his finger in 1835 (see page 43, Chapter 2).[22] The reader may leaf through the inner pages of each of these issues and find more than a dozen other Crockett faces as well, because the almanacs are not consistent in their portrayals within a particular volume, much less between years. His fictional features never closely correspond to the actual and in their extreme variation, whether due to artistic intent, license, or laziness on the part of the illustrators, they graphically demonstrate the almanac Crockett's affinities with the shape-shifting trickster characters of folklore — the coyote of American Indian tradition, the spider of African tradition, and the rabbit of Afro-American tradition.

The "'Go Ahead' Reader" section of the 1837 almanac, which Dorson omits, is quintessential Crockett in its bald lies even though it does not overflow with the outrageous coinages of his idiom. Here Davy tells the reader that he is going to Texas to "go through the Mexicans like a dose of salts" and, to keep the illusion of the authenticity of his authorship of the almanacs alive in light of his death in 1836, notes that he has left behind enough material for several more issues. This section also contains an expanded version of the story in which Crockett wrings the tail off Halley's comet to save the United States from destruction. Unlike the newspaper variants of several years earlier, this tale focuses upon the aftermath of the deed. Davy notes that he has again secured help, this time that of "a *lit*-arary friend . . . to git the '*Gastronomical* calculations.'" He wants "nothing more to do with Gastronomy," and the "see-less-tial bodies" for, as he says,

> I was appointed by the President to stand on the Alleghany Mountains and wring the Comet's tail off. I did so, but got my hands most shockingly burnt, and the hair singed off my head, so that I was as bald as a trencher. I div right into the Waybosh river, and thus saved my best stone blue coat and grass green small clothes. With the help of Bear's grease, I have brought out a new crop, but the hair grows in bights and tufts, like hussuck grass in a meadow, and it keeps in

such a snarl, that all the teeth will instantly snap out of an ivory
comb when brought within ten feet of it. (1837, p. 2)

Although Dorson does include a number of tales on the women
in Crockett's life, "A Tongariferous Fight with an Alligator" from
the 1837 almanac is not among them. Davy is confined to bed with
a fever, his sons are not home, and the giant bull alligators have
squared off and again chosen his rooftop to do battle for the females
in their mating ritual, at least those who were not too busy trying
to get the family pigs out of the hollow log in which Crockett stop-
pered them up at night. Davy and his wife snared one of the com-
batants by the hind leg from his sickbed. In the morning,

> The women then slacked the rope a little and made it fast round
> a hickory stump, when my oldest darter took the tongs and jumped
> on his back, when she beat up the "devil's tattoo" on it, and gave
> his hide a real "rub a dub" [see page 58]. He found it was sharp work
> for the eyes, as the devil said, as a broad-wheeled waggon went over
> his nose. My wife threw a bucket of scalding suds down his throat,
> which made him thrash round as though he was sent for. She then
> cut his throat with my big butcher knife. He measured *thirty seven
> feet* in length. (1837, pp. 8, 10)

The first of two other hidden tales in the 1837 almanac also shows
the "true grit" of Davy's family and friends. In "Perilous Adventure
with a Black Bear," Crockett is unarmed and nearly overtaken by
a large bear before he can reach his cabin, but his demise is delayed
first when his dog Rough seizes onto a hindquarter of the animal,
then by an axe-wielding neighbor, and finally by his loyal spouse
(see page 59). Davy could not have been prouder:

> My wife, although she could but just use her left hand as it was hardly
> healed, as she had lost her thumb and fore finger. They were bit off
> by a cat fish as she attempted to skin one alive. But she caught up
> a hickory rail, and as the bear rushed at her with his mouth wide
> open she ran it down his throat. He corfed as if he had swallowed
> something the wrong eend first. His attention was now taken from
> me, and although completely broken winded, I turned and jumped
> on to the varmint's back, when I reached his vitals with my big
> butcher; and after a most desperate contest, in which we were all
> more or less bitten and my wife had her gown torn nearly off of her,

"A Tongariferous Fight with an Alligator," from *Davy Crockett's Almanack, of Wild Sports in the West, Life in the Backwoods, & Sketches of Texas. 1837* (Nashville, Tennessee: Published by the heirs of Col. Crockett), p. [9]. (University of Tennessee Library.)

we succeeded in killing him. He was a real fat one and weighed six hundred lbs. (1837, p. 19)

The second tale is a fine Crockett yarn entitled "Colonel Crockett's Account of his swimming the Mississippi," which is accompanied by the woodcut "Col. Crockett Annoyed by Varmints when Crossing the Mississippi" (see page 60). Trying to retrieve a goose with a broken wing to add to the three others already gathered for his dinner, Davy strips, dives in, and gives chase, only to find himself pursued by a bear and a wolf. He thought he had taken the necessary precautions by rubbing himself "thoroughly with skunk's grease" to keep "the Alligators and wild cats at a distance as they can't bear the smell of this crittur," but was proved wrong:

> How to get rid of these critturs was the next thing. I div down in a slantindicular direction so as to come up beyond them. When under water an amphibious river calf saw me, and chased me to the surface. Upon breaking water they all began to chase me; luckily there

"A Desperate Contest with a Great Black Bear," from *Davy Crockett's Almanack, of Wild Sports in the West, Life in the Backwoods, & Sketches of Texas. 1837* (Nashville, Tennessee: Published by the heirs of Col. Crockett), p. [18]. (University of Tennessee Library.)

was a planter a few rods distance. I made towards it, and grasping one arm round it caught up a stick of drift wood and prepared to defend myself; upon the wolf's coming within reach, with a good blow over the nose he went off howling. The bear came on, in the most rageriferous manner, so that I was obliged to dodge round the planter, but I gave him some startling raps, when luckily a steam boat seeing this strange sight bore down upon us and just before they reached me the engineer put a rifle ball through the bear's head, and one of the boatmen speared the wolf with a boat hook. And I stunned the River Calf with a blow of my club, so that he was taken. I was invited on board, but as there was ladies on board I did not like to appear in a state of natur, so I dove under the boat and swam ashore. (1837, p. 20)

It should be noted that my selection of tales in which Davy is "in a state of natur," his wife's gown is "torn nearly off her," and his pants are torn off both by the stage driver and the "monstracious great Cat-Fish" had nothing to do with the presence of nudity in

59

"Col. Crockett Annoyed by Varmints when Crossing the Mississippi," from *Davy Crockett's Almanack, of Wild Sports in the West, Life in the Backwoods, & Sketches of Texas. 1837* (Nashville, Tennessee: Published by the heirs of Col. Crockett), p. [21]. (University of Tennessee Library.)

the stories. These were simply the tales that Richard M. Dorson chose not to print. The possible correlation of nakedness to exclusion continues, although on a diminished scale, in the 1838 to 1841 Nashville almanacs and suggests that Dorson's Davy hides something of the more primordial, savage Crockett behind civilization's cloak.[23]

1838 was, in fact, a poor year for Crockett tales in the Nashville almanacs (see page 61), even though the legendary Davy raises sparks once again in the "Go Ahead Reader" introduction to the volume as he explains his difficulties as an author:

> I was born in a cane brake, cradled in a sap trough, and clouted with coon skins; without being choked by the weeds of education, which do not grow *spontinaciously*—for all the time that I was troubled with *youngness*, my cornstealers were *na'*trally used for other purposes than holding a pen; and *rayly* when I try to write my elbow keeps coming round like a swingle-tree, and it is easier for me to tree a varmint, or swallow a nigger, than to write. (1838, p. 2)

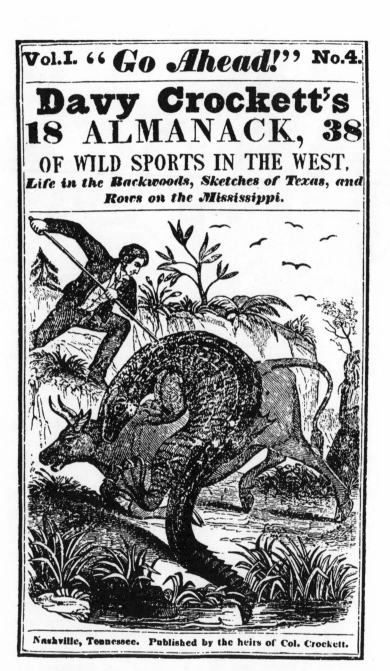

[Crockett Skewers an Alligator Feeding on a Steer.] Cover page of the 1838 *Almanack*. (Caxton Club, Chicago.)

"A Narrow Escape from a Snake," from *Davy Crockett's Almanack, of Wild Sports in the West, Life in the Backwoods, Sketches of Texas and Rows on the Mississippi. 1838* (Nashville, Tennessee: Published by the heirs of Col. Crockett), p. [25]. (University of Tennessee Library.)

In addition to this section, only two full-length dialect tales were printed. Dorson records "A Riproarious Fight on the Mississippi River," in which Crockett instigates a fight and is fought to a draw by Jo Snag, but omits "A Snake Fight and Chase" (see above). In this story, Crockett recounts the herculean battle between two huge rattlesnakes, one brown and one "yaller," but is rousted from his admiring observations after he cuts the rattle off the defeated "yaller" snake for a trophy. For

> to my surprise, as I did so, I felt his tail slip through my fingers, and saw that the poor fellow had come to, and was moving off. But cutting them off, I made 'em rattle, and such another squall as the old brown did set up. He hadn't been mad before; he now doubled himself up in a hoop, and made after me. I streaked it; the faster I run, the more noise I made, and looking behind, I saw him rolling on; every time he turned over, his eyes come up like two coals of fire in a dark night. He gained upon me, so I dropped the rattles, and

as I did so, he settled down upon 'em, and spun round just like he was a top. I thought it was a good time to get clear, so I slipped off, and continued my way home. (1838, pp. 24, 26–27)

The motif of the hoop snake is a familiar one in folklore and helps to elongate the already tall descriptions of the fight Crockett termed a "rough, roar, and tumble for life" (1838, p. 26).

The 1839 almanac initiated the second series of Nashville imprints, those cited as "Published by Ben Harding" (see page 64). Crockett's screamer of a friend, formerly a congressman from Kentucky, is now a peg-legged sailor whose later adventures compete and, in the opinion of some critics, outdo those of Crockett himself at his own audacious game.

Due to certain thematic consistencies, it is useful to treat the 1839, 1840, and 1841 almanacs together. The 1839 almanac is Dorson's favorite of the Nashville issues; however, he still omits a number of excellent tales including the one depicted on the cover, "Col. Crockett and the Elk." Davy's shot missed the elk at ten paces and he was taken for a ride on its antlers.

I wish I may be shot if the way he carried me through the prairie war not a caution to steamboats and rail roads. I never had such a ride in my life. It war not long before I got out my butcher, to make an experiment on his jugular; but I war so ashamed of missing him that I couldn't use it. Now I'm not exactly a feather on a scruple of conscience, and my gentleman soon found that if he war a hoss I war a rough rider, and so he lay down with me and I got off. "Stranger," sez I, "I never said the hard word yet, and so I wont give up whipt; but if you're satisfied so am I, and we wont say another word about it." I thought this was doing the civil thing by him, but he gave a snort like a safety valve and streaked it with his tail up, as much as to say he didn't like my company; which in my mind was a kinder Natchez-under-the-hill spessimen of his broughten up. This was the only thing in my life I ever war ashamed of, for the critter war as big as a four year old colt. I might as well have missed the broadside of a barn. (1839, pp. 25–26)

Two years later in the 1841 issue Davy vindicates his performance in another run-in with an elk. Although entering the contest is the farthest thing from Crockett's mind, he acquits himself fairly well as an unintentional combatant. The tale is rendered here in full be-

Vol. 2.] "GO AHEAD!!" [No. 1.

THE CROCKETT ALMANAC
1839.

An Unexpected Ride on the Horns of an Elk. See Page 25.

Containing Adventures, Exploits, Sprees & Scrapes in the West, & Life and Manners in the Backwoods.

Nashville, Tennessee. Published by Ben Harding. See Page. 2

"An Unexpected Ride on the Horns of an Elk." Cover page of the 1839 *Almanac*. (University of Tennessee Library.)

cause it is just the type of story that seems to fall short of Dorson's notion of "the best." There are no godlike heroic deeds or adventures, no epic battle, and no exaggeration on a grand scale. Yet "A Ride" is a delightfully preposterous cumulative tale that shows Davy in less than complete control.

Thar war a little ditty that happent the fust time I war sot up for Kongress, that I never telled noboddy nothing about; partly bekase every boddy knowed it, and partly bekase I war intermined to keep it a secret. Davy Crocket never duz any thing he is ashamed on, this I did not do myself, for I tried not to do it. I war going to election and had my rifle with me, with my dog Tiger, with two bottles of white face in my pockets. When I got about ½ way thar, and war in the forrest, I seed a cattymount up in a tree, and I clum up to git a fare shot at the cretur, and told tiger to be on hand if he war wanted. I war got on to the nixt branch to the won that the varmint war on, when he jumped down on to the limb and lit close to my elbow with his mouth to my ear, as if he war going to whisper sumthin mity private. I thort I war a gone sucker, but jist at that minnit the limb cracked and snapped off. I didn't stop to see what becum of the cattymount, but I went down, and wood ha' gone into the mud, only thar war a big elk under the tree, and I lit upon his hind parts, and he give a rankantankerous jump which slid me down betwixt his horns like a gal in a sighed saddle, and then he put in all he knew. I like to ha' got my branes nocked out by the branches, and the way he went thro the forrest war like a driving snow storm.— All the trees and rocks seemed to be running the tother way; and Tiger couldn't keep up with us, and his pesky noise only maid the cretur run faster. I held on upon my rifle, and I couldn't help thinking of Kurnill Tonson's mounted riflemen only I shood ha' found it hard work to taik aim, bekase the cretur woodn't give me a chance. Howsever he soon begun to git out of the forrest, and then I war terribly ashamed for feer sum human wood see me, but I coodn't see them as every thing looked streeked as if the American flag war spred over all natur. We went ahed this way till all at wonst I seed thar war sumthing befour us, but I didn't have time to xamine it as we war jumping on like chain litening when it skips down the Mississippy. I soon found what it war, for we dove thro the door of a house, and when the door flew off its hinges, it went agin the wall so hard it stuck thar.—Then the elk pitched agin the door opposite, and tho it war locked, yet that flew into the middle of the flore, and upset a cat, and a table, and a candle that had been used to melt seeling wax. A young feller and a gal that war korting thar jumped up haff skeered to deth.

I railly thort this war the eend of my travels, but the pesky varmint wheeled about, and went hed fourmost out the door agin, and shot ahead on the jump, four mile further, till he cum to the little eend of the Little Fork of Great Skunk's Liver River. We went rite thro the mob for the poles war held ther, and every boddy pulled off their hats and gin 3 cheers for Krockett, and that made me wrathy, and graniverous as a parched corn; bekase they didn't try to stop the varmint at all. But they all hurried out of the way, and bauled— Hurrah for Crockett! Won feller from down East sed he sposed that war the way that our candydates war *run for Kongress.* I spose the elk war so skeered that he didn't no what he war about. But it helped my lection, for they all thort it war an invention of my own, for to gratify the public. The elk had only gone a small peace further when we past by a store whar I war in dett a few dollars, and it war kepp by a Yankee, and he thort I war running away from my creditors. So he razed a hue and cry arter me, and in a minnit the hole village of Apple Toddy Creek war razed. They skeered the elk fust won way and then the tother, and he swang about and jostled me so that it skraped all the skin off my hinder eend, and I begun to feer if I got a seat in Kongress it wouldn't be of no use to me. Howsever the court war settin at the time, and the people skeered the cretur so that it run that way, and as the court house door was open, it run rite in. As soon as the judge seed me, sez he, "Thar's Crockett now! We war jist wanting yer for a witniss in this ere kase of the Widder Strapup. You've cum in the nick of time."

The lawyer that war pleeding agin the widder stared open his eyes, and sez he, "I bleeve it is the Nick o'time, for the devil must ha' brot him to spile my kase."

I jumped rite off the elk, and gin my evidence, and that saved the widder's property; so she took the elk under her protexion, and arter he war broke, she used to ride him to meetin. (1841, pp. 21–22)

Interestingly, the cover story of the 1840 almanac also carries the theme of Crockett's less than stellar heroic performances. Imagine his ignominy when he is scared by an owl (see page 67). In the dead of night, Davy is startled by the bird's cry and "jumpt seven foot high." Thinking back on the fright, he stated: "I cant say that I run so fast as I have run afore now; but it coodn't hardly be said that I waulked, for I stradled so wide that I tore my trousers." After he

Vol. 2.]   "GO AHEAD!!"   [No. 2.

THE CROCKETT ALMANAC
1840.

Whoo-Whoo-Whoop!

Crockett scared by an Owl....See page 2.

**Containing Adventures, Exploits, Sprees
& Scrapes in the West, &
Life and Manners in the Backwoods.**

Nashville, Tennessee. Published by Ben Harding.

"Crockett scared by an Owl." Cover page of the 1840 *Almanac*. (University of Tennessee Library.)

killed it by shooting at the sound of the cry and discovered the nature of his mortal foe, Davy said: "I spose awl the oaths I swore then,
if they war straitened out, wood reech cleen acrost the Mississippi.
It war the fust time that I had run from a cretur not so big as myself;
and I felt stripid as a rainbow" (1840, p. [2]).

In "Tussel with a Bear," the cover story for the last Nashville almanac, Davy recovers from his defeats to show his true grit when
wrestling with a bear in "Rattle-snake Swamp" (see page 69). He has
set out to kill something for the next day's dinner, when a Methodist parson is coming to call, but is grabbed from behind, as he tells
it, by "a great bear that war hugging me like a brother, and sticking
as close to me as a turcle to his shell." His satisfaction at having
his future meal literally in hand quickly dwindles, however, for
"though there war to be won dinner made out between us, it war
amazing uncertain which of us would be the dinner and which would
be the eater." The ensuing rough-and-tumble looks bad for Davy:
"the bear had no notion of loosening his grip on me. He shoved
his teeth so near my nose that I tried to cock it up out of his way,
and then he drew his tongue across my throat to mark out the place
where he should put his teeth." Davy manages to free his right hand,
pull out his "big butcher," and the "way it went into the bowels of
the varmint war nothing to nobody. It astonished him most might-
ily. He looked as if he thought it war a mean caper, and he turned
pale. If he didn't die in short time arterwards, then the Methodist
parson eat him alive, that's all. When I cum to strip, arter the affair
war over, the marks of the bear's claws war up and down on my
hide to such a rate that I might have been hung out for an American flag. The stripes showed most beautiful" (1841, pp. 9–10).

While the conclusion of this particular tale has the naked Crockett revealing the marks of violence from his "tussel" with the bear
in terms of a savage nationalism, there is little political partisanship
in the Nashville almanacs. The story, however, is similar in form,
outcome, and language to many of those included in Dorson's edition.[24] Davy is in danger, but in charge. He is in an aggressive direct
role in this hand-to-claw combat rather than an unwilling passen-
ger on the horns of an elk. The humor of the piece, as such, springs
not from an inherently funny situation, but from the disproportion
arising between the "frontierese" that Davy uses to describe on the
one hand both the bear's death in terms of the parson's meal and

Vol. 2.]   "GO AHEAD!!"   [No. 3.

THE CROCKETT ALMANAC 1841.

Tussel with a Bear. See page 9.

Containing Adventures, Exploits, Sprees & Scrapes in the West, & Life and Manners in the Backwoods.

Nashville, Tennessee. Published by Ben Harding.

"Tussel with a Bear." Cover page of the 1841 *Almanac.* (American Antiquarian Society.)

his wounds in terms of the flag and the savage action of the battle on the other. The language of the story itself is rather conservative. The inept pomposity and fumbling backwoods attempts at grandiloquence that turn on coinages such as "Gastronomer," "slantindicular," "tetotaciously," "exflunctified," "rageriferous," "spontinaciously," and other, even wilder, concoctions and concatenations are all but absent. This type of "dialect" humor and the humor of extreme exaggeration are two of the mainstays of the Crockett tales and rightly hold a strong place in Dorson's edition. What is often missing in Dorson's *Davy Crockett* is the humor that grows as the tale progresses, the humor that marks Davy's second ride on the elk. Subtler only by comparison, it too deserves attention. Note, for example, how the humor builds in the following extract from "Scrape with the Indians." The necessary background is that Davy is in pursuit of a peddler whom he fed and sheltered only to have the "spektakle" salesman talk him out of his money, use his provisions and whiskey like a "famine manufacturer," and then steal his powder horn and shot bag to boot. When Davy discovered the deed he said:

> That made me so mad that I split every button off my trowsers, and I swore so hard that it like to ha' lifted the roof of the house rite off. I sallied out arter the feller. I had a smart chance of small shot in my rifle, and ment to make his rump look like a huckkleberry pudding.
>
> I had gone a good peace thro' the forrest before noon, when I heered a noise behind me. I lookt and seed a passel of Injuns. They war a good ways off, but they war cumin rite toward the place where I sot. At last they seed me, and gave a whoop and run to where I war like a whole herd of buffaloes. I cut dirt around amongst sum bushes, and then I seed that one eend of a log was open, and the open eend war hid in the bushes. But I found the hole war very small. So I stuck my finger down my throte and threw up all the vittles that war in my bowels. But I war not small enuff yet, and I tride to think of the meanest thing I ever did, so as I might feel small. By them means I got in a proper fix for squeezing in, but arter all it war like spiking a cannon. They flew around in a blusteriferous temper when they seed I war gone, and then they sot down on the log. Jist at that moment I felt I war going to sneeze, and I war afeared if I did it would split the log rite open. By good luck I had a little tract in my pockit put out by the Anti-snuff-taking Society. I stuffed one leef of it up my nose and that hindered me from sneezing. (1840, p. 29)

As the Indians push the log into the river, sit astride it, and make for the opposite shore, Crockett rolls the log over and reaches land first. The episode eventually ends in a standoff with Davy and the Indians hurling insults at each other (see page 72).

The reason that Dorson does not treat this tale of the literally shape-shifting Crockett likely also hinges, as it does with a number of the previous stories, on its less than satisfactory conclusion. This story has no struggle, no victor, and essentially no hero, not even one who outwits the enemy. Davy knows that when he and the log are saturated with water that he would "swell, so thar would be no gitting out, for I war wedged pritty tight already" and he is also under water holding his breath. Not wishing to drown, he must strike out for the shore. His only choice is the way in which he exits the log. He believes he cannot slip out unnoticed; his sole alternative is to dump the Indians into the river and reach the riverbank before they realize that their prey capsized them. To credit Davy with great craft or guile in selecting the one course of action actually available to him is rather farfetched. Here he is simply not the comic superman that Dorson evidently found so appealing in his reading of the almanacs and it is not surprising that the Davy who runs and hides from Indians only to secure a draw in the encounter does not appear in *Davy Crockett: American Comic Legend.* Recall Dorson's second stated reason for his selection of material: "to represent the more popular anecdotal themes of the almanacs by the chapter groupings." The hidden Nashville Crockett finds no home in chapters entitled "The Legend Full-Blown," "Ring-Tailed Roarers," "Davy Conquering Man," "Davy Conquering Beast," and "Davy in Lighter Moments,"[25] for the themes this Davy expresses are other than those that Dorson features as "more popular" and "anecdotal."

There are certain other patterns that emerge from Dorson's discrimination of which tales are "the best." In "Ride on the Back of a Buffalo" in the 1839 almanac, the reader is introduced to a Crockett who saves Indians' lives (1839, p. 10). Davy even goes so far in "Indian Notions" as to describe a brave and his small daughter as more than "varmints": "They lookt more like human creturs with human feelings, than any of the breed that I ever noed before." Furthermore, when the Indian tells Davy the sentimental tale of his profound grief over the loss of his wife and his momentary but satisfactory reunion with her when he temporarily penetrated the other

"Scrape with the Indians," from *The Crockett Almanac, 1840. Containing Adventures, Exploits, Sprees & Scrapes in the West, & Life and Manners in the Backwoods* (Nashville, Tennessee: Published by Ben Harding), p. 24. (University of Tennessee Library.)

world because of his great love, the Colonel could only say: "Davy Krockitt is none of your whimperers, but if I didn't drop tears as big as a bullet, I hope I may be shot" (1840, pp. 12–13). This compassionate Crockett was one that Dorson chose to ignore.

Also omitted are certain tales with vulgar expressions and offensive scenes. In "Colonel Crockett and the Mud Turtles," for example, Davy comes upon Indians cutting the heads off a nest of snapping turtles and is bitten by one of their dogs who won't let go of his leg. He looked at the still-snapping severed heads, "picked up one of the biggest heads on the eend of my rammer and cum behind the dog and put it to his tail, and it cotched hold and hung on like grim death to a dead nigger." The end of the story has Davy responding to an Indian's challenge to eat the still-beating heart of a turtle if he is not too squeamish to do so and culminates in a less offensive slur. Davy "swallered three of the turkles harts right off" and said "I'd done it if I'd knowed they'd been rank pisen. They didn't kill me, though I own I feel pretty considerable squawmish every time I think of a snapping turkle, and I felt as if all the Paddies in Murphy Land war dancing an Irish jig in my belly for three days arter" (1839, pp. 30–31).[26]

One of the groups which Davy has the least use for are Yankees. In "Rare Economy" he rails against them all as cheapskates, especially peddlers and preachers, and understandably bristles when "an oncivilized Ingin savage" mistakes him for a Yankee in the conclusion to the second part of the story.

You see, stranger, I war out on the trail of a Cherokee war party, what had been seducing away our hosses and cavorting among our wimmen with their tomahawks and skalpers, and sich like innocent amusements as cums nateral to 'em, and we cum up to 'em jist as they had crossed Red Warrior Creek whar it ar all of a quarter of a mile wide, and we coodn't get across at 'em no way we cood fix it. So they cum down to the edge of their convenient namesake and dared us to cum over and hav our hair cut, which made us hugaceously mad, as who woodn't be, to heer himself abused when his hands war tied? Thar war won devil's kitchen tho', that made me more savagerous than all the rest, for he got into a pecan tree, and shewed us his posterum, if it ar not ondecent to say so, and very politely asked us to kiss it. Now I've known of many such invites being given, but I never knowed noboddy accept none on 'em. Howsever I felt amazen wolfy at what he said and done, and took a blizzard at him. It war a long shot and all depended on luck, and I had my own share on it and another man's too. The screeching varmint tumbled out of the tree and never stirred agin, and his brother rogues ran away, arter they had a comfortable howl over him. When we crossed over we found that the Ingin's hide war not broke and not a drop of blood had cum from him [see page 74].

Sum time arter, when peace war made with 'em, I war at the council, and one of the painted pagans talked the skimmage over. One of the beloved men, said that he had always heered the Yankees war a transcendental saving people; but he never knowed how stingy they war till he seen one on 'em shoot his brother Cockahoop Zigzacker across the Red Warrior without spiling his skin. He'd seen the ants and the bees lay up corn and honey for the winter, he sed, "but he a kind o' thort thar war no kritter but a Yankee that wood hav been

"Rare Economy," from *The Crockett Almanac, 1841. Containing Adventures, Exploits, Sprees & Scrapes in the West, & Life and Manners in the Backwoods* (Nashville, Tennessee: Published by Ben Harding), p. 7. (American Antiquarian Society.)

so particklar about his leather." The brute thort I meant to tan his brother's skin or sell it, as he had seen the Yankees do by all other skins. Now, stranger, I'll leave it to you if sich ignorant wretches ort to be suffered to live. (1841, pp. 4, 6)

Of the two major components of the dark side of Davy, the modern reader probably accepts his violence and savagery more easily than his lack of social conscience. The former is the forerunner of some of the standard television cartoon fare each Saturday morning, but the other component – the Davy who hates and often kills these subhuman "ignorant wretches," whether they are "red niggers" or black without a thought, and takes great glee in insulting and beating "Yankees" and "Paddies" – sometimes makes the reader squirm. A face-to-face confrontation with the blatant racism, chauvinistic humor, and comic stereotypes that many nineteenth-century Americans found appealing is a disturbing experience for those who prefer to hide from history. Dorson does present several of these stories in his edition, but only one from the Nashville almanacs. Although in this instance he superficially covers Davy's tracks by changing the title of "A Scentoriferous Fight with a Nigger" to "A Black Affair," he leaves intact all the other racial slurs that the piece contains (1839, p. 18).[27]

In the main, however, there is a Crockett in the Nashville almanacs who is significantly different than the swaggering, legendary hero that Dorson portrays. By selecting "the best" of the tales and woodcuts, he creates his Crockett in much the same way that John Filson's "autobiography" of Daniel Boone created Filson's Boone.[28] Each compiled the first organized vision but merely one version of a highly visible public property—a volatile, transitory symbol that is always open to reevaluation, reinterpretation, and change. Similarly the Crockett of this essay is but a wider vision of part of the legend's full range. No mention has been made of the hidden stories of Ben Harding, those of Davy's other male friends, or those of fearsome "she-males" like the bear-riding Judy Finx (1839, p. 10), Grace Peabody, "the horowine of Kaintuck" (1840, p. 20), and Zipporina, "the wild cat of the forrest" (1840, p. 14). There are likewise more tales by and about Crockett, such as his surviving the Alamo only to toil as a captive laborer in a Mexican mine, the deputation of screamers who set off to rescue him, and his own escape and recapture, that remain untold. All these stories would still not totally reconstruct the world of the Nashville Crockett almanacs and its singular protagonist. Yet the outlines of Davy's picture are clearer. Compare Dorson's unconquerable "ring-tailed roarer" with the Crockett who wishes to avoid a fight with a stage driver, who runs from Indians, saves their lives, and weeps over their misfortunes. Examine his nakedness, his savage, vulgar, racist behavior in the light of the "hero" who is saved by his wife, chased by a snake, shamed by an elk, scared by an owl, and duped by a peddler. This is the hidden Crockett of the Nashville almanacs. Sometimes compassionate, sometimes cowardly, often crude and often funny, he adds a realistic underpinning to Dorson's superman by emphasizing his loutish origins and propensities and, in so doing, broadens the already epic base of the premier tall tale hero of the American frontier.

NOTES

1. Constance Rourke, "Davy Crockett, Forgotten Facts and Legends," *Southwest Review*, 19 (Jan. 1934), 153. Catherine L. Albanese, "Savage, Sinner, and Saved: Davy Crockett, Camp Meetings, and the Wild Frontier," *American Quarterly*, 33 (Winter 1981), 486. Richard M. Dorson, ed., *Davy Crockett: American Comic Legend* (New York: Spiral Press for Rockland Editions, 1939), [iii]. Daniel G. Hoffman, "The Deaths and Three Resurrections of Davy Crockett," *Antioch Review*, 21 (Spring 1961), 13. Carroll Smith-Rosenberg, "Davey [sic] Crockett as Trickster: Pornography, Liminality, and Symbolic Inversion in Victorian America," *Journal of Contemporary History*, 17 (Apr. 1982), 331, 346. Of the five opinions, only Rourke's can be considered as inaccurate. The materials that undercut her position may have been unavailable to her in the early 1930s. Although Albanese does mention the existence of political almanacs published by Turner & Fisher to celebrate the Whig party's candidates in 1840 (Harrison), 1844 (Clay), and 1848 (Taylor), neither she nor any other scholar to my knowledge has investigated the most overtly political of the Crockett almanacs, *Crockett's Harrison Almanac, 1841* (New York: Elton), in which Davy narrates in dialect the heroic achievements of "Old Tippecanoe." The issue contains no tales about Crockett.

2. Walter Blair, "Six Davy Crocketts," *Southwest Review*, 25 (July 1940), 443–62. Blair's analysis was, of course, completed well before Walt Disney's Davy Crockett first reached the television public on December 15, 1954.

3. In the preceding chapter, John Seelye provides a thoroughgoing view of the publishing history of the early almanacs. See also Catherine L. Albanese, "King Crockett: Nature and Civility on the American Frontier," *Proceedings of the American Antiquarian Society*, 88, Pt. 2 (1978), 230–31.

4. The exception is *Crockett's Comic Almanac. '40* (Albany: A. Skinflint), which exploits Crockett's fame by placing his name upon the cover of an English-style joke almanac. It contains no Crockett stories.

5. The seven Nashville almanacs considered in this study are: *Davy Crockett's Almanack, of Wild Sports of the West, And Life in the Backwoods, 1835* (Nashville: Snag & Sawyer); *Davy Crockett's Almanack, of Wild Sports of the West, And Life in the Backwoods, 1836* (Nashville: Published for the Author); *Davy Crockett's Almanack, of Wild Sports in the West, Life in the Backwoods, & Sketches of Texas, 1837* (Nashville: Published by the heirs of Col. Crockett); *Davy Crockett's Almanack, of Wild Sports in the West, Life in the Backwoods, Sketches of Texas, and Rows on the Mississippi, 1838* (Nashville: Published by the heirs of Col. Crockett); *The Crockett Almanac, 1839. Containing Adventures, Exploits, Sprees & Scrapes in the West, & Life and Manners in the Backwoods* (Nashville: Published by Ben Harding); *The Crockett Almanac, 1840. Containing Adventures, Exploits, Sprees & Scrapes in the West, & Life and Manners in the Backwoods* (Nashville: Published by Ben Harding); and *The Crockett Almanac, 1841. Containing Adventures, Exploits, Sprees & Scrapes in the West, & Life and Manners in the Backwoods* (Nashville: Published by Ben Harding). The range of the astronomical calculations is indicated on the title page of the 1835 and 1836 almanacs and on page [3] of the 1840 and 1841 almanacs. Subsequent citation of

the Nashville almanacs will be given parenthetically in the body of the text by year and page.

One other Nashville almanac has recently surfaced. *The Crockett Almanac, 1841* (Nashville: Berry & Tanhill) appeared as one of nine Crockett almanacs offered as lot 35 in Sotheby's auction catalog for May 23, 1984 (Sale No. 5187). Its cover, however, is identical to the Turner & Fisher Crockett almanac for 1841. It is very likely one of the almanacs which Turner & Fisher provided to other, usually smaller, publishers and who, in turn, sometimes also replaced a woodcut with their own local advertising. Since it is a Turner & Fisher variant and not a part of the two Nashville series of almanacs, which bore consecutive volume and number designations, this item is not included in the present study.

I wish to thank John Dobson of the University of Tennessee Library, and the American Antiquarian Society, The Huntington Library, and the Caxton Club, Chicago, for their kindness in supplying copies of the Nashville almanacs.

6. *Crockett Almanac, 1856* (Philadelphia, New York, Boston, and Baltimore: Fisher & Brother), p. [4]. Also, "The Calendar page in this Almanac is adapted for use in every part of the United States" (p. [2]).

7. Six of the tales are reproduced in Dorson's *Davy Crockett*, 15–16, 40–41, 96–97, 97–98, 116, and 161–62. Others of interest from the *Crockett Almanac, 1856* include: "Crockett's Recipe for Consumption," p. [9]; "What a Tree Can Bear; Or, how Crockett rescued his pet Bear 'Death-hug,'" p. [12]; "A Bear-Thief and a Thief Laid Bare; Or, Crockett splitting up 'A Grizzly,'" p. [25]; and "Crockett's Escape from a Prairie on Fire," p. [30].

8. Constance Rourke, *American Humor: A Study of the National Character* (New York: Harcourt, Brace, 1931), and *Davy Crockett* (New York: Harcourt, Brace, 1934). For Dorson's *Davy Crockett*, see n. 1, above.

9. The almanacs are almost always snatched up quickly by collectors and seldom now reach the catalogs of rare book dealers. Dorson noted that about 1958 an 1835 Nashville imprint sold for fifty dollars ("The Sources of *Davy Crockett: American Comic Legend*," *Midwest Folklore*, 8 [Fall 1958], 144). A defective copy of that same issue that was lacking the last two leaves was offered to me in 1982 for eight hundred dollars. The nine almanacs offered at the 1984 Sotheby Auction (n. 5 above) bore a projected price tag of from seventy-five hundred dollars to ten thousand dollars. Indeed, even those recent volumes that reprint the almanac tales are relatively scarce and expensive. Franklin J. Meine's, *The Crockett Almanacks: Nashville Series, 1835–1838* (Chicago: Caxton Club, 1955), was a limited edition of six hundred copies. Copies of it and of Dorson's *Davy Crockett* (1939) will fetch in the neighborhood of one hundred dollars in fine condition. The Meine edition, although not a facsimile and omitting some of the non-Crockett narrative material, does reprint the Crockett tales and woodcuts from the first series of the Nashville almanacs.

10. Richard M. Dorson's original intent in his selections was twofold: "first, to present the more striking aspects of the central legendary personality, the peculiar quality of humor, the blend of human and superhuman elements; second, to represent the more popular anecdotal themes of the almanacs by the chapter groupings" (*Davy Crockett*, p. 168). Only his first point is here of concern, since the sec-

ond deals with the arrangement of the materials selected rather than the reason for that choice. Some sixteen years later in a letter to the editor, in the *Saturday Review* (Aug. 6, 1955, p. 23), Dorson simplified the explanation of the criteria contained in his first point: "In 1939 I selected the best of the fabulous tales and fearsome woodcuts in the almanacs for publication." In early 1981, he again used the term "the best" to designate his selection of the stories (personal communication).

11. Dorson, *Davy Crockett*, 168n. The usual "liberties" include changes in paragraphing, titles, and spelling, with the occasional deletion of a section of a story.

12. *Davy Crockett: American Comic Legend* is currently available from Greenwood Press and from Ayer Company according to the 1983–84 edition of *Books in Print*.

13. See the articles by John Seelye and Catherine L. Albanese, Chapters 2 and 4 in this volume. See also Richard Boyd Hauck's *Crockett: A Bio-Bibliography* (Westport, Conn.: Greenwood Press, 1982), 79–83, passim; Albanese's "Savage, Sinner, and Saved" and "King Crockett"; and Smith-Rosenberg's "Davey [*sic*] Crockett as Trickster."

14. Such a work is being edited by this author.

15. This eastern origin of western myth in nineteenth-century America is a fascinating tale that is told succinctly by John Seelye in Chapter 2. The issue of the origin of the Crockett almanacs, however, is immaterial to the present discussion. Of the Nashville series, only the 1835 and 1836 almanacs have a copyright.

16. The last category contains a sizeable number of stories about Davy's seagoing sidekick, Ben Harding, that Ben supposedly told to Davy. Crockett's presence, however, serves as little more than the initial stimulus to Ben's narrations; Davy does not take part in those adventures of Ben Harding that fall into this classification. Usually they are stories told by Ben about himself.

17. David Crockett, *A Narrative of the Life of David Crockett of the State of Tennessee* (Philadelphia: E.L. Carey & A. Hart, 1834). A facsimile edition edited by James A. Shackford and Stanley J. Folmsbee is presently available (Knoxville: Univ. of Tennessee Press, 1973). *Sketches and Eccentricities of Col. David Crockett of West Tennessee* (New York: J. & J. Harper, 1833) is a reprinting, but bears the most frequently cited title for the work originally issued as [Mathew St. Clair Clarke], *Life and Adventures of Colonel David Crockett of West Tennessee* (Cincinnati: For the Proprietor, 1833).

18. Dorson, *Davy Crockett*, v.

19. The term *Kentuckian* denoted the "ring-tailed roarer" breed of frontiersman, rather than someone necessarily from Kentucky.

20. The theme is admirably developed in Richard M. Dorson, "Davy Crockett and the Heroic Age," *Southern Folklore Quarterly*, 6 (June 1942), 95–102.

21. See Richard Boyd Hauck's "Making It All Up: Davy Crockett in the Theater," Chapter 5 in this volume, especially pages 106 and 107, and his *Crockett: A Bio-Bibliography*, 67–79, passim.

22. The broad nose and lips featured on the 1835 almanac figure may link it to the comic depiction of blacks, but it appears under Crockett's name. It may well have been taken as a caricature of the frontiersman by the readers who would have no idea of what the real Crockett looked like.

23. The best discussions of Crockett as the noble savage, the significance of his nudity, its relationship to the violence of the tales, and the themes of order versus disorder and civilization versus the wilderness occur in the work of Catherine L. Albanese. See Chapter 4 in this volume and "Savage, Sinner, and Saved," 486–92; "King Crockett," 234–49; and (although dealing with the *Narrative* rather than the almanacs) "Citizen Crockett: Myth, History, and Nature Religion," *Soundings*, 61 (Spring 1978), 94–102.

24. See, for example, the "Davy Conquering Beast" selection of tales in Dorson, *Davy Crockett*, 103–20.

25. Dorson, *Davy Crockett*, 158, v–ix. I exclude the chapter headings that do not deal specifically with Davy: "Doughty Dames," "Ben Harding," and "Pedlars and Pukes." Some of the hidden tales would seemingly suit the chapter devoted to "Davy in Lighter Moments," but are not included with "Crockett Boiling a Dead Indian," "Drinking Up the Gulf of Mexico," and "The Colonel Treeing a Ghost." This last chapter seems designed by Dorson more as a catchall for those stories that did not fit in the other chapter groupings yet were too good to omit in his opinion.

26. Davy is never bashful about what he considers the bad traits of others. In "Colonel Crockett and the Honey Bees" he notes:

> It must be allowed that bees are curous creturs, speshally for making honey. Thar's but two things more curouser, and that ar a Yankee and an Irisher. The Yankee may be all his life making honey, or money, and that's all the same thing in Dutch, but you never ketch him eating any on it himself, which shews he haint got so much sense as a bee, with all his industriousness and ingenuity. Not he – none of his honey is of no use to nobody till grim death has smoked him out of his hive.
>
> Thar's this difference between a Yankee and an Irisher – a Yankee always thinks before he speaks, and an Irisher always speaks before he thinks. You have to hammer a Yankee to a red heat before he strikes, and you must hammer an Irisher dead before he is cool. A Paddy is suspicious his own country is better than enny other, and a Yankee calkilates enny country is better than his own. (1841, p. 22)

27. Dorson, *Davy Crockett*, 86–88.

28. The editorial process is, of course, by nature an imperfect synthesis. For an examination of the early evolution of Boone's image, see Michael A. Lofaro, "The Eighteenth Century 'Autobiographies' of Daniel Boone," *The Register of the Kentucky Historical Society*, 16 (April 1978), 85–97. See also J.A. Leo Lemay's "The Frontiersman from Lout to Hero: Notes on the Significance of the Comparative Method and the Stage Theory in Early American Literature and Culture," *Proceedings of the American Antiquarian Society*, 88, Pt. 2 (1978), 187–223.

4. Davy Crockett and the Wild Man

OR, THE METAPHYSICS
OF THE *LONGUE DURÉE*

Catherine L. Albanese

.

> What is the American, this new man? . . . *He* is an Ameri-
> can, who leaving behind him all his ancient prejudices and
> manners, receives new ones from the new mode of life he
> has embraced, the new government he obeys, and the new
> rank he holds. He becomes an American by being received
> in the broad lap of our great *Alma Mater.*
> —J. Hector St. John Crèvecoeur[1]

These often-quoted words sum up the ideology of newness that surrounded the settlement of the North American continent by Europeans. Indeed, it is almost trite to notice this "New World" ideology, so pervasive is it in the character and culture of the United States and so well documented in American history.[2] Euro-Americans, emigrants who had left their ancient moorings behind them to set out for an unknown land and lifetime, needed to define themselves as a people. They were heirs to a history and tradition from which they were separated by the distance of an ocean and the increasing distance of passing years, and so they learned to celebrate newness. Their chosen land was fresh and innocent, unlike the fleshpots of the corrupted Europe they had fled. It was vigorous and alive, unlike the fatigue to which the Old World had succumbed. In such an environment, these wanderers and colonizers became new people. They had left antiquity and exhaustion behind them to become, as Crèvecoeur's metaphor almost literally suggests, babes in the wilderness. They were sitting, newborn infants, in the lap of a New World Mother Nature. They would grow to be adults and Americans from their adopted seat.

Still, Crèvecoeur and others found a serpent in the Edenic garden. In spite of the apparent security of the lap of *"Alma Mater,"* danger lurked in the New World forests. There people became wild, and "men appear[ed] to be no better than carnivorous animals of a superior rank, living on the flesh of wild animals when they can catch them." A "new set of manners" was "grafted on the old stock" and there produced "a strange sort of lawless profligacy." In fact, Crèvecoeur went on to note, "the manners of the Indian natives are respectable, compared with this European medley." For Europeans, he insisted again, the "eating of wild meat" was inclined "to alter their temper." Articulating the stance and values of the farmer, Crève-coeur could only point to the evils of living too close to the raw edge of the new. "Our bad people are half cultivators and half hunt-ers, and the worst of them are those who have degenerated alto-gether into the hunting state. As old ploughmen and new men of the woods, as Europeans and new made Indians, they contract the vices of both."[3]

Purity and danger were perfectly poised in this myth of the New World.[4] If the new land was a sanctuary, a sacred space in which life, liberty, and prosperity would increase, it was also a boundary place that, with its strange and alien power, could overwhelm the civilized heritage of the European. So it was that Euro-Americans found themselves—at the very center of the ideology of newness—engaged in an extended debate over the relative merits of "civilized" and "savage" existence. The nineteenth-century literary flowering from James Fenimore Cooper's Leatherstocking tales to Herman Mel-ville's romantic narratives of the sea and aboriginal shores is an ex-pression of the depth of American involvement in the question.[5]

Perhaps even more interesting as an expression, though, is the nineteenth-century figure of Davy Crockett. This Davy Crockett is a fictional character who develops from the persona of the histori-cal David Crockett and, also, from a deposit of cultural baggage that extends beyond the life and livelihood of the historical congress-man from Tennessee. The fictive Davy Crockett, much more than a Crèvecoeur or a Cooper or a Melville, takes us, in his newness and civilized savagery, past the world of privilege and high culture to an encounter with the collective mental world of many Americans of the period.

Davy Crockett does this especially as we find him, on the popu-lar level, in the "comic" Davy Crockett almanacs. At the same time, with their strong caricature of the "savage-civilized" debate and their blatant celebration of excess, these Crockett almanacs provoke questions about the innocence and "newness" of their protagonist. Is Davy Crockett (and, standing behind him, Crèvecoeur's new American) really a man without a past? Is he, with his ideological scorn for Indians, blacks, and a host of others including Yankees, a man without European forethoughts and forebears? Are we to join with him in a communion feast to recency without casting a critical eye on the long shadow of history? In fact, if we follow the trajectory of these questions with some concern for issues of historical method, we turn up some surprising answers—and ancestors—for the almanac Crockett. When we think of history not merely as a chronicle of clearly defined events that signal change but also as an account of enduring cultural continuities (*la longue durée*), Davy Crockett's cultural baggage becomes very old indeed. Hidden within are the primordial materials of a mythic European demiworld and the wild creatures who inhabited it.

The Davy Crockett almanacs, produced from 1835 to 1856 in various cities of the United States, packaged standard almanac information with a series of extravagant, and often brutal, anecdotes concerning the fictional Crockett. They were evidently widely read. With editions purportedly published in Nashville, New York, Philadelphia, Boston, and Baltimore and printed using (mass-production) stereotype, the almanacs had both eastern and western audiences. This was, in itself, not particularly surprising, for it was common for almanacs at this period to be widely distributed. Thus, the Crockett almanacs made it clear that they aimed to travel, publishing postage rates for delivery, including those for over four hundred miles. In the same fashion, they ambitiously printed astronomical and meteorological data for all sections of the United States and its territories. With a number of the almanacs available in several imprints, internal evidence argues that they were directed both to a rising middle class of business-minded city dwellers and to more traditional rural and farm folk.[6] Hence, when viewed critically, they provide significant insights into the ideas and attitudes of ordinary Americans of the time.

For these people, as for their more sophisticated compatriots, culture and nature each had its alluring and dangerous elements. Culture brought the assurance that ordinary Euro-Americans felt they lacked: it spoke of centuries of survival and enrichment; and in their case it included the heritage of political dominance and elitist pride through membership in the community of those who raised empires and made history. Remembering the heritage could offer an effective antidote to the roughness and lack of civilized refinement Crockett's contemporaries saw surrounding them, even when they dwelled, as many almanac readers did, in middle-class residences in eastern cities. Meanwhile, in the rising tide of the Industrial Revolution and the ebbing one of hierarchy, the decadence of Europe—and of the eastern seaboard—seemed particularly manifest. So nature, as New World wilderness, held out the promise of democratic regeneration for readers of the almanacs and their kind, and they turned toward the frontier often in imagination, if not in act. What concerns us here, however, is the combined fear and fascination with wildness that followed these Euro-Americans as they entered New World forests, albeit mostly in imagined ways. This fear-fascination, if traced to its ancient roots, discloses a tremendous irony in the New World myth and metaphysic. It reveals, standing solidly beneath the cloak of innocent newness, the complicity of age-old European imaginings and anxieties. Seen from the perspective of what hides under the cloak, the myth of the New World dissolves in the myth of European antiquity.

In the Davy Crockett almanacs, with language that obliquely echoes Crèvecoeur, the chief symbols for the alluring temptation of the wilderness are American Indians and, like to them, the Euro-American Davy Crockett. Onto the persons of Crockett and the Indians, as caricatured in the almanacs, writers and readers could project sides of themselves they chose not openly to own. They could articulate their fears of losing the civilization they had so painfully acquired over centuries and, in the meantime, could identify ambiguously with the wildness they repudiated. Hence, in numerous, flamboyant anecdotes written by unidentified authors, Indians function thoroughly as savages, and Davy Crockett shows himself to be of corresponding temper. Indian adventures with Crockett, who straightway subsumes their traits into his own character, form a symbolic cluster. Recurring throughout the slender almanac booklets, the duet of Crockett and the Indians captures a pornography of racism and violence that hides beneath itself an epistemology of fear and fascination. Some examples will suffice to illustrate the pattern.

83

Fear of Indians and their world, often metamorphized into belligerence and aggressive menace against the wild and alien enemy, runs through Crockett's accounts. In one instance, not unaware of other forms of literary discourse, Crockett stated his case outright, confronting the "noble-primitive" school of Indian interpretation. "You romantic an full head o' steam authors, what write with such a perfect looseness on the bravery of the Injuns," he harangued, as he described "the true circumstantial caracter of these upright squadrupeds." Distancing himself from what he feared to acknowledge as human, he declaimed against Indian humanity, which was "a little bit thinner than city milk." Even further, Crockett adumbrated his final fear of cannibalism, opining that Indians liked a "drink of white baby's blood nearly as well as whiskey"; the only reason that they did not eat each other was "bekase they're of the buzzard disposition, and couldn't begin to stomach their own carron acrousness." Indians cheated, lied, and stole; and once an Indian who had successfully begged some whiskey from Crockett and his friend Ben Harding rewarded them both by carrying off a powder horn from one and a jackknife from the other. Indians walked naked and resembled the wild beasts that they hunted. They did not possess refinement or manners of any sort and, the secret and gnawing source of Crockett's discomfort and fear, could not be fit subjects for civilization. When Crockett discovered an Indian in sore distress with a snake wrapped around his body, he denied his plea for help, telling the Indian "the sarpent war a civilised cretur compared to him." In fact, when his pet bear, Death-Hug, was treed by Indians who were preparing to eat the bear, Crockett came to the rescue, and together they killed the Indians. Indians, in the metaphysical taxonomy Crockett used to express and control the menace, were "red niggers" and "as jolly a squad o' the red rango-tangs as ever barked a skull."[7]

Most of all, as Crockett had intimated, Indians killed — and when they did, they often ate their victims. Here was the ultimate act of wildness and the ultimate inner horror for a Euro-American — the fear of what one might become projected, as a parody, onto "savages." So it was that on one occasion Crockett's daughter was captured by Indians who were "determined to cook half of her an eat the other half alive," out of revenge, Crockett said, for the lickings he had given them. This time the girl was lucky because some pan-

84

thers, recognizing her "true grit," "formed a guard around her, and wouldn't allow the red niggers to come within smellin distance, an actually gnawed her loose, an 'scorted her half way home." In similar fashion, Sal Fink was carried by Indians to "Roast flesh Hollow, whar the blood drinkin wild varmints determined to skin her alive, sprinkle a leetle salt over her, an' devour her before her own eyes"; and Ben Harding found himself bound to a tree with a fire lighted as "the principal savages held their wooden bowls up to catch the blood and gravy for their greedy chops." Both Sal and Ben survived to tell the tale, giving voice at once to themes of fear and deliverance; but others were not so fortunate. Crockett told how he and Ben encountered "a hull flock o' these upright painters [who] had been out on a midnight plunder an blood drinkin, among some poor human people." One chief, named Wild Cat, headed "the sassiest tribe o' sausage colored niggers, that ever split a skull, or breakfasted on the warm blood o' white faced human nater."[8]

Surrounded by creatures of such inclinations, Crockett spent his days engaged in active combat. Once, as he related, a Cherokee Indian "shewed us his posterum, if it ar not ondecent to say so, and very politely asked us to kiss it." Feeling "amazen wolfy," Crockett fired and hit him but did not, he added, break the Indian's hide[9] (see page 74, Chapter 3). The incident was revelatory, disclosing by innuendo the other side of the coin of fear. In the anecdote, the "savage" was acting as a savage should. Although there is the business of his politeness, suggesting the complexity of the symbolic and mythic process for the anonymous almanac authors, the Cherokee was being crudely arrogant and at least a trifle prurient.[10] But more important, in the act of putting an end to the Indian's savagery, Crockett had taken a physical step that articulated, through the language of the body, the fundamental cause of his fear. There was, beneath the veneer of civility, a metaphysic of fascination that ruled and nourished him. Crockett, therefore, *became* what he sought to extinguish: incarnating the old adage that the hunter must imitate what he hunts, he was allured by the savage wildness he saw and, bringing out a side of himself that lay ready within, came to resemble his Indian foe. In fact, it is not too much to claim that his wolfishness and his killing were the external manifestations of a resonating inner state. Davy Crockett, in short, had shown himself to be a wild man.

In anecdote after anecdote, the almanacs present a Crockett who could be ignorant as an Indian, naked as an Indian, hungry as an Indian, and bestial as an Indian. When he rescued Sal Fungus from an Indian about to scalp her, Crockett wanted to skin the "uncarcumsized cretur alive." In the fight that followed, Crockett described how the Indian "put his hand into my mouth to haul out my tung; but I held on his hand with my teeth, and took his wrist about half off." Not without a touch of savage gallantry, he gave the Indian's eye to Sal after it came out. Again, in still another account of a struggle with a half-breed, Crockett recalled: "I glued myself to him and after a half-hour's tussel I walked my grinders into his throat and spilt a little of his mixed blood. My wife keeps his scalp fastened to a stick, to brush the flies off the table when we are at dinner."[11]

As this incident and others hint, the culmination of the savage transformation—and its final fascination as well as fear—was cannibalism. Crockett, indeed, had proclaimed himself a cannibal in the almanac version of his introductory speech before the Congress. After a beginning testimonial to his wildness ("Who-Who-Whoop-Bow-Wow-Wow-Yough"), he had launched into a bombastic declamation in which he established his credentials for his fellow congressmen. Significantly, he summarized by proclaiming that he could "walk like an ox; run like a fox, swim like an eel, yell like an Indian, fight like a devil, and spout like an earthquake, make love like a mad bull, and swallow a nigger whole without choking if you butter his head and pin his ears back."[12] If we are to believe the innuendos of other almanac episodes, "red niggers" were just as appealing for satisfying Crockett's gargantuan appetite. In one episode, witnessing to his superiority to Moses, who struck water from a rock, he told how, after a meal with some Indians, he got into a contest with their chief. The "reglar injun war breakdown" went on until "his brother an sisters red hides begun to shout and whoop all kinds o' triumph and used-up-ness at me." Crockett's response was typical and telling:

> So I jist spirted a gallon or two o' tobacco gravy on the rock, an went at it, savage an beautiful; dreckly the old rock begun to smoke an snap like a hemlock back log; arter that, the fire begun to fly about, an the tarnal big stone ware so all baken hot, that the red Chief's feet begin to singe, but haven on a parr o' fire-proof shoes, I didn't

86

begin to feel it, but kep on dancin, till the Chief fell down half cooked, an his party run off whoopin with thar blankets all in a light blaze.[13]

In another incident, Crockett hinted at the nourishment to be derived from Indian blood as he told of "mowing down" a group of Indians caught stealing his horse fodder. He had "made their heads an legs fly about," and "the red nigger's sap both watered an manured my field, till it war as red an striped, as Uncle Sam's flag." The results were noteworthy. "Thar's a stack o' thar bones standing in the medow to this very day; an from the large majority o' thar blood that watered it all over, I have had a treble crop o' the tallest injun grass every summer, but mow me for cow fodder, if every single clover head was not as copper colored as an injuns hide."[14] On this occasion, Crockett had not soaked in the nutriment that came from Indian flesh and blood; only the meadow had. Yet he was already symbolically contemplating what Richard Slotkin has called the "savage eucharist." Slotkin has masterfully shown us the meaning of this primordial communion feast and its violent fascination for Euro-Americans.[15] Here was a way to ingest the virtue and power of one's foe in an act of assimilation and identification through which one became more truly oneself. Here was a way to absorb the world, to conquer fear by expanding oneself in a symbolic act that complemented and completed the expansionist act by which the American Hunter stalked the prey of a continent.

In Crockett's case, the virtues of savage blood were apparent in a series of anecdotes that, structurally, escalated from one to the other. If Davy Crockett had proclaimed his identity as cannibal to the Congress, had prepared Indian flesh for consumption by half cooking it, and had duly noted its nutritional advantage, he also began to use it as food—at first for his pet bear, Death-Hug. Although, to be sure, Crockett and Death-Hug had once before scalped four Indians "in the natural way with our teeth," now Crockett deliberately killed and boiled an Indian to nourish the bear when he was suffering from a "bowel complaint."[16]

Then, finally, in a climactic episode we meet Crockett the cannibal unambiguously. Symbol and innuendo give way to explicit proclamation as the veil is lifted and we see, without equivocation, the truth of Crockett's identity. Walking, with expansionist signifi-

"Crockett's Patent Gouging; Or, Using Up Two Indian Chiefs," from *Crockett Almanac, 1849* (Boston: James Fisher), p. [9]. (American Antiquarian Society.)

cance, "along the Oregon, in the neighborhood of the big Rocky," Crockett met two Indian chiefs and fought them "about an hour an a half, arter feeden time." When he began to "feel the appetite of a double run mill stone," the solution to the problem was simple. One Indian became gravy for the other, and dinner was served for Crockett and his dog. The meal, as Crockett testified, was "super-licious."[17] As we read of the exploit, Crèvecoeur's "eating of wild meat" comes back to haunt: it was, after all, the eating of Indian meat (see above).

In this context, it is illuminating to follow Crockett down the dramatic road to cannibalism. Communion of flesh created an ultimate reference for the many ways in which he and his readers debated the merits of the savage and civilized states even as they embraced the ideology of newness. The savage eucharist suggested the strength of their identification with the New World metaphysic, for the Crockett of the almanacs and the readers of the almanacs felt themselves inexorably drawn to savages. They themselves were like "red niggers," and they esteemed and admired even as they feared and condemned. Their tension between the poles of attraction and repulsion was expressed in the Crockett tales and their popularity. Savages, despite Euro-American fears or because of them, were "good for thinking" and "good for feeling."[18] They also offered models for everyday action and became foci for rituals of avoidance and communion; e.g., taboos against interracial marriage but veiled celebrations of cannibalism.

It is, of course, common to treat such attitudes sociologically, psychologically, and anthropologically, and this discussion has implied all three. But it is also possible to treat them historically. Such an approach has, indeed, already been suggested by introductory allusions to historical method and by reference to the ancient European roots of the fear-fascination regarding wildness. The New World metaphysic, if pursued far enough, becomes an Old World metaphysic, and the myth of America hides behind itself the ancient mythologies of Europe. A consideration of contemporary French historical writing will throw important light on these statements and yield useful historiographical results.

In his *Mediterranean and the Mediterranean World in the Age of Philip II* (far, but not so far, from Davy Crockett and the wild places he inhabited in North America), Fernand Braudel, the great historian of the French *Annales* school, aspired as one of his goals to present "a history in slow motion from which permanent values can be detected." He wanted to "rediscover the slow unfolding of structural realities, to see things in the perspective of the very long term." Using geographical space as a concept to unify the first section of his massive work, Braudel pondered the role of environment and climate, of boundaries and human communications through trade and in cities. This was *la longue durée*, the study of the "recurrent features of Mediterranean life." When Braudel turned from this continuing base in his second section, he considered social history in which, he said, structure and conjuncture combined. Here was the slow-moving, but also the ephemeral, as Braudel tackled the complexities of economic and political systems, of class strata, cultural groups, and techniques for waging war. Finally, after a now lengthy exposition of nine hundred or so pages came the chronicle of short-term events and the politics and people leading to and from the Battle of Lepanto in 1571. Braudel had explored "history in depth" in the preceding chapters, and he thought that the ways in which he had done so had provided "the essentials of man's past." By contrast, events were the "ephemera of history," which passed "across its stage like fireflies, hardly glimpsed before they settle back into darkness and as often as not into oblivion."[19]

Despite his misgivings about short-term crises, however, in the finished work, *la longue durée*—the study of long duration—joined analysis of events of medium and short duration to form what *Annales* scholars have called *histoire globale*. In this vision of total history Braudel had identified three kinds of time with which historians must be concerned—all three of them, as we shall see, relevant to Davy Crockett and the era of the Crockett almanacs. As *Annales* student Traian Stoianovich has summarized, these kinds of time are: "duration at a quasi-immobile level of structures and traditions, with the ponderous action of the cosmos, geography, biology, collective psychology, and sociology; a level of middle-range duration of conjunctures or periodic cycles of varying length but rarely exceeding several generations; a level of short duration of events at which almost every action is boom, bang, flash, gnash, news, and noise, but often exerts only a temporary impact."[20]

Applied to the Crockett almanacs, Crockett's "superlicious" meal on the flesh of two Indian chiefs was surely the "news" and "noise" of a short-term event. The economic organization of Crockett's world, with its emphasis on self-sufficiency and subsistence through skill in the hunt—this was, in Braudel's terms, a conjuncture. As a middle-level event, it lasted only for several generations until the pressures of population turned the frontier territory into part of the more highly organized agro-economy of the succeeding era. (Indeed, the almanacs, as popular fiction, were a reflection of the fact that the transformation had in large part already occurred.) But finally, when we come to events of long duration in the world of the Crockett almanacs, historiographical scrutiny sheds revealing light on Davy

Crockett and the mentality that structures his "red niggers" and his cannibalism toward them.

While Braudel viewed *longue durée* mostly in environmental and economic terms, it is possible to transpose his insights, as Stoiano-vich's "collective psychology" hints, to the inner chronicle of European and Euro-American peoples. In doing so, "red niggers" become part of an enduring history of images of the "other" through which Europeans defined their own values. Even more, Crockett, by him-self becoming wild and "other," exposes the long story of the inner drama of temptation and acquiescence to the savage state. "Savage" Indians reveal themselves as so much paraphernalia by which Euro-Americans historically defended themselves against inner and outer demons they chose not to own, even as they subtly and subcon-sciously sheltered them. An equally savage Crockett celebrates de-monic fascination owned and appropriated; now, indeed, overtly regarded and embraced. Viewed in this light, a brief glance at the ancient European heritage of the wild man casts the figure of Davy Crockett into strange and ironic relief. The long ages of cultural continuity, in all their fear and violence, claim him; and he is linked to an ancestry of wild men as old as Europe. The New World meta-physic turns out to be, after all, the metaphysic of Braudel's *longue durée*.

In his now classic study *Savagism and Civilization*, Roy Harvey Pearce wrote that "in spite of the nationalism which forced its growth, the American understanding of the Indian depended on an idea of savagism whose main structure derived from European sources."[21] Pearce went on to analyze these sources in the work of the eighteenth-century historians who followed the school of Scottish common-sense philosophy. But both Scottish common sense and the Ameri-can Davy Crockett with his "red niggers" stood in the shadow of centuries. Indeed, even older than Europe, in one of the earliest documents to emerge from the Mesopotamian cradle of civilization, we find the wild man Enkidu, who, in *The Epic of Gilgamesh*, was friend and equal to the sacred king. As he first emerged from clay and water at the hand of the goddess Aruru, "his body was rough." It was "covered with matted hair like Samuqan's, the god of cattle." Enkidu, in fact, "ate grass in the hills with the gazelle and lurked with wild beasts at the water-holes."[22]

However, it would be difficult, if not impossible, to trace a link between Enkidu and the European tradition of the wild man. Hence it is to the ancient Greeks that we turn to see the wild man's ancestor securely ensconced on the European continent. Significantly, he manifests himself first as an anthropomorphic god. He is Cronos of Hesiod's *Theogony*, who in an act of divine cannibalism swallows his own children as they come from the womb of Rhea. Or he is, collectively, the giant Titans, who in Orphic poetry trapped the infant god Dionysus, "tore him to bits, boiled him, roasted him, ate him, and were themselves immediately burned up by a thunderbolt from Zeus; from the smoke of their remains sprang the human race."[23] In Homer's *Odyssey*, he is the one-eyed Cyclops Polyphemus, giant son of the god Poseidon, who sought to devour Odysseus and his comrades as they returned from the Trojan War. In an uncanny likeness to Crockett's sometime treatment of Indians, "two of them at once he seized and dashed to the earth like puppies, and the brain flowed forth upon the ground and wetted the earth. Then he cut them limb from limb . . . and ate them as a mountain nurtured lion, leaving naught."[24]

By the fifth century B.C., the wild man has become historical, appearing in the writings of Herodotus as he describes the people of the Sahara, "the dog-headed men and the headless that have their eyes in their breasts . . . and the wild men and women" of western Libya. Others of the ancients speak of the anthropophagi, man-eaters who, as among the Sauromatae and the Scythians, shock elite European authors with their barbarousness.[25] According to primordial myth, Rome is founded by the twin brothers Romulus and Remus, the sons of the war-god Mars, who in their infancy are suckled by a she-wolf. By the time Rome "falls," however, the wild man, now historicized, has moved, like Crockett's later denizens of the forest, to the frontiers of the empire: he is a barbarian whose savage ways drag down the citadel of the city. He continues to survive, too, in traditions and beliefs regarding "monstrous races," such as the Cynocephali noted by the Christian saint Augustine, "whose dog-like head and barking proclaim them beasts rather than men."[26] And he survives vigorously, as Richard Bernheimer's study shows, in the wild men of the Middle Ages.[27]

By now, as Bernheimer tells us, the wild man is "a hairy man curiously compounded of human and animal traits." He is naked but covered with fur except, usually, for face, hands, and feet, and frequently he carries a weighty club or tree trunk. Sometimes, in a bow to civilization, he wears a bit of foliage twisted around his loins. "In the case of the wild man," Bernheimer observes in a statement that for us evokes Crockett, "the testimony from the thirteenth century is often identical with that from the nineteenth." Just as important, Bernheimer seeks the heritage of the wild man among the old Graeco-Roman gods. There the wild man is a demon, a faun, and a satyr; a relative of Silvanus, associated with gardens and trees, and of Silenus, deity of mountainous woods. He is master of animals, dominating them with his physical violence and, besides, with the intuitive kinship they find in his company. But he also has affinities with Orcus, the native Italic god associated with death and the underworld, and he is linked, too, by philological evidence to Lamia, the ancient Greek ghoul who devoured children. Thus, as Bernheimer argues persuasively, the wild man who "so often appears in medieval literature and art as less than human, may very well at a time beyond the reach of written sources have commanded the stature and honor of divinity."[28]

Through the medieval encyclopedists, Margaret T. Hodgen notes, stories of wild men "enjoyed a vitality and longevity impossible to exaggerate."[29] That vitality only increased during the age of discovery —and, like his later progeny in the nineteenth century, the wild man continued to be linked to cannibalism. Thus, on the enchanted island of *The Tempest*, probably suggested by a shipwreck in the Bermudas, William Shakespeare's Caliban carried in his name an anagram for *cannibal*. Meanwhile, other English and European voyagers were bringing home reports of savage and cannibalistic peoples in the New World. Here, no longer dwelling among the gods, the wild man had become, with Caliban, a demonic brute. In the earliest book on America that was printed in English (1511), we learn that Indians, as Crockett's savages, are "lyke bestes without any resonablenes," that "they ete also on(e) a nother," that "the man etethe his wyf his chylderne" and "they hange also the bodyes or persons fleeshe in the smoke as men do with us swynes fleshe."[30] Later, in Richard Hakluyt's *Voyages* (1598–1600), accounts of cannibals and other savage peoples in the New World flourished. "There remaine some among the wild people, that unto this day eate one another," wrote Henry Hawks. "I have seene the bones of a Spaniard that have bene as

93

cleane burnished, as though it had bene done by men that had no other occupation."[31]

Hence, when Europeans gazed at the Americas, they perceived these lands and their peoples, overwhelmingly, in the terms of the mythology of the *longue durée*. As Hodgen summarizes their descriptions of what they saw, "the strange and bizarre was emphasized at the expense of the prosaic and carefully examined." "Meanwhile," she elsewhere observes, "to compound the anxieties of the onlookers as a new image of the universe began gradually to take shape, and the old one withered away, mankind itself no longer appeared to be a single homogeneous species or unit. It was cleft to the core into at least two cultural categories, the civil and the barbarous, the polished and the savage."[32]

Nor did the wild man, within the new setting, eschew a scientific appearance. By the tenth edition of his *Systema naturae* (1758–59), the Swedish taxonomist Carolus Linnaeus had divided humankind into five distinctive races. There were "Europaeus," "white, sanguine, muscular"; "Asiaticus," "sallow, melancholy, stiff"; and "Afer," "black, phlegmatic, relaxed"; all preceded by "Americanus," "reddish, choleric, erect," and, initiating the series, "Ferus" (wild), "on all fours, mute, hairy." Linnaeus had introduced this category to accommodate some nine reported cases of "feral" humans or "beast"-children who had wandered into the gaze and control of civilized society. Thus, *Homo sapiens ferus* emerged as a subspecies of *Homo sapiens*.[33]

It is worth noting that in his classification, however ethnocentric, Linnaeus had clearly separated the wild man from the Indian. Meanwhile, from a different perspective the Enlightenment was heralding the incarnation in the Americas of the "noble savage"–the gallant and uncorrupted prince of the wild for whom the Old World expressed its nostalgia and esteem. So the eighteenth century kept the wild man, but–different from the earlier explorers and conquistadores of the age of discovery–new images of both wild man and savage distinguished the wild man from the peoples of the New World. Still, the unconscious fusion of Indian and wild man did not disappear in the light of the age of reason. Learned taxonomists and their admirers could distinguish between races, and elites of enlightened and, then, romantic leaning could discourse on noble savages. But, as Gary B. Nash has reminded us, new images of the savage were the product of the "upper stratum of society." For frontier people in the contact situation (and, we could add, for an insecure urban middle class still spiritually close to them), "the old stereotypes remained basically unchanged throughout the eighteenth century."[34]

To return to Davy Crockett and the Crockett almanacs after this encounter, however brief, with the wild man of European myth and story is to see Crockett with different eyes. His cannibalism, his sometime violence toward animals (the savage hunter) and other-time affection for them (his pet bear, Death-Hug), even his "hairy" frontier uniform with its fur cap look less distinctively American now. The familiar has become estranged, the "comic" and grotesque distorted by a larger incongruity. Crockett's alternately negative and ambivalent imaging of Indians, with all its racism and jingoism, discloses itself as an expression of the abiding metaphysic of the *longue durée*. This metaphysic, in its antiquity, belies the glib enthusiasms of the rhetoric of an innocent New World, and it shows us an original, fearful wildness in the European enterprise. Seen from this perspective, both Hector St. John Crèvecoeur and Davy Crockett are old in mind and spirit. If they are brothers under the skin—the farmer and the hunter, the educated writer and the rough-edged populist— they are brothers in their mutual affirmation of the European categories regarding "otherness," which shape and control them despite and even through their language of newness.

And this is not all. Throughout this study, religious language has made its appearance again and again. The New World was a sacred space, a place of both purity and danger, in which Davy Crockett could celebrate the savage eucharist in the final act of cannibalism. Crockett's wild ancestors, in the mental world of generations of Europeans, were linked in their origins and mythic attributes to early epiphanies of the Graeco-Roman gods. Beyond that, the history of the encounter of the wild man with the cultured European and his progeny has been tied to the growth and triumph of Christendom. It is, indeed, the expression of an identity struggle that is essentially religious.

The centuries of Judaeo-Christian heritage had brought with them allegiance to a god of history and further allegiance to the values of historic destiny as passed on by Graeco-Roman culture. Church and empire, together as Christendom, had stood at the center of the world, the redemptive beacon of civilization in the darkness of the frontier outposts of the barbarians. To be identified with culture meant to participate in the citied traditions of church and empire. To be savage, on the other hand, meant to revert to the original chaos, to the "weeping and gnashing of teeth" that apostles and saints had warned against. The choice was clear: it lay between heaven and hell, salvation and sin/damnation.[35]

In the context of such a past, identity questions about savagery and civilization were, for Crockett and the almanac readers, at a deep level religious. There were unchristened (read "uncivilized") barbarians abroad in the American landscape (one wonders if entering throngs of immigrants were not also obliquely included here by writers and readers?); and surely their acknowledged savagery was an exterior expression of interior form. It followed, therefore, that identity questions involved, at the other pole from the savagery of the "red nigger," the demands of manifest destiny in the New Israel of America. The Crockett of the almanacs, like his real-life model, was, we remember, a congressman—and a patriot; but he went further than the original Crockett, who died at the Alamo in 1836. The fictional Crockett sounded his expansionist message throughout the decade of the 1840s. Texas, Oregon, California, they all were to be part of the United States, and Crockett boasted he could show Americans "the chap fit to send to Congress, and one that knows how to talk about Oregon, annex Texas, flog Mexico, swallow a Frenchman whole, and lick John Bull clar out of his breeches!"[36]

Hence, the cannibalism of the savage eucharist was a symbolic act that signaled the assimilation of a continent. The boastfulness of Crockett was fitting because, as a wild man, out of the constructions of the *longue durée* he was also a god. If in conquering wildness Crockett had himself been wild, what he lost in Christian civility he gained in Christian and unchristian fury: now, like a born-again Crusader who was also a berserker, he could exterminate demonic beings who threatened the growth of his kind of American society. Paradoxically, what he lost in Christian civility he could gain in an ecstasy of power and control, extending civilization to encompass the continental "other."

All of this is to point to the complexity of the figure of Crockett in the almanacs. The classical wild man had been an expression of European fear and fascination with "otherness"—the wildness that was the unconscious counterpoise to Western civility and the embodiment of one side of a tension that was mostly kept hidden from view. When the terms of the debate became manifest with the exploration of the Americas and other lands and with the Enlightenment, new possibilities for the wild man emerged. Crockett seized these possibilities, in his own person articulating the debate between savagery and civilization even as he favored savagery. The traditional wild man did not *in himself* express both sides of the question: Crockett does. Thus, although he epitomizes wildness, throughout the almanacs he concerns himself, with thematic regularity, with issues of civility and politeness. (Recall the Cherokee whom we met earlier *politely* showing his posterior to Crockett.) More than that, Crockett's political involvement as a congressman is an anomaly in the classical character of the wild man. In the image handed down in the European *longue durée*, barbarians were, for the most part, those bereft of the power to organize and act politically.[37] By contrast, Crockett's overriding nationalistic ambitions and imperialisms reflect a distinctively American pattern in which the ideology of nature thrives as part of the political ideology of the United States.[38] Indeed, the gross politicization of the wild man in the case of Crockett and in other American examples is an instance of movement — of the slow chart of change — passing into the *longue durée*.

Nevertheless, to notice Crockett's departures from the classical image is not to yield to American exceptionalism and the New World metaphysic. The record of Crockett's activity as a wild man speaks for itself. He wears the badge of his wild identity too obviously to be ignored once we have made the acquaintance of his European forebears. "What is the American, this new man?" In Crockett's case and in the case of the almanac readers, as we have seen, he was really very old. Beyond that, he was at least covertly religious. Because the deep structures of his language and action were mythic, they had access to sacred power. The *mysterium tremendum* that Crockett and his readers touched was, it is true, more demonic than sanctified; but in understanding its origins, we glimpse the compelling force that drew humans to dreams and deeds of savagery. The demonic divinity that lurked in the unconscious of the anonymous writers and readers of the Crockett almanacs was, in his era, a strong and commanding presence. Under the enduring sign of the *longue durée*, we can surely suspect that the wild man continues to be present in ourselves.

NOTES

Research on the Davy Crockett almanacs was carried out at the American Antiquarian Society in Worcester, Massachusetts, and with the assistance of a Fred Harris Daniels Fellowship from the society. Portions of this paper were first presented at a National Endowment for the Humanities seminar conducted by Professor Walter H. Capps at the University of California, Santa Barbara, during the summer of 1977 and at a symposium at Arizona State University in Tempe, Arizona, in January 1978. I am grateful to the society, the seminar, and the symposium for their help. I also wish to thank Professor Charles H. Long, who first introduced me to *Annales* history and whose discussions of wild men, "primitives," and "others" have greatly aided me.

1. J. Hector St. John Crèvecoeur, *Letters from an American Farmer* (1782; Gloucester, Mass.: Peter Smith, 1968), 49.

2. For a classic account based on the literature of the nineteenth century, see R.W.B. Lewis, *The American Adam: Innocence, Tragedy, and Tradition in the Nineteenth Century* (Chicago: Univ. of Chicago Press, 1955). For an anthologized collection of documents that explore the meaning of the "New World" in religious terms, see Giles Gunn, ed., *New World Metaphysics: Readings on the Religious Meaning of the American Experience* (New York: Oxford Univ. Press, 1981). (The phrase "New World Metaphysics" comes from Walt Whitman in *Democratic Vistas* [1871].)

3. Crèvecoeur, *Letters from an American Farmer*, 52, 57–59.

4. The language and the interpretation here owe something to the thought of Mary Douglas. See Douglas, *Purity and Danger: An Analysis of Concepts of Pollution and Taboo* (London: Routledge and Kegan Paul, 1966).

5. James Fenimore Cooper's novel *The Last of the Mohicans* (1826) is an especially clear example of the debate about savagery, here in terms of American Indians. Herman Melville's first novel, *Typee, A Peep at Polynesian Life* (1844), introduces the theme of the debate, which appears repeatedly in his work. His later novel *The Confidence-Man* (1857) contains a chapter, "The Metaphysics of Indian-Hating," that is particularly germane to the character of Davy Crockett explored in this essay.

6. For further discussion of the Davy Crockett almanacs, see Catherine L. Albanese, "King Crockett: Nature and Civility on the American Frontier," *Proceedings of the American Antiquarian Society* 88, Pt. 2 (Oct. 1979), 230–39; and Albanese, "Savage, Sinner, and Saved: Davy Crockett, Camp Meetings, and the Wild Frontier," *American Quarterly* 33 (Winter 1981), 485–92.

7. *Davy Crockett's Almanac, 1844* (New York: Turner and Fisher), 5; *Crockett's Almanac, 1850* (New York, Philadelphia, Boston: Fisher and Brothers), 17; *Fisher's Crockett Almanac, 1843* (Buffalo: Sold by Eli Hollidge [probably published in New York City]), 10; *Crockett Almanac, 1856* (Philadelphia, New York, Boston, Baltimore: Fisher and Brother), 12; *Davy Crockett's Almanac, 1844*, 20. (Most of the Crockett almanacs did not have numbered pages, but I have supplied them, as necessary.)

8. *Crockett's Almanac, 1851* (Philadelphia, New York, Boston: Fisher and Brother), 25; *Crockett Almanac, 1854* (Philadelphia, New York, Boston, Baltimore: Fisher and Brother), 21; *Crockett Almanac, 1856*, 29; *Crockett's Almanac, 1846* (Boston: James Fisher), 5; *Davy Crockett's Almanac, 1845* (Boston: James Fisher), 8.

9. *The Crockett Almanac. Containing Adventures, Exploits, Sprees & Scrapes in the West, & Life and Manners in the Backwoods* (Nashville: Published by Ben Harding, 1841), 6. Ben Harding is fictional, and we do not know the real publisher of this almanac. There was evidence that the issue had actually been produced in Boston, since the signatures on woodcuts were those of Boston artists and engravers. See Franklin J. Meine, ed., *The Crockett Almanacks: Nashville Series, 1835–1838* (Chicago: Caxton Club, 1955), xviii.

10. There were clear sexual innuendos within many of the Crockett anecdotes. S.N. Dickinson's Crockett almanac of 1842 ceremoniously announced to proper Americans that it would substitute new articles for those of a "less elevated character." "Nothing," said the nameless author, would "be introduced into its pages at which the most fastidious in morals can take offence." On the same page, under the title "Indian Barbarity," was an article that described a female captive stripped naked and bound to the stake by Indians until rescue. To make the point still more explicit, an accompanying graphic showed the hapless woman tied, with breasts exposed (*Crockett Improved Almanac, 1842* [Boston: S.N. Dickinson], 2). For a discussion of the sexual themes of the Crockett almanacs, see Carroll Smith-Rosenberg, "Davey [*sic*] Crockett as Trickster: Pornography, Liminality and Symbolic Inversion in Victorian America," *Journal of Contemporary History* 17 (Apr. 1982), 325–50.

11. *Crockett's Almanac, 1848* (Boston: James Fisher), 24–25; *Crockett Awlmanaxe for 1839* (New York: Turner and Fisher), 21.

12. *Davy Crockett's Almanack, of Wild Sports in the West, Life in the Backwoods, & Sketches of Texas* (Nashville: Published by the heirs of Col. Crockett, 1837), 40. (There is no evidence that Crockett's "heirs" did, indeed, publish this almanac.) See, also, *Crockett's Yaller Flower Almanac, for '36* (Snagsville, Salt-River: Boon Crockett, and Squire Downing [New York: Elton]), 20. Were the fictional Crockett to offer a response to this essay, he would probably object that he was never cannibalistic, since blacks (as Indians) were simply species of wild animals. For our purposes, however, the distinction is more important for what it tells us about the implicit ethnocentrism—and here, racism—of inherited ideas about wildness than as a logical point in an overt argument. Still further, this analysis proceeds from what, in the "objectivity" of the fiction, Crockett was doing.

13. *Crockett's Almanac, 1846*, 12.

14. Ibid., 20.

15. See Richard Slotkin, *Regeneration through Violence: The Mythology of the American Frontier, 1600–1860* (Middletown, Conn.: Wesleyan Univ. Press, 1973), 48, 124–25, 518–20, et passim.

16. *Crockett's Almanac, 1846*, 16 (cf. *Davy Crockett's Almanac, 1844*, 18); *Davy Crockett's Almanac, 1847* (New York and Philadelphia: Turner and Fisher), 25.

17. *Crockett Almanac, 1849* (Boston: James Fisher), 9.

18. This analysis is indebted to the structuralism of Claude Lévi-Strauss. See, especially, Lévi-Strauss, *Totemism* (Boston: Beacon Press, 1963), 89 et passim. Here,

however, I extend Lévi-Strauss's understanding to include, with Émile Durkheim, collective sentiment. (See Durkheim, *The Elementary Forms of the Religious Life* [1915], trans. Joseph W. Swain [New York: Free Press, 1965], esp. 29.)

19. Fernand Braudel, *The Mediterranean and the Mediterranean World in the Age of Philip II* (1949; 2nd rev. ed., 1966), trans. Siân Reynolds, 2 vols. (New York: Harper and Row, Torchbooks, 1975), 1: 23, 353; 2: 901. Significantly, Braudel confessed, "It was only after much hesitation that I decided to publish this third section . . . it has strong affinities with frankly traditional historiography." He thought Philip II and his contemporaries were "possibly, probably even . . . under an illusion" when they felt "that they were participating in a mighty drama" (2: 901). The *Annales* "school" received its name from the influential French journal established by Lucien Febvre and Marc Bloch in 1929. Braudel joined the *Annales* Committee in 1937, became a member of the board of editors in 1946, and continued as director of the journal after 1956. But *Annales* was a movement and not simply a periodical, and at the heart of the movement lay a new model for doing history.

20. Traian Stoianovich, *French Structural Method: The Annales Paradigm* (Ithaca, N.Y.: Cornell University Press, 1976), 109.

21. Roy Harvey Pearce, *Savagism and Civilization: A Study of the Indian and the American Mind*, rev. ed. (1953 as *The Savages of America: A Study of the Indian and the Idea of Civilization*; Baltimore: Johns Hopkins Press, 1965), 82. More recently, Robert F. Berkhofer, Jr., has gone further in identifying the wild man's European sources in terms germane to this essay. Berkhofer has argued that the usage *savage* "probably derives from the ancient one associated with the [medieval] 'wild man,' or *wilder Mann* in Germany," quoting and citing Richard Bernheimer's *Wild Men in the Middle Ages* (n. 27, below, and cf. discussion later in this section of the essay). See Robert F. Berkhofer, Jr., *The White Man's Indian: Images of the American Indian from Columbus to the Present* (New York: Knopf, 1978), 13, 14–15. I am indebted to Professor James Ronda for calling this work to my attention.

22. *The Epic of Gilgamesh*, trans. N. K. Sandars, rev. ed. (Middlesex, Eng.: Penguin Books, 1972), 63.

23. Hesiod, *Theogony*, trans. Hugh G. Evelyn-White, 453–62; E.R. Dodds, *The Greeks and the Irrational* (1951; rpt. Berkeley: Univ. of California Press, 1971), 155.

24. Homer, *Odyssey*, trans. A.T. Murray, 9.290–93.

25. Herodotus, *Historiae*, trans. A.D. Godley, 4.191. For the Sauromatae and the Scythians, see the extracts from Strabo (*Geographia* 7.301–3) and Tertullian (*Adversus Marcionem* 1.1) respectively, in Arthur O. Lovejoy and George Boas, *Primitivism and Related Ideas in Antiquity*, Contributions to the History of Primitivism (1935; rpt. New York: Octagon Books, 1965), 327, 343. For other observations on anthropophagy, or cannibalism, see Lovejoy and Boas, *Primitivism*, 121, 135, 213–16, 260; and for a useful discussion of the ancient history of "monsters" and its transmission to medieval and early modern Europe, see Rudolf Wittkower, "Marvels of the East: A Study in the History of Monsters," in Wittkower, *Allegory and the Migration of Symbols* (Boulder, Col.: Westview Press, 1977), 45–74.

26. Augustine, *City of God*, trans. Marcus Dods, 16.8. For a good, short account of Romulus and Remus, the legendary founders of Rome, see Mark P. O.

Morford and Robert J. Lenardon, *Classical Mythology* (New York: David McKay, 1971), 422–23.

27. Richard Bernheimer, *Wild Men in the Middle Ages: A Study in Art, Sentiment, and Demonology* (Cambridge, Harvard Univ. Press, 1952).

28. Ibid., 1, vii, 93–100, 26–32, 42–43, 21.

29. Margaret T. Hodgen, *Early Anthropology in the Sixteenth and Seventeenth Centuries* (Philadelphia: Univ. of Pennsylvania Press, 1964), 68. The seventh-century Isidore of Seville is probably the best known of the encyclopedists, but others include, in the thirteenth century, Bartholomaeus Anglicus, Albertus Magnus, and Vincent of Beauvais, and, in the fourteenth, Sir John Mandeville.

30. The source of this quotation from Hodgen, *Early Anthropology*, 409, is anonymous. For a discussion of Shakespeare's *Tempest* and Caliban in the context of a study of the wild man, see Earl Miner, "The Wild Man through the Looking Glass," in Edward Dudley and Maximillian E. Novak, eds., *The Wild Man Within: An Image in Western Thought from the Renaissance to Romanticism* (Pittsburgh: Univ. of Pittsburgh Press, 1972), 94–97.

31. Richard Hakluyt, *The Principal Navigations, Voyages, Traffiques, and Discoveries of the English Nation*, 12 vols. (1903–5; rpt. New York: AMS Press, 1965), 9:397. For other accounts of cannibalism, see, for example, 8:100, 120; 10:18, 473.

32. Hodgen, *Early Anthropology*, 113, 376. For a brief, insightful discussion of American "savages" as wild men, see John Block Friedman, *The Monstrous Races in Medieval Art and Thought* (Cambridge: Harvard Univ. Press, 1981), 200–7.

33. For the relevant extract of Linnaeus's *Systema naturae*, translated into English, see J.S. Slotkin, ed., *Readings in Early Anthropology*, Viking Fund Publications in Anthropology, No. 40 (Chicago: Aldine Publishing, 1965), 177–78. For the discussion of the passage with specific reference to the wild man on which this account is based, see Robert M. Zingg, *Feral Man and Cases of Extreme Isolation of Individuals*, in J.A.L. Singh and Robert M. Zingg, *Wolf-Children and Feral Man* (1942; rpt. Hamden, Conn.: Archon Books, 1966), esp. 177–78.

34. Gary B. Nash, "The Image of the Indian in the Southern Colonial Mind," in Dudley and Novak, *Wild Man Within*, 84 n. 66.

35. For a useful discussion of Graeco-Roman and Christian understandings of the barbarian and their mingling, see W.R. Jones, "The Image of the Barbarian in Medieval Europe," *Comparative Studies in Society and History* 13 (1971), 367–407, esp. 380–92. For "weeping and gnashing of teeth," cf., among other instances, Matt. 22:13 and Luke 13:28 (King James Version).

36. *Davy Crockett's Almanac, 1847*, 13.

37. See, for instance, Hayden White's discussion of the barbarian who, without speaking Greek, lacked the power to achieve political life (White, "The Forms of Wildness: Archaeology of an Idea," in Dudley and Novak, *Wild Man Within*, 19).

38. For a longer discussion of the imperialism of history and politics over wild nature in the Davy Crockett of the almanacs—and its relation to issues of civility and politeness—see Albanese, "King Crockett," 225–49.

5. Making It All Up

DAVY CROCKETT IN THE THEATER

Richard Boyd Hauck

．

This is truly the very thing itself—the exact image of its
Author, DAVID CROCKETT.
—Preface to A Narrative of the Life of
David Crockett of the State of Tennessee

The Davy Crockett legend can be thought of as a large set of variations upon an extremely malleable public property, continuously
expanded by creators who reshape it according to their understanding of their audiences' values and expectations. This dynamic collective fabrication has its own life, independent of the historical facts
of David Crockett's life. Crockett himself bent the facts when he
wrote his autobiography. The most important of his many inventions is his artfully contrived persona: he presents himself as a simple, commonsensible, honest man who resists party influence so that
he can properly represent the folks back home by always doing what's
right. His plain way of talking is recapitulated by literary devices that
suggest the backwoods idiom. The book provides a stable, permanent core of story, but none of the makers of Crockett's legend has
ever felt particularly bound by it. Like the legend's other artifacts,
the Crockett dramas have departed drastically from the core story,
mixing pieces of it into new plots that support the rhetorical purposes of the writers, producers, and actors. Furthermore, the stock
features of each genre demand that the figure of Davy be modified
as needed: he is the romantic male lead in Murdock and Mayo's
melodrama Be Sure You're Right, a role model for children in Disney's
television series.

But of all the exploitations of Davy's story, the plays—nineteenth-
century comic melodramas and twentieth-century films—have been
by far the kindest. In contrast, for instance, the two prose narratives

commonly published together with the autobiography as *The Life of David Crockett* were constructed by promoters who took advantage of Crockett's burgeoning reputation by attaching to it all sorts of jury-rigged devices of political aggrandizement: *Colonel Crockett's Tour to the North and Down East* was an instrument of Whig party ambitions; *Col. Crockett's Exploits and Adventures in Texas* was a call for chauvinistic support of American expansionism.[1] Likewise, the infamous Crockett almanacs, which at first simply pirated material from the autobiography, soon recast Davy as the ignoble savage of the western woods, a nasty caricature conjured up by hack writers grubbing for a living in eastern cities.[2] The melodramas and movies have instead sustained the legend's more admirable potentials. They reflect Crockett's own theatrical style as a yarn spinner, campaigner, and humorist. They poke friendly fun at his naiveté, and they are sympathetic to his egalitarianism. In the theater, Davy Crockett has consistently been portrayed as an American hero, the straight-shooting backwoodsman.

The history of Davy in the theater begins in a remarkable fusion of two early nineteenth-century avatars of the backwoods type, one the public image of Crockett, the other a comic stage character developed by the author James Kirke Paulding and the actor James Hackett. The stage character is Nimrod Wildfire, and the play is *The Lion of the West*, first produced in April 1831, in New York, and seen by the congressman himself in December 1833, in Washington. Though initially Crockett took offense and Paulding and Hackett claimed the resemblance was only a coincidence, the legendary man and the comic character reaped reciprocal benefits. The play boosted Crockett's popularity even as it parodied his backwoods mannerisms, and Crockett's reputation as the irreverent, funny, no-nonsense representative of the common folk helped bring audiences out to see the play. The key to this fortunate match is that both figures were successful amplifications of a young but widespread tradition. By 1830 the backwoodsman—a scout, Indian fighter, and hunter—was already established as a stereotype in the theater. Crockett was not the sole inspiration for Wildfire; the characterization of Wildfire enhanced Crockett's image but did not define it.

Crockett was in fact an authentic backwoodsman. He had been a scout and Indian fighter and enjoyed a monumental local reputation as a bear hunter. But from the beginning of his political career, he promoted his image by adopting artifices of the stereotype that were not necessarily indicative of his usual behavior. For campaigning he chose clothing that was associated by the public with the backwoodsman, and he gave seemingly naive speeches designed to ingratiate himself with his unschooled constituents. To make sure he devised exact signals for dialect in his autobiography, he enlisted help from Thomas Chilton of Kentucky, another congressman who knew the lingo.[3] His motto "Be always sure you're right, then go ahead" might well be revised to read "Be always sure you look right, then you'll be ahead." After all, as the model for his autobiography Crockett had Benjamin Franklin's, and it is Franklin who teaches us that commanding the art of virtue is not enough—we must also make our virtues visible to others. Crockett knew that he was a type, and he labored to master the role. The type was in turn improved by his contributions to it.

When, early in 1830, James Hackett advertised a prize for a new play featuring an original American character, he did not have a specific parody of Crockett in mind. He was working within the tradition of the stage type of the backwoodsman: his repertoire already included four such characters (with names like Solomon Swap), and he was looking for a fifth.[4] The earliest variant of this figure, the rude Yankee bumpkin (a Down-East character), has a history that goes back at least to 1787 and the role of Brother Jonathan in Royall Tyler's *The Contrast*. In his western guise as the irreverent, tall-talking, straightforward, good-hearted braggart, he is nearly that old. This "gamecock of the wilderness" or "ring-tailed roarer" had already reached a theatrical zenith in 1822, in New Orleans, when Noah Ludlow stepped out in buckskin shirt and leggings, moccasins, and fur cap to sing Samuel Woodworth's "The Hunters of Kentucky."[5] The song celebrated the sharp-shooting prowess of Andrew Jackson's Kentucky and Tennessee militiamen in the Battle of New Orleans; the name *Kentucky* stood for the whole mythic West of the 1820s. In one of the song's stanzas we hear that every man among them was "half a horse and half an alligator."[6] The phrase "half horse, half alligator" is the hallmark of the frontier braggart, and for a while James Hackett was to make it Nimrod Wildfire's exclusive property—until Davy Crockett inherited it by way of the serendipitous association that Hackett was promoting. Paulding won the prize in November of 1830, and Hackett's role in the deliberate development of the similarity between Wildfire and Crockett began. By the time Hackett and Crockett staged their wonderful confrontation at the Washington Theater in 1833, it was widely taken for granted that Wildfire mirrored Davy. As the actor and the congressman exchanged bows, the audience gleefully acknowledged the recognition.[7]

Likewise, Paulding did not initially design Wildfire to be primarily a parody of Crockett. He wrote to the painter John Wesley Jarvis, who was famous as a practical joker and yarn spinner, and asked for "a few sketches, short stories & incidents, of Kentucky or Tennessee manners, and especially some of their peculiar phrases & comparisons. If you can add, or *invent* a few ludicrous Scenes of Col. Crockett at Washington, You will be sure of my everlasting gratitude."[8] Thus we see that Paulding was seeking information useful to a general characterization of the traditional backwoodsman, and that he knew the comic side of Crockett's public image provided a good example. Joseph J. Arpad has demonstrated that Jarvis's contribution to Paulding's research was not so much to "invent" Crockett stories as to furnish some of the hyperbolic phrases from the long-winded school of backwoods yarn spinning.[9] In December of 1830, Paulding denied that he intended specifically to burlesque Crockett, and supposedly he exchanged friendly letters with the congressman to set everything right.[10] But the fact is that by then he had combined his knowledge of the backwoods stereotype and a great many "ludicrous" impressions of Crockett to formulate his final portrait of Nimrod Wildfire. Hackett took it from there. (See pages 106–107.)

The success of *The Lion of the West* was due to the public's enthusiastic verification of the association of Wildfire and Crockett, and this accounts for the persistence of Wildfire's role through several drastic revisions of the play. The scripts of the earliest versions are lost. A version dated 1833 was discovered by James N. Tidwell and published in 1954. For once, censorship served posterity: the play had been submitted to the Lord Chamberlain's Office before being approved for production at the Theatre Royal, Covent Garden; Tidwell found that copy in the manuscript collection of the British Museum. It had been censored to remove all disparaging jabs at the character Mrs. Wollope, a burlesque upon that famous critic of Americans and their behavior, Mrs. Trollope. (In the censored text cleared for presentation in London, her name was changed to

Engraving of James Hackett as Nimrod Wildfire in James Kirke Paulding's *The Lion of the West* made from a portrait by Ambrose Andrews. The caption reads: "Come back, stranger! or I'll plug you like a watermillion!" (Harvard Theatre Collection.)

Cover page of *Davy Crockett's Almanack, 1837,* with the woodcut of Davy apparently copied from Andrews' portrait of Hackett. (Caxton Club, Chicago.)

Mrs. Luminary.) A primary element of the play's satire was thus gutted. Fortunately, the deleted material was visible in the manuscript and is restored in Tidwell's edition. The 1833 version has a different title, *The Kentuckian, or A Trip to New York*, and two new writers had made contributions to its revision—the Massachusetts actor, playwright, and novelist John Augustus Stone and the English dramatist William Bayle Bernard. Earlier forms of the play were summarized in various contemporary reviews, and information about these variants is in Tidwell's introduction and in Vera Jiji's recent casebook, which includes several such summaries.[11]

In the summarized versions, as in the extant text, the play centers on a contrast between the manners of Americans and of English visitors. Both are targets of satire, but by the final curtain the play has rhetorically affirmed the superiority of the American style of straightforward behavior and common sense uncorrupted by elaborate schooling or allegiance to worn-out institutions. If the Americans are rude and naive, the English are immersed in self-deceiving formalities. In the version for which we have the whole text, Mrs. Wollope is the main representative of the English attitude. She does not appear in the earlier summaries, so her character is apparently a Stone-Bernard innovation. Mrs. Wollope has come to America not only to observe the citizens but to ameliorate (her first name is Amelia) their behavior. The title of her projected book, *Domestic Manners of the Americans*, is of course the title of Frances Trollope's, published in 1832. Mrs. Wollope finds Americans, Wildfire in particular, all too "horridly familiar." By this she means they do not respect class distinctions—she is shocked when they audaciously address her as an equal.

Wildfire's manners are in fact atrocious. Everything he does is slapstick comedy. In Mrs. Wollope's presence, he flops himself down in one chair and puts his feet up in the other, blocking her attempt to sit; he gets roaring drunk and brags about it; he thinks his ostentatious dispensation of dollars can solve any problem. If he is a lout, however, Mrs. Wollope is a fool. Assuming that all Americans are barbarians, she sets about raising money to establish an academy for the reform of their manners. Blinded by her prejudices, she fails to see the evil machinations of her brother Jenkins, who is the melodrama's villain. He is posing as Lord Granby, having taken the name of a deceased companion, and is now perpetrating a scheme to marry the heroine, Caroline Freeman, for her money. In contrast, Wildfire no sooner meets the villain than he knows him for what he is.

Caroline's mother is satirized as a bourgeois American social climber who worships that European delusion, inherited nobility. Mr. Freeman, however, articulates the play's support of the American idea of natural nobility. He approves of Caroline's wish to marry Percival, an honest English merchant; his wife insists that Caroline shall marry "Lord Granby."

> Mrs. Freeman. Is not this the man to enlarge her ideas?
> Freeman.   Yes, my love, and to contract her fortune.
> Mrs. Freeman. Would you refuse your consent to a nobleman?
> Freeman.   Mrs. Freeman, this is not the place to discuss the merits of an European institution. In our social system, rectitude and talent confer the only titles. If the result has been the people's happiness, why should I not rather give her to a man whose nobility is in his conduct, not his name?[12]

Caroline herself sees that Percival is "Affable, intelligent, and generous," but her mother scornfully asks "Has nobility no charm?" and commands her daughter to encourage his lordship.[13]

A reading of the text shows us that Wildfire's loutish act is to be played strictly for laughs. *The Lion of the West* is a standard sentimental melodrama with a hilarious American original superimposed upon it. The play's romantic plot does not dictate Wildfire's inclusion, but its success as staged absolutely depended upon it, since without him it would be a very boring drawing-room comedy and nothing more. The basic tensions in the plot are between the customs of Europe and America and between the manners of Easterners and Westerners; Wildfire's comic characterization magnifies these distinctions, reinforces the satire, and deflates the pomposity of the play's rhetorical passages.

When Caroline and Percival finally get together, Wildfire plays angel to their future by offering to set them up on a big homestead carved out of his holdings in "Kaintuck," for "the ground's so rich there that if you but plant a crowbar over night *perhaps* it will sprout tenpenny nails afore mornin'." By then, of course, Jenkins has been exposed, and driven off by Wildfire's threat, "I'll swallow you whole." Mrs. Wollope has huffed offstage, none the wiser for her experiences in America. Freeman delivers the moral of the story in a speech that reconciles the cultural conflicts that have been the basis of the play's rhetoric. "Percival, if you and Caroline wish to be united, you have my consent; we ask but to be looked at like other people, not with the eye of prejudice or interest, but of candor. We have our evil with our good, but we feel that there are affinities between the Briton and American which should quench the petty fires of dissension and establish on the basis of their mutual freedom the glorious altar of fraternity."[14] With the words "we ask," Freeman must have turned to address his message to the audience. In the decade of America's fierce new nationalism, the statement was both rational and bold.

For the student of Crockett's legend, the most valuable feature of the play is Wildfire's tall talk. In fact, until Tidwell unearthed the script, a scattered few of Wildfire's roaring declamations were all we knew of it. One of these is the famous "brag" in which the frontiersman threatens to punish the villain in a duel. But Wildfire does not brag about his fighting ability as much as he brags about his ability to brag! On the banks of the Mississippi one day, he recalls, he felt "wolfy" because he hadn't had a fight in ten days and was thinking "I must kiver myself up in a salt bin to keep." When he met a riverboatman who might give him a contest, he says, he started right in to outbrag him. The stranger answered the challenge with "Mister, I can whip my weight in wild cats." Wildfire retaliated, "My father can whip the best man in old Kaintuck, and I can whip my father. When I'm good natured I weigh about a hundred and seventy, but when I'm mad, I weigh a *ton*." This ferocious exchange ends with Wildfire's famous line, "Why, I'm the yaller flower of the forest. I'm all *brimstone but* the *head*, and that's *aky fortis*."[15] The first Crockett book, the half-spurious, half-authentic *Sketches and Eccentricities of Colonel David Crockett of West Tennessee* (1833), subsequently appropriates Wildfire's language and claims that his thundering boasts were originated by Davy. In Chapter 13, we are told that the legendary congressman introduces himself with "I'm that same David Crockett, fresh from the backwoods, half-horse, half-alligator, a little touched with the snapping-turtle; can wade the Mississippi, leap the Ohio, ride upon a streak of lightning, and slip without a scratch down a honey locust; can whip my weight in wild cats,—and if any gentleman pleases, for a ten dollar bill, he may throw in a panther, —hug a bear too close for comfort, and eat any man opposed to

Jackson."[16] In a deliberate falsification, the key phrases of both Wildfire's and his opponent's boasts are here fused into one and assigned to Crockett. For at least twenty years, innumerable variations upon Wildfire's speech appeared in books like this, as well as in the Crockett almanacs, the newspapers, and "sporting" or "literary" periodicals such as the New York *Spirit of the Times*. This is why Wildfire's way of talking was known to modern scholars even when the play was lost.

Clearly *The Lion of the West* served primarily as a vehicle for Hackett. Wildfire not only monopolizes all the chairs, he gets all the good lines: the young heroine, for instance, has only forty words in the whole play. Hackett readily drew audiences by staging Wildfire monologues in a one-man show of his original characters, and it was such an excerpt that Crockett saw in Washington. In Frank Murdock and Frank Mayo's *Davy Crockett; Or, Be Sure You're Right, Then Go Ahead*, however, our backwoodsman is an integral part of the melodramatic formula. He is, of all things, the romantic hero of a classic sentimental comedy complete with a heroine whose happiness is threatened by a weak-willed uncle, a wimpy fiancé, and a wicked villain.

Be Sure You're Right was written in 1872 and is now available in Volume 4 of *America's Lost Plays*. The editors of this collection record that it was "probably the best-known of the American frontier melodramas." Murdock wrote the play especially for Mayo, who starred as "Davy Crockett, aged twenty-five," according to the opening night playbill.[17] Of the many reincarnations of Davy they discuss in their book *America's Humor*, Walter Blair and Hamlin Hill found Mayo's to be funniest, mainly because so much of the humor seems to be unintentional. In the last scene of Act 2, which takes place in a remote cabin in the woods during a fierce blizzard, Davy saves the heroine from a pack of wolves by barring the door with his arm. He has had to use the heavy wooden bar for firewood. Act 3 opens the next morning with Davy still standing at the door, his swollen arm stuck in the brackets. His first line is "This is getting kind of monotonous, this business is." Blair and Hill call this "truly a thing of beauty"—an impeccable judgment.[18] But the humor of the line could just as well have been intentional. The play can be understood as both a conventional melodrama and a parody of a melodrama. Its enormous success is a matter of record: after a bad

start in September 1872, Mayo rewrote the script and reopened at
Woods' Museum in Manhattan, June 1873; it began a long tour in
England at the Alexandra Theatre in Liverpool, June 1879; it closed
at the Broadway Theatre in Denver, June 1896. This twenty-four year
run was stopped only by Mayo's death. Presumably, the play was
not staged each and every night, so he acted in others as well, but
in keeping track of the performances of *Be Sure You're Right*, Mayo
lost count at two thousand! Obviously, people went to see it because it was a great deal of fun. (See frontispiece.)

Almost nothing from the factual history of Crockett's life is re-
tained in Murdock and Mayo's play. Only our hero's legendary common sense and backwoods style of talking remain. When the curtain rises, we see him as a bachelor living in a mountain cabin with
his mother, Dame(!) Crockett, his nephew Little Bob, and his niece
Little Sally. Soon we are introduced to Davy's childhood sweetheart
Eleanor, whose rich father took her away long ago for travel and
education. Now Eleanor's father has died and she has returned to
the mountains with her uncle, Major Royston, her fiancé, Neil, and
her fiancé's father, Oscar Crampton. The hard foray from the city
to the woods has exposed Neil's lack of character, and Eleanor has
begun to think that marrying him will be a mistake. Royston is deep
in debt to Crampton, who also has evidence of irregularities in Royston's affairs and is blackmailing him. Like Nimrod Wildfire, Davy
sees straight through the villain the first time he lays eyes on him.
The plot's crisis is resolved by the heroism of both Davy and Eleanor. Eleanor saves her uncle by generously relinquishing her inheri-
tance to dissolve his debts and boldly burning Crampton's letters
of evidence. Davy scares the villain away by threatening him with
mountain justice—a trial before "Judge Lynch."

Much of the play's humor derives from the contrast between Davy's
backwoods talk and Eleanor's schoolbook speech. The peak of this
comic interplay is a scene in which she reads Walter Scott's "Lochinvar" to him, and he becomes emotionally distraught because he sees
a parallel between Lochinvar's romantic dilemma and his own. He
loves Eleanor and has been pining away, certain that he is beneath
her notice. "Well," says Davy, "there's something in this rough breast
of mine that leaps at the telling of a yarn like that." Eleanor apolo-
gizes, thinking she has somehow offended him. He replies, "Oh, don't
mind me. I ain't fit to breathe the same air with you. You are schol-

arly and dainty, and what am I, nothing but an ignorant backwoodsman, fit only for the forests and the fields where I'm myself hand in hand with nature and her teachings, knowing no better?"[19] In loving sympathy, Eleanor offers to teach Davy to read and write. It was this sentimental hilarity that tickled Hamlin Garland, who many years later reminisced about the play in his introduction to an edition of the Crockett books. "The playwright," he observed, "had made of Davy a young Lochinvar of the Canebrake, endowing him with all the romantic virtues."[20] This exactly describes the alterations wrought upon the legendary figure by the formulas of the melodramatic genre.

The rhetoric of *Be Sure You're Right* strongly supports the notion that living with nature redeems the soul from the corruptions of civilization. This theme is of course central to all of American popular culture. "Nature" is outdoors, in the forest or the country, and one's "living" must be simple. Urban life, socially approved manners, and wealth in excess of need are hazardous to spiritual health. In the city one is surrounded by con artists and parasites; money is a magnet for trouble; a mask of good manners hides every deceiver. Eleanor has learned these lessons by hard experience. When Neil asks her if she knew the Crockett family when she was a girl, she replies, "Yes, and I am proud to know them still. I love their honest simplicity, rugged though it be. It refreshes me like a draught of pure spring-water, or a breath from this fresh mountain air." Later, when she yields her fortune to save her uncle, Davy asks her if she won't find it difficult to give up the fine life, for "this is all I've got to offer you, and you've been used to better." She replies, "Used to what? Gaudy jewels that please the eye when the heart is empty? Oh, I have been so lonely amidst all these splendors." She has found her true wealth in the woods and mountains, and in "the heart and home of Davy Crockett."[21] Curtain.

That the sentimental humor of *Be Sure You're Right* was still vivid to Hamlin Garland several decades after he saw it is a clue to its popularity. To our delight, we find that the play also persisted in the memories of the first producers of films about Davy Crockett. They turned for their inspiration, not to the Crockett books, as later moviemakers have, but to Murdock and Mayo's story line. Fortunately, we have a source of information about the plots of these films: summaries and narratives published in periodicals like *Mov-*

ing Picture World and *Motion Picture Magazine*. The first two films, released in 1909 and 1910, were melodramas in the classical mold. The third, released in 1915, was a slapstick comedy, a farcical takeoff on the original. And the fourth, in 1916, was nothing less than a full-scale cinematic version of the Murdock and Mayo play.

Early in 1909, the New York Motion Picture Company brought out *Davy Crockett—in Hearts United*. The story opens in Davy's home, and we see the arrival of two citified young people: Anna, who has the role equivalent to Eleanor's in the Murdock and Mayo play, and Blake, who substitutes for Neil. They have come to the cabin to see if anyone can mend a broken saddle girth; there is a similar detail in Act 1 of *Be Sure You're Right*. Davy does the mending while Anna reads "Lochinvar" to him, and they fall in love, but Anna is still betrothed to Blake, whom she has come to detest. After Anna and Blake depart, they are lost in a storm and threatened by wolves. Davy, who has followed, rescues them. Later, on the lawn in front of Anna's father's house, the desperate heroine is about to be married to Blake, but at the last moment Davy rides his horse across the yard, scoops her up, takes her off to his cabin and marries her.[22]

Less than a year later, Selig Polyscope Company released *Davy Crockett*. In this, the heroine's name is Mary. She is the daughter of "a humble trapper in the mountains," and she is pressed by "another suitor more favored by the parents." (The suitor is not named in *Moving Picture World's* summary.) Davy spirits her away from a barn dance, however, and on their way home, they are attacked by wolves. They take refuge in a cabin, where Davy endures a night with his arm stuck in the door, just as in the play. When Mary gets home, she finds that her parents have prepared her wedding. She is "upbraided" for loving Davy and rushed at once into the nuptials, "to wed her mother's choice." Davy rides in and carries her off, this time "emulating Lochinvar's ride."[23]

The slapstick farce, *Davy Crockett Up-to-Date*, was released in 1915 by United Film Service. The heroine has become a "blonde young lady," and both the unwanted rival and the wolves are displaced by a band of Indians. While foolishly walking in the woods alone, the blonde is "surprised and kissed by one of her red-skinned lovers." This makes her "so indignant that she stops to thrash him." His enraged companions grab her and attempt to scalp her, but "losing her forelock does not seriously injure her health." She escapes, meets

Davy, and the two run to his home. There, the Indians attack the cabin as the wolves did in the play, and the film collapses in its slapstick climax as the Indians are repulsed by hardtack biscuits thrown at their heads.[24]

The full-scale film version of Murdock and Mayo's play appeared in 1916, released by Pallas (Paramount) and starring Dustin Farnum as Davy and Winifred Kingston as Eleanor. It was titled simply *Davy Crockett*, and the author of the screenplay was Frank Mayo, the actor's grandson. A narrative version of the screenplay appeared in the September 1916 issue of *Motion Picture Magazine*, and is reproduced, complete with some wonderful stills from the movie, as Chapter 6 in the present volume. The film had been reviewed in *Variety* a month earlier: the critic admired its scenery, Farnum's spectacular bronco riding, and the scene where Davy bars the door with his arm, but was less than impressed with the "drawn-out and padded story."[25]

The narrative version in *Motion Picture Magazine* shows that the movie follows the general plot outline of the play, but there are a few important alterations. In the story's first scene, we meet Davy's childhood sweetheart, Eleanor, before she leaves with her father for Europe; the first scene of the play occurs at the time she returns, after her father's death. In the narrative, it is Eleanor who inadvertently puts the bar to the cabin door into the fireplace; in the play, Davy uses it to start the fire because there is no other fuel in the cabin. In the play, therefore, Davy has made a stupid mistake, but in the film, Eleanor, who is a mountain aristocrat brought up in the manor house, can be forgiven because she is understandably ignorant of log cabin machinery. For the screen story's conclusion, the writer turned away from the play entirely and borrowed the rescue scene from the earlier movies. Davy rides his horse straight through the manor house and into the drawing room, where Eleanor's wedding is under way. She has turned toward the door in anticipation of her release, for the two have planned it all, in the style of "Lochinvar." Davy scoops up his bride, and together they gallop out the door and are "gone down the path of the moon" that leads "into the wide world." The story says that Davy's daring rescue leaves the wedding party looking on "pallid with amaze."[26] Surely this splendid phrase describes the impact the film itself had upon its audiences in 1916.

The makers of these movies saw nothing to be gained by referring to historical facts. Like the play, the films were sentimental and
humorous, and people went to see them for the fun of it. But other
early moviemakers were attracted to a piece of history that included
Crockett—the events at the Alamo. Davy is a minor character in
The Immortal Alamo, released by Melies in 1911, and in *The Martyrs
of the Alamo,* from Fine Arts-Triangle, 1915; he is the lead character—
as played by Cullen Landis—in a possibly interesting film that has
been lost, Sunset's *Davy Crockett at the Fall of the Alamo,* 1926.[27] A
lively later film is *Heroes of the Alamo,* produced by Sunset and released by Columbia in 1937. Lane Chandler plays Crockett in this
one, and at least one scholar has noted a strong similarity between
Chandler's relaxed, lanky Davy and Fess Parker's.[28] The film treats
Davy's death ironically: wounded, he tries to crawl away but is clubbed
to death by a Mexican soldier.[29]

The portrayal of Davy that has most influenced our contemporary popular idea of Crockett's legendary image is Fess Parker's, in
the famous Walt Disney series. (See page 146, Chapter 7). In late
1954, Walt Disney Productions shot three segments of its Davy Crockett story for the weekly show *Disneyland.* While assembling the film,
the studio discovered that there was not quite enough footage to
fill the time alloted, so *Disneyland's* musical composer, George Bruns,
and the scriptwriter, Tom Blackburn, whipped up a song—with seventeen stanzas—to bridge the gaps between scenes. This was "The Ballad
of Davy Crockett," with the notorious refrain that every kid in the
United States sang at the top of his or her lungs throughout, it
seemed, the whole of 1955. The first segment of the show, "Davy
Crockett—Indian Fighter," was shown in December 1954; the second
and third, "Davy Crockett Goes to Congress" and "Davy Crockett
at the Alamo," were shown in January and February 1955. These
three were edited and assembled for the movie version, *Davy Crockett,
King of the Wild Frontier* (the title comes from the ballad's notorious
refrain). When the movie was released in May 1955, the famous fad
was at its height. Two follow-up shows were made, "Davy Crockett's
Keelboat Race" and "Davy Crockett and the River Pirates." These
were shown in November and December 1955, and released to theaters
as *Davy Crockett and the River Pirates* in July 1956. By then the fad
had burnt itself out, and few people who saw the first movie when
they were children can remember that there was a second. However,

one of Walt Disney's profitable insights into the nature of popular culture was that films made for children have a continually renewed audience, and all five of the Davy Crockett television segments are regularly rerun.[30]

Fess Parker's portrayal stresses natural nobility and common sense, qualities that are close to the core of the Crockett legend. When he has to fight, he fights heroically, and all viewers remember the final shot of Davy swinging his broken rifle Betsy to knock down his attackers inside the ruined walls of the Alamo. In Disney's film, Davy doesn't die—he fades out. Parker does an especially good job capturing Crockett's humorous style. His talk is down-home and funny. "I'm plumb flutterated by the honor," he says. He bites his tongue when he has to write his name. The first time we see him, he is grinning at a bear, and sure enough, his grin compels the critter's submission. In the legend, Crockett's grin stuns raccoons and knocks the bark off trees. Later, when Parker's Davy tries to grin down a hostile Indian, he loses—the Indian can't see the humor in it.

Parker's role is supported by several other interesting portrayals, among them Basil Ruysdael as a gruff, tough Andrew Jackson; Helene Stanley as a brave and intelligent Polly (David's second wife, Elizabeth, is not in the series); and Hans Conried as the cynical, fastidious, and effete Thimblerig, a character invented by Richard Penn Smith in 1836 for his spurious *Col. Crockett's Exploits and Adventures in Texas*. Every fan remembers Davy's sidekick Georgie Russel, played by Buddy Ebsen. Georgie has as many comic lines as Davy, and the series launched Ebsen's long career in television, which included lead roles in *The Beverly Hillbillies* and *Barnaby Jones*. Though the studio borrowed the name of George Russell (with two *l*'s), a companion Crockett mentions in his autobiography, the character is otherwise an invention. One surprise is that he is made the innovator of media publicity promoting Davy's legend. It is he who, in the story, has composed "The Ballad of Davy Crockett," which he sings in an off-key croak. One day, Davy, who has been puzzled by the wildfire spread of his reputation, discovers a pamphlet filled with tall stories about his bear-hunting adventures. The author is Georgie. Now Davy understands why, wherever he goes, everybody already knows him.

Rhetorically, the plot underlines the utility of folk wisdom, plain talk, and unhesitating remedial action. Greed, cruelty, slick politics, and bigotry are the enemies. Everything in the film shows that children are the implied audience. In one memorable scene, Davy Crockett stands up in Congress to defend the human rights of Indians. His fierce opposition to Jackson's Indian Removal Bill costs him his congressional career, but he has lived up to his motto by doing what's right. History tells us that the real David Crockett did oppose the Indian Removal Bill but tried to keep his position quiet. He knew it would spell political ruin back home in West Tennessee, where most of the settlers favored Indian removal. The news leaked out, and he lost the next election anyway (for this and other reasons).[31] But to anyone who has a strong memory of Davy on the floor of the House in Disney's film, the historical reality doesn't have enough Truth in it to matter.

In Disney's interpretation of Davy's story, as in virtually all previous Crockett drama, the legend was shaped to meet the demands of the form, and the form was shaped by the producer's perception of the expectations and tastes of the audience. These principles are also at work in John Wayne's portrayal in *The Alamo*, from United Artists (1960), but this image of Crockett is unique in that it is also shaped by a legendary actor who is a member of the same mythic type. Whether he plays a pilot or a Marine, a cowboy or a prospector, John Wayne is always the Westerner—like Crockett, a man of strong words backed by a ready will to act, a straight shooter with a rifle or a truism, a humorous good fellow to his friends and a disaster to his enemies. As the stereotype of the Westerner has grown, so has the popular idea of Crockett's legendary appearance. A man who was in reality about five feet, eight inches tall has become in our collective imagination six feet four in his stocking feet. John Wayne *was* a big man, and his physical appearance in *The Alamo* suggests the popular idea of Crockett's stature. Wayne evokes Crockett simply by dressing the part and acting like himself. The Crockett legend and the Wayne legend are made of the same stuff, and this fusion of the two is the only three-dimensional representation of the legendary Crockett ever to appear in the theater.[32] (See page 119.)

In *The Alamo*, his name is *Crockett*. He is Davy occasionally, but only to his closest friends; he is seldom called David. In the newspapers and magazines of the 1830s, he was most commonly called Crockett or Colonel Crockett, so the film has rung a note of authenticity in this simple detail. Wayne wears a buckskin jacket and

John Wayne as David Crockett. From the United Artists release "THE ALAMO."

either a coonskin cap or a rounded felt hat. The buckskin and the coonskin are the fictional clothes of the legend; Crockett himself wore a buckskin shirt only to reinforce his image on the campaign trail, and he may never even have owned a coonskin hat. It is John Wayne's presence that carries the picture. His Crockett is boastful, swaggering, intelligent, crafty, humorous, flirtatiously courteous to women, hard drinking, straight shooting, and straight talking. Most important of all, he is self-conscious: he knows he is a legend in his own time, and he knows that his stand at the Alamo may well turn out to be a suicidal fulfillment of his artificially wrought public character.

Though it contains admirable work by Richard Widmark as Bowie, Laurence Harvey as Travis, and Richard Boone as Houston, this is not a great film, but for any student interested in the long history of Crockett's legend, it is a touchstone. One of its best moments captures both the absurdity and the courage of the self-conscious hero when Travis accuses Crockett of making it all up—his clothes, his speech, his reputation, everything. John Wayne produced and directed this film—far be it from him to have his Crockett deny the invention.

NOTES

1. The autobiography is *A Narrative of the Life of David Crockett of the State of Tennessee* (Philadelphia: E.L. Carey & A. Hart, 1834). *Crockett's Tour* (E.L. Carey & A. Hart, 1835), was probably written by William Clark; *Crockett's Exploits* (E.L. Carey & A. Hart, 1836) was assembled by Richard Penn Smith. The three are often combined as *The Life of David Crockett, the Original Humorist and Irrepressible Backwoodsman* (e.g., New York: Lovell, Coryell and Co., n.d.; or New York: A.L. Burt, 1902).

2. See John Seelye and Michael A. Lofaro's essays, Chapters 2 and 3 in the present volume, for information on the curious history and contents of the almanacs; for discussions of the political background of the various Crockett books, see James A. Shackford, *David Crockett: The Man and the Legend* (Chapel Hill: Univ. of North Carolina Press, 1956), and Richard Boyd Hauck, *Crockett: A Bio-Bibliography* (Westport, Conn.: Greenwood Press, 1982)—hereafter cited as *Crockett*.

3. Shackford, *David Crockett*, 89–90, 265; *Crockett*, 4–8.

4. Marilyn Miller, "Yankee Theatre," in *Showcasing American Drama: A Handbook of Source Materials on "The Lion of the West,"* ed. Vera Jiji (Brooklyn: Humani-

ties Institute, Brooklyn College, 1983), 3; see also the handbill reproduced in James Kirke Paulding, *The Lion of the West*, ed. James N. Tidwell (Stanford: Stanford Univ. Press, 1954), 52; hereafter cited as *Lion of the West*.

5. See Chapter 2 of Constance Rourke, *American Humor: A Study of the National Character* (New York: Harcourt, 1931), and V.L.O. Chittick, ed., *Ring-Tailed Roarers: Tall Tales of the American Frontier, 1830–60* (Caldwell, Idaho: Caxton Printers, 1941); *Crockett*, 67–79.

6. The words and music for "Hunters of Kentucky" can be found in Benjamin A. Botkin, ed., *A Treasury of American Folklore* (New York: Crown, 1944), 9–12.

7. See my earlier essay in the present volume (Chapter 1) for an account of this meeting.

8. Ralph M. Aderman, ed., *The Letters of James Kirke Paulding* (Madison: Univ. of Wisconsin Press, 1962), 113.

9. Joseph J. Arpad, "John Wesley Jarvis, James Kirke Paulding, and Colonel Nimrod Wildfire," *New York Folklore Quarterly*, 21 (1965), 92–106.

10. *Letters of Paulding*, 112; Crockett's reply is in note 2, pp. 112–13. Shackford (*David Crockett*, 254–55) makes a good argument that the Crockett letter is a fake whipped up by Whig party lackeys, and that Paulding may have known this.

11. Tidwell, Introduction to *Lion of the West*, 7–14; Jiji, *Handbook*, p. 4.

12. *Lion of the West*, 19–20.

13. *Ibid.*, 37.

14. *Ibid.*, 61–62.

15. *Ibid.*, 54–55.

16. *Sketches and Eccentricities of Colonel David Crockett of West Tennessee* (New York: J. & J. Harper, 1833), 164. The author was probably Mathew St. Clair Clarke.

17. Isaac Goldberg and Hubert Heffner, eds., *America's Lost Plays*, 4 (Bloomington: Indiana Univ. Press, 1963), xviii–xix.

18. Walter Blair and Hamlin Hill, *America's Humor: From Poor Richard to Doonesbury* (New York: Oxford Univ. Press, 1978), 144.

19. *America's Lost Plays*, 4: 133.

20. Hamlin Garland, ed., *The Autobiography of David Crockett* (New York: Scribners, 1923), 3.

21. *America's Lost Plays*, 4: 125, 146–48.

22. *Moving Picture World*, May 8, 1909, p. 609.

23. *Moving Picture World*, Apr. 23, 1910, p. 657.

24. *Moving Picture World*, May 22, 1915, pp. 1261, 1336.

25. *Variety Film Reviews, 1907–1920*, Vol. 1 (New York: Garland, 1983), for Aug. 4, 1916.

26. *Motion Picture Magazine*, Sept. 1916, p. 98. The same issue has an article by Peter Wade titled "Unto the Third Generation" that is billed as "A Chat with Frank Mayo," 119–20 + 168. Many thanks to Michael A. Lofaro for sharing with me these serendipitous discoveries.

27. *Moving Picture World*, May 27, 1911, p. 1204; and Oct. 30, 1915, pp. 864, 1155; Kenneth W. Munden, ed., *The American Film Institute Catalogue of Motion Pictures Produced in the United States: Feature Films, 1921–1930*, F2 (New York: Bowker, 1971), 174.

28. Richard B. Dimmitt, *A Title Guide to the Talkies* (New York: Scarecrow Press, 1965), 716; letter to the author from Don Graham, University of Texas, April 24, 1983.

29. Accounts of the controversies surrounding Davy's death are in Dan Kilgore, *How Did Davy Die?* (College Station: Texas A. & M. Univ. Press, 1978), and *Crockett*, 50–54.

30. Christopher Finch, *Walt Disney: From Mickey Mouse to the Magic Kingdoms* (New York: Abrams, 1973), 361; *Crockett*, 91–96; letter to the author from David R. Smith, Walt Disney Archives, February 10, 1981.

31. For an interpretation of Crockett's opposition to Indian removal see *Crockett*, xvii–xxiii.

32. There is also a three-dimensional characterization of Crockett in a work of fiction: Dee A. Brown, *Raise High the Banner: A Novel Based on the Life of Davy Crockett* (Philadelphia: Macrae-Smith, 1942). In *Who Played Who in the Movies* (London: Frederick Muller, 1979), Roy Pickard says that Fess Parker and John Wayne are "the best-known screen Crocketts," but his choice for "the most accurate" is "grizzled character actor Arthur Hunnicutt" (48). Hunnicutt played Crockett in *The Last Command*, a film about the siege of the Alamo (see Filmography, below).

A DAVY CROCKETT FILMOGRAPHY

The film indexes by Richard Dimmitt, Kenneth Munden, and Roy Pickard, and *Moving Picture World, Motion Picture Magazine*, and *Variety Film Reviews*, mentioned previously, along with Einar Lauritzen and Gunnar Lundquist, *American Film Index: 1908–1915* (Stockholm: Akademibokhandeln, 1976); John Stewart, *Filmarama*, 1 (Metuchen, N.J.: Scarecrow Press, 1975); and the various volumes of the *New York Times Film Reviews* (New York: New York Times and Arno Press, 1970–) provide information that establishes the following Crockett filmography. The order is chronological. Not all the movies listed here are discussed in the article. Films about the Alamo are included, since Crockett is usually featured as an important character. Old reviews sometimes failed to list actors and, when they did cite the names, they often failed to connect the actor with the character played; if known, the actor playing Davy is named here in parentheses. My thanks to Allen Ellis, Indiana University Reference Library, for his indispensable assistance in running down Crockett characterizations in long-forgotten movies.

Silents

Davy Crockett—in Hearts United. New York Motion Pictures, 1909. (Charles K. French.)

Davy Crockett. Selig Polyscope, 1910. (Probably Hobart Bosworth.)

The Immortal Alamo. Melies, 1911.
Davy Crockett Up-to-Date. United Film Service, 1915. (Probably W.E. Browning.)
The Martyrs of the Alamo. Fine Arts–Triangle, 1915. (A.D. Sears.)
Davy Crockett. Pallas (Paramount), likely produced by the Oliver Morosco Photo-play Co., 1916. (Dustin Farnum.)
Davy Crockett at the Fall of the Alamo. Sunset, 1926. (Cullen Landis.)

Talkies

Heroes of the Alamo. Columbia, 1937. (Lane Chandler.)
Man of Conquest. Republic, 1939. (Robert Barrat.)
Davy Crockett, Indian Scout. Reliance, 1950. (George Montgomery played Davy Crockett, "cousin" of the hero.)
Man from the Alamo. Universal, 1953. (Trevor Bardette.)
The Last Command. Republic, 1955. (Arthur Hunnicutt.)
Davy Crockett, King of the Wild Frontier. Walt Disney, 1955. (Fess Parker.)
Davy Crockett and the River Pirates. Walt Disney, 1956. (Fess Parker.)
The First Texan. Allied Artists, 1956. (James Griffith.)
Alias Jesse James. United Artists, 1959. (Fess Parker, in a walk-on part.)
The Alamo. United Artists, 1960. (John Wayne.)

6. A Newly Discovered Silent Film

AN ARTICLE ON *DAVY CROCKETT*
(OLIVER MOROSCO PHOTOPLAY CO.)

by *Norman Bruce*

.

The following article from the collection of Michael A. Lofaro is reprinted from the September 1916 issue of *Motion Picture Magazine*. For a discussion of the film, see Chapter 5, Richard Boyd Hauck's "Making It All Up: Davy Crockett in the Theater."

Davy Crockett

(Oliver Morosco Photoplay Co.)

With DUSTIN FARNUM in the illustrations as
DAVY CROCKETT

By NORMAN BRUCE

his story was written from the Photoplay of
FRANK MAYO, who adapted the
same from the stage play
of that name

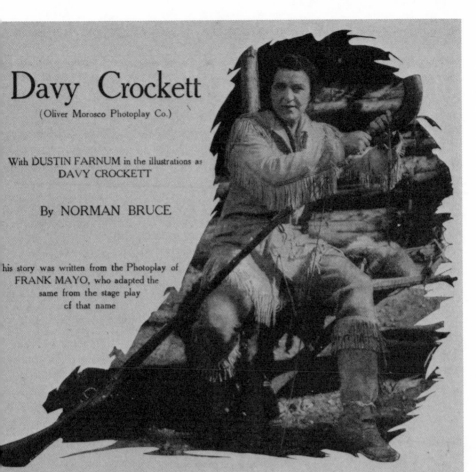

HE was as much a part of the forest as the powerful oaks thru which they were passing, rugged, tough-inewed, a thing of unroofed air and wild torms; she was as much a part of the orest as the playful sun-gleams spattering the leaves, or the delicate bluebells inging fairy tunes atop their slim, swaying stems. Not lovers, these two, for hey were very young, and a gulf of birth ay between them too wide and deep to e bridged by a frail thought of sentiment, but comrades, as the oak is comade to the wind-flower. They walked or the most part in understanding ilence, for the boy had few words at he beck of his tongue, and the girl was oo sensitive to the forest mood to belittle t with the chatter of the manor-house.

Beyond the willows the river rushed y, streaked with gold and carrying on ts current scarlet and yellow leaves, for, n spite of the warm wind and flawless sky, the year was at its turning. Eleanor Vaughn plucked a stalk of goldenrod and held it, a trifle sadly, for him to see.

"That means winter, Davy," she sighed, "and an end to our good times. I could find it in my heart to be very sorry."

"There'll be other summers," said Davy, practically, "and, besides, the woods are full of things to see and hear and learn in winter-tide."

The girl shook her head. "But I shall not be here," she said. "My Aunt Bettina, in England, has written, and father and I sail next week. It seems I am growing up, and must be taught young-ladyish airs and graces, how to hold a fan, and embroider knights on tapestry, and strum the harpsichord." Her face clouded. She raised her wide, childish eyes, blue as harebells under clear water, to the boy's face. "When I think of growing up—I am almost—afraid."

The boy did not speak nor look at her.
He grasped his rifle fiercely and strode
on so fast that she had to run to keep
pace beside him. Beneath the dark skin,
not yet pierced by beard, his jaw was
grimly set and his young eyes were
somber.

"Davy! Where are you hurrying so
fast?" the girl panted, shaking the fine,
golden ringlets back from her moist forehead. "And aren't you a bit sorry I'm
going away?"

"I'm goin' to look at my b'ar-trap,"
answered Davy, briefly. He ignored the
latter part of her question. "You remember the b'ar we saw a ways back.
headed this way? I'm thinkin' maybe
he smelt the bait—the wind was right
for't and the tracks lie that way."

He pointed to the moss at their feet,
printed with a great, blunt paw, but the
girl did not follow his finger. Her eyes,
hurt and wistful, were on his face, and
the corners of her full, child-pouting lips
were quivering.

"You care more about your old bears
and foxes than you do about me!" she
cried, stamping a small, angry foot. "I
thought you'd be sorry, and you aren't!
Why, maybe I'll marry a—a lord or
something, over in England, and never
come back at all!"

"I reckon that's just what will hap-
pen," said Davy Crockett, slowly. He
stood, big, straight, splendid of limb and
muscle, before her, a dark, slow flush
creeping over his set face. "You're
Eleanor Vaughn, daughter of a gentleman. You're rich, you're book-l'arned—
I'm Davy Crockett, son of a trapper.
When you come back they wont let you
speak to me—or maybe you wont want
to. I dont like it, but it's the way of the
world. I reckon it wont do no good to
cry."

The girl's face had cleared during
his speech, and now she burst into a peal
of laughter, dancing up and down and
pelting him with the crumbling gold of
the flower in her hand. Her flowered,
beruffled gown swirled about the imma-
ture grace of her slender figure, a trifle
coltish as yet, with only so much beauty
as the hard, green bud that will later
uncurl and curve into a rose of men's
desire.

"YOU CARE MORE ABOUT YOUR OLD BE..

The boy's thick, black brows drew
together under her dainty mockery

FOXES THAN YOU DO ABOUT ME!" SHE CRIED, STAMPING A SMALL, ANGRY FOOT

d, suddenly, tears of boyish rage stood   she was all contrition, and ran to his side,
is dark eyes.   At the sight of them   taking one big hand in her own.

"There! We wont spoil our last day with bickering," she wheedled. "I dont know why I laughed. I often do things I dont understand myself, and I meant to be so nice, too. See——"

She dived into a capacious pocket in the wide folds of her skirt and took out a small volume, flourishing it triumphantly. "It's a book of poems; they are much nicer than bears. Let's sit down under this tree and I will read them to you."

The forest was very still, as if holding its breath to hear. Full length on the moss the boy lay, chin in cupped hands, rapt in the dream her voice evoked as it swung into the stirring lilt of Sir Lochinvar. On his wild steed, the young knight galloped against a reddened western sky to the towered hall of his lady; the wedding guests whispered; the bridegroom paled, and fair Ellen smiled and sighed. Young Romance, haunting, wistful, sad with the tender grief of evanescent things, stirred their hearts. The girl's eyes were full of tears, as she finished reading, but the boy's gaze flamed, and he sprang with one bound to his feet, head flung back, arms clenched at his sides.

"He was a *man!* Cant you see him— the horse plunging, rearing—a great brute like your father's Devilskin? It makes me feel as tho I could—could do *anything!* It makes me proud to be strong and a man——"

Suddenly he looked at Eleanor, and a startled something sprang into his eyes, a something that had not been there before. It was as tho he had never really seen her till now. Their gaze locked, the forest grew suddenly hushed, and the girl's childish breast rose on the swell of her breath. There was all the purity of the dawn moment in this nascence of sex, passionless, awed and wondering.

"Davy! Davy!" she cried brokenly, and held out her hands. He went on one knee and caught them awkwardly, then dropped them. The touch had broken the spell, and once more they were Eleanor Vaughn heiress, and Davy Crockett the trapper's son. With new consciousness, she pulled her skirt over her slim ankles and rose, avoiding his look.

"I'm glad you liked the poem, Davy," she said sweetly, but there was cruelt in her veiled eyes, for had he not droppe her hands? "I'd leave the book wit you—if you only knew how to read!"

The blood in the boy's cheeks an swered the lash of her words. H stooped, picked up his gun, and set h teeth hard. When he finally spoke, h voice was curt. "I reckon I kin *l'arn*" he said briefly, "an' now, suppose we g look for that b'ar?"

A week later Eleanor Vaughn and h father set sail for England, leaving th manor-house in charge of Vaughn friend, Hector Royston. On that sam day Davy went to the schoolmaster an asked to be taught his letters.

In two years a great deal may hap pen. An awkward hobbledehoy of boy may change into a tall, handsom man; a slip of a girl may bloom into beautiful young woman. But it take more than two years to build a bridg across the chasm between a tiny trapper cottage and a manor-house set like proud jewel among age-old oaks an elms. Something of this thought was i Davy Crockett's mind, as he stood, on moon-plashed evening in spring, lookin over the hawthorn hedge, flowered wit white ghosts of blossoms, in the so dusk, at the lighted windows of th Vaughn library. Within he could se several men sitting about a card-tabl among them Royston, who, rumor sai was too fond of his little game for h own good. The other men at the tabl Davy recognized as a Colonel Crompto and his nephew, Neil, guests since mi winter at the manor-house. With th sure instinct of male-kind, Davy's loo halted on Neil Crompton's handsom florid face with its easy smile and bol eyes under lids a trifle swollen an heavy. He was dressed in an assure swaggering fashion, every article of h apparel just a shade overdone—the flow ered waistcoat too gay, the white nec cloth too tall, the ruffles at his wrists to full and wide—yet withal, Davy admitte bitterly, a fine figure of a man and on to seize a woman's fancy. And no Eleanor was coming home.

"Davy Crockett," he said alou grimly, "you are a fool! What's th doings of the gentry to you with yo

"IT MAKES ME FEEL AS THO I COULD—COULD DO ANYTHING!"

eat, coarse hands and coon cap? And hat's your midnight struggles with hoolbooks and the times you've fought man's temptations and come out clean?

What's that to a lady like her? There's things i' this world that cant be downed —I can kill a wildcat with my bare hands, but I cant strangle what's atween her and me. Oh, God! it isn't fair! It isn't fair!"

He turned abruptly and plunged into the darkness, drawing it around his misery like a cloak. Very like one of the strong, primitive forest creatures was this strong, primitive man—inarticulate, suffering dumbly with the instinct to hide his pain. When, an hour later, he strode

Davy looked at his mother dazedly
"Is Colonel Vaughn dead?" he ask
The old woman nodded, important w news.

"A month ago—rest his soul! It w Bessie Merrill, the chambermaid at t manor-house, told me. An' the you mistress an' her aunt are comin' ho tomorrow. Royston, the gamblin' c

DAVY "L'ARNS" HOW TO READ LOCHINVAR

into the tiny cottage sitting-room, where his mother and father sat, his face was swept of conflict. He tossed his fur cap into a corner and settled down over his schoolbooks, great shaggy head propped on his fists. Across his bowed shoulders the old people's gossip droned unheeded, till suddenly a name caught his attention.

"An' he was full ten year younger 'an ye, feyther, Colonel Vaughn was—a youngish man ye might a'most say. An' him to go so sudden! The ways o' the Lord are queer, to be sure."

rascal, is to be her guardian. Why, Da lad, what's ailin' yeh? It's white as sheet yeh are!"

"Nothing, mother," said Davy, a turned back to his book; but the lette might have been Egyptian hieroglyphi for all the sense they carried to his brai Tomorrow he would see her, and aft that all the tomorrows would be full the need of her and empty with the lac of her. She would be farther from hi at the manor-house than she had bee across the seas. If it had not been f

e helpless old people nodding in their
airs, he would have flung his books
ide, caught up his cap and hurried out
to the night, never to return.

Yet, after all, the meeting was not so
rd. Eleanor came toward him as soon
s he stepped into the hall, the next
'ternoon—a new, beautiful woman—
leanor, with the old frank friendliness
her bluebell eyes. She wore a black
'ess that added inches and stateliness
› her bearing, and her face was a little
orn with the recent tears, but Davy
ought, as he looked at her, that very
arely she was the most beautiful woman
the world.

"Davy!" Eleanor cried, tremulously—
oh, Davy, how big you've grown; how
ig and brown and splendid! Why
ou're a *man*, not the boy who took me
ear-hunting, and I—I suppose I'm
rown up, too."

"You're grown up, too," nodded Davy.
Ie saw Neil Crompton lounging in the
oorway beyond, an amused smile on his
verfull red lips, and suddenly he felt
lumsy and out of place in the white
aneled room with its silken draperies
nd the supercilious family portraits on
he walls.

"He looks at me as tho I were a
ervant," he thought dully; "no doubt
he thinks of me that way, too."

As soon as he decently could, he slipped
way, and thruout all the summer and
utumn that followed he never entered
he manor-house again. He saw little of
Eleanor. Neil Crompton was with her
wherever she went, and gossip had them
etrothed before the first red leaf fell.

Gun over his shoulder, Davy roamed
he forest, seeking difficult peace of spirit
n its strong, calm silences. The shy
wood-folk grew to regard him as one of
heir own kind and peered at him from
ough and underbrush with bright, sym-
athetic eyes, or ran on tiny, silent feet
t his side. So the long summer dragged
y at last, and Davy's forest was aflame
vith scarlet torches of death and decay.

He walked, on an afternoon in late
October, thru a drift of painted leaves
o visit one of his bear-pits at a great
listance from the settlements. A strange
ush was in the air, and the boughs
noved restlessly at the will of a noiseless

wind. Dour clouds scattered across the
sky, snuffing out the chill autumn sun-
shine, scattering a gray, woolly light over
the world.

"Snow!" he muttered, "and soon, too!
Ah——"

A white flake floated by his eyes, then
another; in an instant the air was blind
and breathless with the snow. Davy
laid down his gun to draw his cap more
closely about his ears; when he turned
to look for it, it was gone—erased by
the snow! There was no time to stop
to hunt now. In another hour he would
be lost beyond hope, for the wild swirl
of the storm was wiping out landmarks
on every side. With a flash of joy, Davy
remembered the cabin he had passed a
mile back on the side of a hill.

Ten minutes later, drenched to the
skin, he staggered across the crumbling
sill and jerked at the door with numbed
fingers. Then he stopped, for somewhere
beyond in the maelstrom of the snow he
heard a woman's voice crying hopelessly
for aid.

"Coming!" shouted Davy, hoarsely.
"Keep on calling, so I can find you!"

The thread of sound guided him thru
a narrow strip of pinewoods, across a
field, stumbling at every step, until he
almost ran against a slim, black shape
that rose suddenly out of the snow.
Then the wind caught up his cry and
whirled it over the forest to where, on a
far-away hillside, a pack of lean, gray
shadows ran thru the drifts:

"Eleanor! My God! 'tis Eleanor!"

At his touch, the girl gave a great
gasp and crumpled forward into his
arms. In spite of their danger, and the
pain of his numbing limbs, a fierce joy
shook the man, as he stumbled back to
the cabin carrying the dear weight of
her against his heart. But the first words
she spoke when she opened her eyes
dispelled it.

"Neil," she moaned—"he fell—and
then I could not find him. He may be
dying even now."

Davy's face grew very white and stern.
"Tell me," he said slowly, "you care for
this man's life a great deal?"

In answer she held up one slim hand,
on which a great ruby glowed and flamed
like a naked heart. "It is—his ring,"

she stammered. "I do not know how much I love him, but I do know I would not have him die. Oh, Davy, you must save him! What are you listening to? *What is it you hear?*"

The man turned a quiet look on her that stilled her panic. Then he straightened his great shoulders and flung back his head with a queer little smile. "I will find him and bring him back to you if God will let me," Davy Crockett said solemnly and was gone.

The lean, gray shadows—how near they are! And now they speak with hoarse, howling cries that the wind brings to the ears of the man stumbling thru the snow. He hears them, smiles again that strange smile, and goes on to meet them down the hill.

Eleanor had given up all hope, when, moments or hours later, a staggering, swaying bulk sprawled across the door-sill.

"Quick!" said a hoarse voice she

hardly recognized as Davy's —"bar the door. They're right behind!"

He laid Neil on the floor and sprang to the door, forcing it shut; then the room rang to his cry of horror.

"The bar—it is gone!"

Eleanor pointed a shaking hand toward the chimney-place, filled with dancing flames. "I broke it up—to make a fire," she said huskily. "What frightful thing is coming? Oh, God!"

A deep howl answered her, and the door swayed open under the impact of a dozen panting bodies. Davy forced it back with an effort that brought the veins out on his forehead.

"Wolves!" he said. "I cant hold it against them, unless——"

He was tearing at his coat. She caught his purpose and cried out in protest, but too late. Down had slipped his arm thru the bar-sockets just as the mad-

dened animals outside flung their wei; again on the door. A groan burst tween his bitten lips, but he stifled it a managed a gallant, tortured smile.

"It'll—hold," he gasped; "never—mi me. Look—after him."

The next hour was etched on Eleanc memory forev —the slc coming to l of the stunn man before fire; the baff howling o side; the t figure

HE STUMBLED BACK TO THE CABIN, TH DEAR WEIGHT OF HER AGAINST HIS HEART

crouched against the door, smiling at h with white lips whenever she looked t ward him; the poor, swollen arm wit its great, hanging, helpless hand.

When the rescuers had come at las they had had to cut the door away to se him free, but after that first involuntar tribute to pain not a groan had escape his lips, tho the great drops stood ou upon his forehead. For two weeks afte ward, they told her, he had carried tha arm in a sling—that much and no mor e heard of Davy, but sometimes the bonair Neal caught an absent look in r eyes that disturbed him. "Gad! sir, I think the wench is daft er that trapper fellow," he fretted; ou must prod old Royston and have m hurry the marriage, for I've no mind be jilted for a lout of a woodsman," had urged his uncle, Colonel Crompton.

him she ran forward, holding out piteous little hands. "Your arm, Davy?" she asked tremulously—"your poor, brave arm?" He shook his head impatiently. "I came," he said somberly, "to say good-by. I am going away tomorrow, and I wanted to wish you—happiness—before I went. I *do* wish it, Eleanor, with all my soul."

"IT'LL HOLD!" HE GASPED; "NEVER—MIND ME. LOOK—AFTER HIM"

A few days later Davy heard that the edding date had been set and the guests vited. His mother returned from a call Bessie, with breathless tales of preparation at the manor-house, of a cake iked in a hogshead, flowers ordered om Jamestown, and a wedding dress as ie as the one the Governor's wife wore the last Assembly Ball. Davy listened silence. Then he set the coonskin cap his dark head and went to the manorouse to see Eleanor. She was sitting all one in the great drawing-room when stood in the doorway, and at sight of

"You are going away?" She touched her throat with a small, trembling hand. "Not coming to my wedding? Davy, I cant be married without you there!"

He met her look with the eyes of a suffering wild creature, but no words came. Suddenly she touched his arm and began to speak very low: "Davy, last night I learnt a shameful thing. Colonel Crompton and my guardian were speaking in the library very loudly, tho I would not have heard what they said if I had not crept downstairs after a forgotten book. I caught my name and I listened. I learnt that Crompton won a large sum from my guardian at play—more than he could pay—and so he made a bargain to buy me for his nephew as part of the debt! Davy, do you think I can ever marry that man?"

He passed a bewildered hand across his eyes, as tho to brush away a dream too wonderful for belief. And the sleeve of his fringed hunting-coat slipped back, showing two livid scars on the white skin. Eleanor gave a little, broken cry and caught the hand in her warm, fluttering grasp.

"Davy, do you remember the poem I read you once long ago?" A tender mockery touched her lips. "What would poor Ellen have done if Sir Lochinvar hadn't come out of the west, do you suppose?"

Light leaped into Davy's dark eyes. Yet, still he dared not quite believe. "Eleanor!"—his deep voice caught on the word—"you mean——"

"Oh, blind Davy!" she whispered—"oh, stupid Davy! I have never loved any man but you. And now I dare say no more. There is some one coming. Go quickly, but remember Sir Lochinvar!"

The story was the talk of the countryside for a generation and became the heritage of folk-lore for lovers a hundred years later, to read with clasped hands. And yet, strangely enough, no two versions of it quite agreed as to

details. Some said that Eleanor was death-white bride as she came into tl Vaughn drawing-room that night, on o Royston's arm; others, that her face w rose-tinged and that she wore a triur phant smile. Some say that Neil Crom ton, a personable enough bridegroom his white satin and gold lace, came meet her and tried to take her hand, b she refused it; others, that the bishe himself had joined their hands and ha opened his book before the interruptic came. But all stories unite on what ha pened to prevent the fair Eleanor fro becoming a purchased bride. In tl hush before the first words were spoke the thud of swift hoofs was heard ga loping up the avenue of linden-tree And, at the sound, Eleanor sprang fro her bridegroom and faced the doo way, thru which rode Davy Crockett c the great, unbroken mare, Devilski Straight thru the gaping crowd the blac animal reared and plunged. Stoopir from the saddle, the rider caught tl bride, in her filmy robes, and swept h to the saddle before him with a sing swerve of his splendid body. And the while the onlookers watched, pallid wit amaze, the great horse bounded thru tl doorway and was gone down the pat of the moon that led them thru the lir den-trees into the wide world.

And so, dauntless in danger, mode in the courage of his heart and arm, ar daring in love, Davy Crockett won h heart's desire at last.

7. The Recycled Hero

WALT DISNEY'S DAVY CROCKETT

Margaret J. King

As a public property of the first rank who hails from both history and myth, Davy Crockett is as fine a figure of popular culture as can be imagined. His vibrant and irrepressible life as a popular hero, spanning two centuries and still in progress, is in itself a case study in the career of a popular hero who moves across every stage and through every medium of culture—from tall tale, folklore, journalism, government record, fiction, stage play, historical document, to academic treatise, and, more recently, through the offices of Walt Disney, into the mass media of television, film, and popular song.

It is tempting to confine Crockett's heroic saga to the nineteenth century. But Crockett did not begin as a folk hero and gradually develop into a media hero. From humble origins as a local folk hero, he grew into a national media hero as a political party symbol, progressed into folk legend, then emerged into media form once more in the 1950s. The Disney-inspired Crockett phenomenon is literally a second coming, one even more grandiose than the first.

Crockett's heroic career may be viewed as a multidimensional whole, the product of many changes, large and small, in Crockett's popular interest and interpretation. Most of these developments took place posthumously, and are continuing to unfold, of course, with ongoing shifts in the popular view of America's past. Thus, to limit the study of Crockett to his actual lifetime would be to ignore the greater and more influential stages of his heroic growth.

The entire sequence of events forms a pageant: his early popularization by Whigs for political purposes as the prototype of the "just plain folks" politician; subsequent Crockett legends based on the earlier "media campaign" during his lifetime; fascination with the legends that attached themselves to Crockett after his death, especially in the almanacs, autobiographies, stage plays, and dime novels; study of these popular forms of literature by historians and folklorists; Disney's great popularization of Crockett in 1955; the subsequent renewal of historical, folkloristic, and sociological interest in Crockett; and finally, academic study of the entire "Crockett process" that depicts Crockett as the point of convergence for all these trends. The historical Crockett can now be seen as a "first cause" in an evolutionary life story that yields a very checkered current biography in the popular mind.

This review of the Crockett craze, therefore, will move across a span of two centuries—from the historical Crockett to the gigantic character of legend and folklore to a focus upon the television "renaissance" of the man—with stops along the way to study the steps in his evolution into the paragon of American heroes.

The profile of national character is very much drawn after the profile of our heroes; to see them is to see ourselves. The recycling of history, as much as the writing of history, has much to say about the sensibility of a time and people. Many clues lie in the transformation of a hero out of history. When one era recycles a hero from another, that hero is brought up to date, altered, and molded to the temper of the present. The making-over process can reveal much about how national values, beliefs, and outlooks have changed from one generation to another.

A study of the Davy Crockett craze challenges the conventional definition of *craze* as an ephemeral occasion, something trivial and superficial that passes without leaving any mark. Instead, it suggests that such popular events are at least as strong a force in shaping popular ideas as more official underpinnings of culture, such as the conscious policies of government and of formal education, forms usually regarded as the most influential in shaping public opinion and action.

Although students of popular culture tend to concentrate on twentieth-century media topics, the printed literature of the nineteenth century is crucial to an understanding of the images of Crockett and other popular heroes such as Andrew Jackson in today's popular mind. Crockett's media image took hold during his lifetime within the period of four congressional campaigns, two of which he lost. There is some suggestion that he might have been considered for the presidency had his election record been better.

The "autobiographies" that appeared were in the new tradition of the personal history and in the same vein as Weems's *Life of Washington* (1800) and Wirt's biography of Patrick Henry (1817). In contrast to straightforward factual history, personal histories were human-interest statements that formed the first chapter in the national cult of personality as described by Daniel Boorstin and others.[1]

The four Crockett autobiographies, which are credited at least in part to him, are *Sketches and Eccentricities of Colonel David Crockett of West Tennessee* (1833); *A Narrative of the Life of David Crockett of the State of Tennessee* (1834); *An Account of Colonel Crockett's Tour to the North and Down East* (1835); and *Col. Crockett's Exploits and Adventures in Texas* (1836). These accounts were based on Crockett's backwoods exploits, his observations of city life and national affairs, his campaign tour and congressional career, and his Alamo adventures, including a posthumous account of the siege and his heroic death. Although these rich and evocative sketches of the backwoods and political life have made a contribution to popular literature and social history that far outdistances any partisan motives that may have launched them, they also framed the first installment of the Crockett myth,[1] and did so in a manner that has been compared to Mark Twain's for wit and delivery. That they were, in the main, deliberate fabrications on the part of Washington Whigs who used an embellished version of Crockett's canebreak waggery, his support of anti-Jackson legislation, and the popular success of his East Coast tour for their own ends, was of little consequence. Vernon L. Parrington suggests that Crockett's image was "created at Washington. Not the spontaneous product of the popular imagination, it was the clever work of politicians."[2] An early evaluator of the Crockett saga and of its importance to American character, Parrington further suggests that the power of folklore is not always adequate to the task of hero making, and often requires a large assist from the media. Furthermore, to extend this statement from 1927 fully into the contemporary scene, it should be noted that the channels of traditional folk communication have now been largely supplanted by the powers of television, movies, and the record industry in the formation of heroes.

The legend-building epoch in Crockett's career occurred after his death and was constructed around the previous Whig media campaign with the major addition of Crockett's dramatic death at the Alamo. Also added were continuations of his life taken from ancient mythology, such as the updated tale of Crockett as fire bringer, the hero who now unfreezes the sun by greasing the earth's axle with bear fat and brings back a piece of the sunrise in his pocket for all to see.[3] Parrington notes that "[Politicians who had] exploited Davy as a convenient weapon against Jackson saw their work prosper beyond all expectations, get out of their hands, enlarge itself to a center of backwoods romance, and pass into folklore. It was an unforeseen outcome that must have been vastly amusing to those who set the thing going."[4] The resulting folklore, in turn, provided material for scholarly investigations such as Parrington's critical approach and Richard M. Dorson's appreciative resurrection of the almanac tales in *Davy Crockett: American Comic Legend.*[5]

Crockett's appeal to academics and intellectuals helped to consolidate his previous position as folk hero. Now, in retrospect, this unanticipated development bears comparison with Walt Disney's efforts with Davy, which were successful beyond any estimation or intention of the studios. However superficially or unselfconsciously Disney drew on this complex panoply of forces, he revitalized Crockett and thus mobilized, for the second time, a popular preoccupation with the Crockett myth that in turn led to a revival of academic discussion. (It is a pertinent note on sources of academic debate that its stimulus here was television, although at the time electronic popular culture was seen only as a conduit, not as a source of interest in itself.)

The major contributions of the early Crockett authors, juvenile biographers, historians, publicity agents, and ghostwriters to American history and folklore were the creation, propagation, and analysis of his frontier boast, tall tale, practical joke, a dozen or so colloquialisms, and period atmosphere—particularly regional dialect. Later, at the same time that the intellectual Crockett forum had its flowering, a branch of Crockett "folklore" emerged from Disney's 1955 craze, along with millions of coonskin caps. Dozens of new biographies, concocted to respond to popular demand, along with those reissued for that purpose, favored the writer's fancy over any strictly historical investigation of Crockett's life.[6] Preliminary research also indicated that these juvenile biographies, carried along by the swell of the craze, almost certainly had widespread influence on the American educational system. Treatments of Crockett in grade-school textbooks, a convenient barometer for popular concepts of history, grew in size and emphasis during and after 1955. Disney's recreation of Crockett may have gone beyond popular myth and into the rewriting of frontier history, for he allowed Davy to reach back to transform our view of his own history, region, and era.

The status of our heroes is fluid and changing, the balance between their respective powers over the collective imagination a delicate one. The closing of the frontier had transferred public interest to other projects and other characterizations of American life, particularly industrial urban ones. Disney not only rescued this frontier memory from impending oblivion by removing it from its former folklore niche, but also raised it above the historical enthusiasm Boone enjoyed, reversing the interest ratio between the two men, during the craze, and certainly even now. What mechanisms bring these changes about are still within the range of impressionistic scholarship. To understand their scope and behavior would be, in large part, to understand ourselves in light of the way we view our national past. Parrington put it this way: "Davy was a good deal of a wag, and the best joke he ever played is the one he played upon posterity that has swallowed the myth whole and persists in setting a romantic halo on his coonskin cap."[7]

The number of pedestals in the pantheon of heroes is always limited. Certain historical periods recede further and further into the past, reducing, as distance does, their dimensions and complexity. In the case of the American frontier, which, even at the start of the twentieth century, was relegated to "an historical project,"[8] the separation of heroic and humorous strains of frontier history described by historians such as Parrington had merged and blurred. By the time of the Crockett craze, it seems that only one position assigned to the model frontiersman remained—one that, from the opening of the frontier, had always been occupied by Daniel Boone. Crockett was now developed by Disney into such a forceful symbol of the same period (in reality, some fifty years later than Boone) that Crockett was allowed not only to displace Boone but also to assume characteristics traditionally ascribed to Boone. The television series *Daniel Boone*, similarly, followed in the wake of the Crockett craze, with the same actor (Fess Parker) starring as both frontiersmen.

The lesser pedestal, which Crockett had occupied before the craze, was that of frontier jokester, a "ring-tailed roarer," the "wag of the canebreaks," the master of the frontier boast ("I've got the fastest horse, surest rifle, prettiest sister and ugliest dog in the state of Tennessee"; "I'm half horse, half alligator") and teller of tall tales; a lighthearted, earthy personality, eccentric and personable, a "trickster/transformer"[9] – this is the American character who emerged as a full-scale hero of the same stature as Boone himself.

In a concerned *New York Times* article during the craze, Bernard Kalb voiced his alarm at what he saw as the disappearance of Boone's position in the popular mind resulting from Crockett's pervasive mythic power. Kalb noted that in 1955, for the first time in 136 years, the anniversary of Boone's death on September 26 in his home state of Kentucky went completely uncelebrated. Kalb posed the plaintive question, "America's popular imagination has room for a former tenant, hasn't it, Mr. Disney?"[10]

In sharp contrast to Boone, the "Columbus of the Land . . . Achilles of the West . . . the American Moses who led us into the Promised Land," Crockett, a "TV myth," was, as Kalb quotes Parrington, a "simple-minded frontiersman," whose legend was created by Whig politicians after he had run for Congress "possibly as a joke," and who, compared to Boone, was a Johnny-come-lately to the settling of the frontier. Kalb noted that "Boone had an international reputation years before Crockett kilt even his first b'ar."[11] Boone was the talk of two continents, inspiring versions of American frontiersmen by such luminaries as Lord Byron and James Fenimore Cooper, in contrast to the "lesser literature" of more local interest in the Crockett almanacs and autobiographies, and the more specialized academic audience for the studies of Crockett by folklorists and cultural historians.

Of the two heroes, Crockett was by far the lesser light. In his 1874 biography of Crockett, John Abbott admits that, much as he admires his subject, "Davy Crockett was not a model man. But he was a representative man."[12] Referring to the questionable attribution of the four Crockett autobiographies, E.J. Kahn reported in the *New Yorker*, "David . . . emerges from his own story as a barely literate backwoodsman with a parochial view of the world, an easygoing, if somewhat windy, storyteller, a legislator who was far more politician than statesman, and a man of scant humility."[13]

While Teddy Roosevelt allied both frontier heroes in naming his "Boone and Crockett Club" of gentlemen hunters,[14] it was definitely Boone that Daniel Beard, founder of the Boy Scouts of America, drew upon as the basis for the frontier spirit and motif for his organization. Crockett's eccentric and fanciful reputation, when placed beside the dignity and solemnity of Boone's, which reached its height with the issuance of the 1934 bicentennial Boone memorial half-dollar, provided "a foil for the austere and antisocial Boone"[15] and made Boone look like a cultivated gentleman and scholar by comparison. This view was an extension of the original prototype of the Boone image set down in the 1784 "autobiography" by Filson. This earlier ascetic Boone was less appropriate to the "other-directed" cultural climate of the 1950s than was the congenial, civic-minded Crockett. Perhaps Disney's original choice of Crockett to be a Disney feature over the obvious "favorite son" was in fact a matter of cultural preference rather than any chance personal selection.

With Walt Disney studios as the lever, what forces hurled this humorous regional rake into his fast orbit as a hero of popular culture? What powers transformed this homespun plain-folks pundit into a twentieth-century media hero of television and film, with millions of young followers—all generally unfamiliar with the historical setting, issues, sensibility, or any other index of the times? How could the symbols of ballad and coonskin cap, in a television series introducing an unknown actor in his first leading role as Crockett, set off waves in the national economy, popular thinking, the mass media, the "generation gap," and however briefly or tangentially, the political scene?

The modern Crockett craze, appearing in early 1955, is now considered to be one of the great popular culture events of that decade. It was catapulted into existence by two of America's most formidable media forces—Walt Disney and television—and ignited by the catalyst of a new consumer audience: the baby boom generation. Walter Blair saw in the craze an important case study in popular culture that, if the right questions were posed, would, he suggested, "throw light upon the taste and fantasies of the American people."[16]

Walt Disney himself was unaware of and completely at a loss to explain the mechanisms involved in the $300 million industry that grew up around the symbol of Davy Crockett. After gaining momentum through the winter and spring of 1955, it died as quickly and unexpectedly as it had begun, not only leaving Crockett as an oversized figure in popular history, but also creating a sizeable academic controversy about Crockett's true nature and his meaning for American history, and resulting in a general public inability, even now, to think of Davy Crockett without simultaneously calling up the Disney name.

The craze revealed four central points of interest for the student of popular culture. First, it occurred very soon after the coming of age of television—the widespread ownership of sets and television watching as a major leisure-time activity. It proved dramatically and for the first time the power of television to influence, and even more importantly to determine, behavior on a grand scale with an intensity previously and since unmatched by any fad of its kind and brief duration.

Second, the craze was the key to the discovery by programmers and advertisers of a fabulous new lode in American commercial life: the child market. Never before had a single generation found itself with so much leverage as consumers. The prosperous postwar years yielded a new class of citizens—"consumer trainees" as Riesman, Glazer, and Denney called them[17]—children who from their first years knew spending power and how to use it. The craze generation, spanning the ages of two to twelve, had power of the purse, and the Crockett craze was its first proving ground and coming of age. This first column of the baby boom generation, which would grow up into a population force of millions of college-educated and media-bred consumers, remains the largest single target of business and marketers.[18]

Third, the craze demonstrated the ability of a popularizer such as Disney to mold and manipulate public concepts of history and to change dramatically those that had for generations seemed very stable and immutable. In this case, Disney's version revived from near-obscurity and enlarged substantially a minor American frontiersman much different from, and less distinguished than, the traditional time-tested symbol—Daniel Boone. This transformation of the Crockett character—to the extent that, like Peter Pan and Mary Poppins, he is thought by many to be a Disney creation—supports the idea of the entertainer as educator, as in Max Rafferty's startling reference to Disney as "the greatest educator of this century."[19]

Through his Disneyfication, Crockett was elevated and popularized out of his former secondary position to replace Boone as the central symbol of the frontier, so that in the course of this transformation, many of Boone's most notable characteristics were overtly transferred to the personality of Crockett. Crockett not only eclipsed Boone in the popular imagination but absorbed a generous tinge of the Boone persona as well. One measure of Disney's success in doing this is that even former FCC Commissioner Nicholas Johnson confused Boone with Crockett as the subject of the craze, stating in his book *How to Talk Back to Your Television Set*, "When television's Daniel Boone, Fess Parker, started wearing coonskin caps, so did millions of American boys."[20] Although Parker did play Boone in the 1965–70 series, that show inspired no popular crazes: Johnson was thinking of the Crockett craze.

Fourth, renewed research into Crockett's historical personality and then-current popularity reveals a dynamic process of interpenetration and interplay between areas usually considered separate: history, folklore, and popular culture. The interweaving of these three forces—during and after Crockett's lifetime, during the Disney craze, and since—paint an organic portrait that can shed light on other popular figures whose own recycled careers parallel Crockett's: Jim Bowie, Mike Fink, Nathan Hale, John Brown, and Robert E. Lee, to name a few.

The Crockett craze was, in Bernard Kalb's words, "by far the best-selling myth in America"[21] in its time and serves as a prime example in the history of the "madness of crowds" in its upstart growth and awesome proportions. The movie *Davy Crockett, King of the Wild Frontier* was originally designed by Disney enterprises in 1954 as a three-part television series and as the first installment in a larger series about American folk heroes to be shown on *Disneyland*, the weekly Disney television series aired Wednesday evenings on ABC. (See page 146). "Davy Crockett, Indian Fighter" appeared on December 15, 1954; "Davy Crockett Goes to Congress" on January 26, 1955; and "Davy Crockett at the Alamo" on February 23, 1955. According to *Time*, it was the Disney contract with ABC-TV that "definitely marked the entry of the ABC network into the TV major leagues."[22] In June of 1955 the Crockett series was refashioned for release as a feature-length film to add fuel to the craze. The choice of Crockett to lead the series, according to producer Bill Walsh, was "dumb luck; . . . at that time he was considered just one more frontiersman."[23] (Folklorist Richard Dorson claims to have given Disney his chance at the Crockett legend years earlier, but he had not been able to get past the Disney front office on his California vacation.

Fess Parker starring in *Davy Crockett, King of the Wild Frontier*. (© 1955 Walt Disney Productions.)

Dorson recalls, "I left town that day, and Disney had to wait sixteen years to become rich and famous").[24]

Fess Parker, the actor who came to be identified with Crockett himself (although comparison with historical portraits of Crockett show that no physical resemblance could have been intended) was playing anything but a frontier role when he was seen by Disney as a possibility. Disney was imaginative enough to foresee the Crockett future for Parker when he spotted him in a small movie role as a hospital patient.[25] The film in question was none other than *Them!*, Warner Brothers' science fiction thriller about giant ravenous ants in the New Mexico desert, and Parker happened to be playing a victim of their rampages.

Another kingpin in the craze was the Crockett background score, "The Ballad of Davy Crockett," recorded later in sixteen versions by various vocalists, for a total sale of four million copies. In addition to the more historical nineteenth-century "Davy Crockett March," related musical types stretched to include a "Davy Crockett Mambo."[26] The original "Ballad" was composed as a filler for the television series, fattening the story out to fill three sixty-minute slots. Screenwriter Tom Blackburn and his associate George Bruns went down the hall to the music room and came back thirty minutes later with the song. Christopher Finch, reporting on this incident in *The Art of Walt Disney*, tells us that Blackburn said, "I never wrote a song before in my life," and Walsh added, "I thought it sounded pretty awful, but we didn't have time for anything else."[27] The natural question about the song's great popularity, like other questions of what catches the fancy of a national audience, is moot.

Enjoying instant and enormous success, the ballad became what motivational researcher Ernst Dichter, in his analysis for *Tide*, called the "carrying device" of the craze, which he describes as one of the three essential ingredients—along with subconscious need and symbolism—of any fad.[28] Evidently Dichter was able to develop this rather new definition of a craze on the basis of his confrontation with the Crockett boom.

The "Ballad" was the carrying device, but fads also need to be rich in symbols. The coonskin cap, highly visible and the essential element of the Crockett uniform, was the symbol of the fad's ultimate allure: the fulfillment of a shared subconscious need to identify with national history—especially the long-lived fantasy of the

West. But ballad and cap also allied the craze to more genuinely historical trends. Dichter compared the cap to Christianity's cross and the Nazi swastika alike, claiming that through this cap and ballad, it was possible for children to actually feel that they had "become" Davy Crockett.

The coonskin cap was by far the star product line. Demand for the cap produced the biggest run on raccoon pelts (including tails) since the 1920s. From a standard twenty-five cents per pound, raccoon suddenly jumped to six dollars. When the live raccoon supply flagged behind the galloping demand, raccoon coats from the twenties were converted to do double duty for fad and fashion. One particularly flammable line of hats became the subject of municipal safety bulletins, and all fire chiefs were warned of their potential as fire hazards in a national safety memo.[29]

Three thousand other products associated with the Crockett name only by the loosest link—their label bearing the name Davy Crockett—were displayed in special Crockett sections in department stores. Merchandise included everything from frontier regalia to bath towels, lunch boxes, play telephone sets, baby shoes, ukeleles, athletic equipment, and ladies' panties. Altogether, Crockett products came to account for as much as 10 percent of all children's wear sales.[30] New books about Crockett's life were written and old ones reissued, often in inexpensive paperbound form. Grosset and Dunlap's *The Story of Davy Crockett*, selling at 10,000 copies per year before 1955, made a second debut, with a thirtyfold sales increase during the craze.[31]

The initial open season for manufacturers was occasioned by the public nature of the Crockett name, which had not been copyrighted by Disney. This lack of foresight was key evidence that the studios anticipated no windfall from the TV series. Disney brought but lost a suit against Baltimore garmentmaker Morey Swartz. Swartz had filed and renewed his own patent for a Crockett clothing trademark long before Disney's popularization of the name and capitalized on his good fortune by licensing still other manufacturers to use the trademark for 5 percent of their net sales.[32] Eventually Disney was able to tie up some of the royalties on the Crockett trademark issued by the Disney corporation to manufacturers as "Walt Disney's Davy Crockett," although the Crockett name itself remained, like Crockett himself, a public property.[33] In any case, the battle over the use of the name as a registered trademark should be further explored as a colorful brief on the relationship between mass media, commerce, and the law. This issue is one that haunts all proprietary characters, who, while identified with their creators, may nevertheless be simply "on loan" from real life.

The economics of the craze were impressive. In his recent biography of the baby boom generation, *Great Expectations*, Landon Jones cited the Crockett mania as one proof of "the power of the baby boom, by its sheer size, to make or break an entire product line."[34]

Besides its effect on consumer patterns as "just about the largest merchandising feat of its kind,"[35] the craze led to certain kinds of group behavior among children, particularly the widespread singing of the "Ballad" and playacting of Crockett's career based on episodes in the Disney series. This collective dramatization, in song and impromptu theater, fits Lazarsfeld's postulate that fads fill the need for status and a common experience imperative in the cultural climate of other-directedness described so fully by Riesman, Glazer, and Denney in *The Lonely Crowd.*[36]

At the height of the craze, *Life* described the Crockett phenomenon, with liberal photo illustration, as having "a sudden and shattering impact on the nation's home life," and John Fischer, *Harper's* editor, suggested that the craze had turned children "within the course of a single television program, into Davy Crocketts," displacing creative play formerly based on space cadets and Hopalong Cassidy (a fad of 1950 but very much smaller than Crockett's).[37] (See page 150).

Teachers began to complain that the craze interfered with classroom discipline, claiming that "kids did nothing but play Crockett games, and need to be calmed down." In response, Fess Parker and Buddy Ebsen (who played Crockett sidekick Georgie Russel) wrote and recorded a song based on the Crockett motto, "Be sure you're right, then go ahead" that was "supposed to have a quieting effect."[38]

Children were not the only activists in the craze. As with many another popular phenomenon, such as the crossword puzzle, an amusement first designed for children soon spread into the adult province as well. For everyone concerned with the impact of the past on the present, Crockett's emergence as a full-scale national hero posed the issue of his original social significance, which in Disney's version was excessively idealized. If this version turned sharply from the true "historical" Crockett, it was one in which parents and edu-

Three winners in the Davy Crockett contest for June, 1955, sponsored by the *Philadelphia Evening Bulletin*. When actor Fess Parker arrived in Philadelphia for the opening of the theater release of *Davy Crockett, King of the Wild Frontier*, a committee of contest winners was on hand to greet him at the Philadelphia International Airport. Many such contests were held across the country. (*Philadelphia Evening Bulletin*/Temple University Photojournalism Collection.)

cators could delight. Disney's Crockett, the common man with dignity – congenial, neighborly, civic-minded, and upwardly mobile, or, in short, other-directed – made him a most fitting ideal for the 1950s. His advent was welcomed for another reason as well: he was a real-life hero whose carefully selected attributes were seen as preferable to the superhuman powers of comic fantasy heroes. The *New York Times* commented that "Crockett remained a good-natured superman – salty, humorous, even modest – and his present revival may be taken as a healthy sign by those who have deplored the vogue of the comic-book superman."[39] Ironically, the process of building fictional super-heroes reverses the Crockett process: that of building up an apparently real flesh-and-blood man from the stuff of the popular novel, word of mouth, and the yellow press.

Those with a more neoprogressive outlook, however, were dismayed at the discrepancies between Disney's Crockett and the real thing. John Fischer's *Harper's* editorial denounced the media version as "A Crockett who never was – a myth as phony as the Russian legend about kind Papa Stalin," and added, "we spurn unheroic facts in favor of a simonized, Disneyfied version of history."[47] He was answered with fierce territorial support for Disney's creation by a Tennessee reader: "To those children this man has represented a frontiersman of the highest caliber and a fighter for the good of our country. . . . Even though what you have written is no doubt true, I feel it would have been much better to have . . . allowed the children to continue to believe that Davy Crockett was a hero."[40]

In furnishing the youth of America with a hero who was brave, intelligent, stalwart, and kind, Disney excited a brief but heated academic debate over the character of Crockett as a national ideal, centered around John Fischer's editorial and John Haverstick's article in *Saturday Review*, and augmented by newspaper editorials and a radio broadcast by William F. Buckley, Jr.

Letters to the editor, even from nonacademics, showed a remarkably detailed knowledge of Crockett's role in the Texas Revolution, as well as his larger role in American history than Boone's. But the most vehement commentaries were aimed at confirming or discrediting Crockett's good moral character. This remains the most intriguing, contradictory, and elusive phase of the Crockett question.

The craze was invested with surprising political energy, from Kefauver's coonskin cap, sported as part of his vice-presidential campaign of 1956, to the more serious approach of the education director of the United Auto Workers, Brendon Sexton, who denounced Crockett in a Detroit radio address; evidently Crockett's portrayal as a rugged individualist was ill-suited to union interests. Labor columnist Murray Kempton wrote a four-part debunking series, "The Real Davy," in the New York Post, claiming that Davy was "a fellow purchasable for no more than a drink." Children picketed the Post offices with placards asking, "Who you gonna expose next? Santa Claus?"[41]

William Buckley answered these attacks on Mutual Broadcasting's "State of the Nation": "The assault on Davy is one part traditional debunking campaign and one part resentment by liberal publicists of Davy's neurosis-free approach to life. He'll survive the carpers." The Communist Worker questioned the attackers as well, although presumably for different reasons: "It is all in the American democratic tradition, and who said tradition must be founded on 100% verified fact?"[42]

There was some talk of the Republican party making use of the Crockett image as the Whigs had in Jackson's era. If this intention was at all genuine, then Kefauver's identification with Crockett was sagacious enough to keep this from happening, if not to win the election. It is ironic, too, that during his campaign Kefauver appropriated the Crockett symbol popularized by television, while five years earlier, the 1951 Kefauver Hearings on Interstate Crime had ascribed to television the role of an agent of corruption.

Writing in Southwest Review, Joseph Leach claimed that Crockett lore had promoted a picture of Texans as "blood-thirsty braggarts stemming directly from the Crockett character,"[43] an image Disney had the opportunity to temper with heroism and dignity in the romanticized staging of Jim Bowie's dying words to Crockett in the Alamo sequence.

An additional aspect of the Crockett controversy was the matter of his actual physical appearance, which came to be academic as Fess Parker became the model of Crockett in the popular mind. The New York Times included several portraits of the historical Davy with long Indian-style braids, deep-set, skulking eyes, and a long sallow face.[44] A John Neagle painting of Crockett as a freshman congressman with flowing tie (1828) was displayed in the Boston Museum of Fine Arts, and "just in case any small fry failed to recognize their hero as he really looked,"[45] museum director Perry Rathbone made sure the older portrait kept company with a cardboard cutout of the Disney version. Once again, a "simple" craze, first and foremost by and for children, went on to engender a wider adult concern about national hero-worship, regional pride, and issues of truth in history.

But these controversies faded when the craze went into a sharp decline and fall, unpredicted and most unwelcome by the many who had made new careers and fortunes in its momentum. In May of 1955 a *Time* article had reported "U.S. retailers see no reason why the Davy Crockett boom should not keep going at least until Christmas," and a Detroit buyer flatly declared, "Davy Crockett is bigger than Mickey Mouse."[46] Optimism proved fatal, especially for the fur trade. "Many were caught with warehouses full of raccoon tails and buckskin fringe, when, almost without warning, the Crockett craze lost its lure." By fall of 1955, the craze went into a sudden tailspin that left retailers in the lurch. One manufacturer summarized for the rest the rule of crazes: "When they die, they die a horrible death."[47]

Not even the tools of motivational research were able to save the Crockett industries from sudden ruin, although Alfred Politz later explained the fad's demise to be the result of the "downward mobility" factor of trends in general as they "fall" from older to younger, richer to poorer, stylish to unstylish groups. In this case, older children, who adopted the fad first, quickly let go of their allegiance to Crockett as younger children, "an age class they no longer wish to be identified with,"[48] took it up from their seniors.

Ernst Dichter, founder of motivational research and coauthor with Politz of the in-depth Crockett study in *Tide*, felt that with the right techniques a fad even of Crockett dimensions could be spontaneously and consciously generated, its course plotted, and its end foreseen and perhaps even avoided indefinitely. Politz thought that an absolute scientific rule could be derived for this purpose.

This confidence in the social psychologist's ability to understand and control public behavior on a scale similar to that of advertising —which might be seen as a succession of small-scale fads, but greatly enlarged, extended, and accelerated—was largely wishful thinking advanced by hindsight. The desire to turn Disney's "dumb luck" success, through ad-man expertise, into something more calculable and manipulable, reflected the researcher's dream of selling irresistible symbols of ultimate persuasion centered around some relentless sub-conscious collective need. Dichter and Politz issued this statement to the profession: "[The] challenging job for the future—creating fads of the first magnitude for our children—is the combined job of the researcher and the creative man [professional ad man]."[49]

This challenging job for the future persists. Even with the tireless work of motivation researchers in studies of trends, we are still only on the brink of discovering the collective American unconscious. Our best ad men cannot hope to create great crazes until they can understand the ones we have already experienced. Until a satisfactory analysis of the Crockett craze is developed as the test of this ability, the most difficult "why" and "how" questions remain.

Good answers can be expected to draw a dynamic profile of the volatile encounter between our mass media, national history, and popular consciousness. But more importantly, the 1955 Crockett craze, unlike its predecessors, stirred up an interest and an inquiry into a basic issue in American experience and character. It caused us to question the real nature of the early frontier hero and to investigate his symbolic value in defining and judging the American past in the same way that investigation into the intentions of the Founding Fathers and into the legends that surround some of them underlie judgments concerning the nature and image of American government.

The mass media have become powerful but subtle forces in the workings of the American mind. Television, film, popular music, and mass commercial culture, added to the mainstay channels of scholarship—history, literature, folklore—indicate how complex and interwoven the meaning of one man can come to be for American life. From newspaper accounts to Disney films, from documentary to oral history, the migratory saga of Davy Crockett over the last one hundred and fifty years argues persuasively for the study of our heroes in terms of popular culture. The recycling of Davy Crockett for generation after generation of a public eager for heroism makes clear that the understanding of the history of America as the American people understand it must go well beyond the straightforward review of the historical record or of biography based on that record.

NOTES

1. See a discussion of this issue by Robert Penn Warren in "A Dearth of Heroes," *American Heritage*, 23 (Oct. 1972), 4–7.

2. V.L. Parrington, *Main Currents in American Thought* (New York: Harcourt, Brace, 1927), II, 173.

3. Dixon Wecter, *The Hero in America* (New York: Scribner's, 1941), 191.

4. Parrington, II, 174.

5. Richard Dorson, *Davy Crockett: American Comic Legend* (New York: Spiral Press for Rockland Editions, 1939).

6. E.J. Kahn, Jr., "Be Sure You're Right, Then Go Ahead," *New Yorker*, (Sept. 3, 1955), 64–70. The limitations of these juvenile books, best-sellers during and following the craze, raise some serious questions about the genuineness and seriousness of any primary and secondary resources for the study of the phenomenal success of Disney's Crockett. Seen in this way, the biographies are an outgrowth of the folkloristic tradition set up in the outlandish comic adventures of the Crockett almanacs, though far less consciously so. In his survey of accounts of Crockett's life in this sudden generation of literature, Kahn found basic discrepancies regarding the key factual events in Crockett's life: the killing of his first bear; the origin of the motto "Be Sure You're Right, Then Go Ahead"; his famous rifle, Betsy; his death at the Alamo; and like all heroes, regarding the importance of his last words.

7. V.L. Parrington, quoted in John Haverstick, "The Two Davy Crocketts," *Saturday Review*, July 9, 1955, p. 19.

8. Howard Mumford Jones, Foreword to Dorson, *Davy Crockett*, xi–xiv.

9. Paul Radin, *Trickster: A Study in American Indian Mythology* (New York: Schocken, 1956).

10. Bernard Kalb, "Dan'l, Dan'l Boone," *New York Times Magazine*, Oct. 9, 1955, p. 42.

11. Ibid.

12. John Abbott, *David Crockett, His Life and Adventures* (New York: Dodd, Mead, 1874), v.

13. Kahn, "Be Sure You're Right," 66.

14. Peter J. Schmitt, *Back to Nature* (New York: Oxford Univ. Press, 1969), 13.

15. Marshall Fishwick, *The Hero, American Style* (New York: David McKay, 1969), 82.

16. Walter Blair, "R.I.P.: King of the Wild Frontier," review of *David Crockett: The Man and the Legend*, by J.A. Shackford, *Saturday Review* (July 21, 1956), 26.

17. David Riesman et. al., *The Lonely Crowd*, quoted in Vance Packard, *The Hidden Persuaders* (New York: David McKay, 1957), 141.

18. Landon Jones, *Great Expectations: America and the Baby Boom Generation* (New York: Ballantine, 1980), 50–51.

19. Max Rafferty quoted in Herbert J. Schiller, *The Mind Managers* (Boston: Beacon Press, 1973), 99.

20. Nicholas Johnson, *How to Talk Back to Your Television Set* (New York: Bantam, 1970), 24.

21. Kalb, "Dan'l, Dan'l Boone," 42.

22. "Disneyland," *Time*, Nov. 8, 1954, p. 95.

23. Christopher Finch, *The Art of Walt Disney* (Burbank: Walt Disney Productions, 1973), 361.

24. Richard Dorson, Letter to the Editor, *Saturday Review*, Aug. 6, 1955, p. 23.

25. "U.S. Again Is Subdued by Davy," *Life*, April 25, 1955, p. 27.

26. Ibid. The subject of Crockett's name in music history, is, of course, a study in itself. Disney studios credits a lyrical piece sung at the end of the Alamo siege, "Farewell to the Mountains," to Crockett himself.

27. Finch, *The Art of Walt Disney*, 361.

28. Vance Packard, *The Hidden Persuaders*, 142, referring to Ernst Dichter, "Fads: What Starts Them, What Keeps Them Going, Why They Die," *Tide*, Nov. 1958, pp. 20 ff.

29. "Davy Crockett Craze on the Wane," *New York Times Magazine*, Dec. 11, 1955, p. 27.

30. "The Wild Frontier," *Time*, May 23, 1955, p. 92.

31. John Haverstick, "The Two Davy Crocketts," *Saturday Review*, July 9, 1955, p. 19.

32. "The Wild Frontier," 92.

33. "Davy Crockett Craze on the Wane," 27.

34. Jones, *Great Expectations*, 50–51.

35. "U.S. Again Is Subdued by Davy," 27.

36. Paul Lazarsfeld, quoted in "Davy Crockett Craze on the Wane," 27; D. Riesman, N. Glazer, and R. Denney, *The Lonely Crowd* (New Haven: Yale Univ. Press, 1950).

37. "U.S. Again Is Subdued by Davy," 24; John Fischer, "The Embarrassing Truth about Davy Crockett," *Harper's*, 211 (July 1955), 16.

38. "U.S. Again Is Subdued by Davy," 24.

39. "Coonskin Superman," *New York Times Magazine*, April 24, 1955, p. 24.

40. Fischer, "The Embarrassing Truth," 16; John P. Wright, Lookout Mountain, Tennessee, "In Defense of Davy," Letter to the Editor, *Harper's*, 211 (Sept. 4, 1955), 4.

41. "Davy: Row and a Riddle," *Newsweek*, July 4, 1955, p. 56.

42. Ibid.

43. Joseph Leach, "Crockett Almanacs and the Typical Texan," *Southwest Review*, 35 (Spring 1950), 88 ff.

44. Kalb, "Dan'l, Dan'l Boone," 42.

45. "Davy in Bean Town," *Time*, Aug. 8, 1955, p. 59.

46. "Davy Crockett Craze on the Wane," 27.

47. Packard, *Hidden Persuaders*, 142.

48. Politiz quoted ibid., 142.

49. Ibid., 143.

THE DAVY CROCKETT CRAZE: A BIBLIOGRAPHY

Blair, Walter. "R.I.P. King of the Wild Frontier." *Saturday Review*, July 21, 1956, p. 26.

"Braggarts of the Backwoods." *Life*, April 11, 1960, pp. 99–100.

"Coonskin Superman." *New York Times Magazine*, April 24, 1955, p. 20.

"Crockett and Circulation." *Newsweek*, July 18, 1955, p. 60.

"Davy: Row and a Riddle." *Newsweek*, July 4, 1955, p. 56.

"Davy Crockett Craze on the Wane," *New York Times Magazine*, Dec. 11, 1955, p. 27.

"Davy Crockett 'Elected'." *New York Times*, May 19, 1955, p. 32, col. 4.

"Davy in Bean Town." *Time*, Aug. 8, 1955, p. 59.

"Decline of a Hero." *Collier's*, Nov. 25, 1955, p. 102.

Dichter, Ernst. "Fads: What Starts Them, What Keeps Them Going, Why They Die." *Tide*, Nov. 1958, pp. 20ff.

Dorson, Richard. Letter to the Editor. *Saturday Review*, Aug. 6, 1955, p. 23.

Finch, Christopher. *The Art of Walt Disney*. New York: Harry Abrams, 1973.

Fischer, John. "The Embarrassing Truth About Davy Crockett." *Harper's*, 211 (July 1955), 16–18.

Haverstick, John. "The Two Davy Crocketts," *Saturday Review*, July 9, 1955, p. 19.

Jones, Landon. *Great Expectations: America and the Baby Boom Generation*. New York: Ballantine, 1980.

Kahn, E.J., Jr. "Be Sure You're Right, Then Go Ahead." *New Yorker*, Sept. 3, 1955, pp. 64–70.

Kalb, Bernard. "Dan'l, Dan'l Boone." *New York Times Magazine*, Oct. 9, 1955, p. 42.

"King Davy and Friends," *Time*, Aug. 1, 1955, p. 30.

King, Margaret J. "The Davy Crockett Craze: A Case Study in Popular Culture." Ph.D. dissertation, University of Hawaii, August 1976.

———. "The Disney Sensibility." M.A. Thesis, Bowling Green State University, March 1972.

Letters. *New York Times*, May 8, 1955, Sec. 4, p. 4, col. 4.

Maltin, Leonard. *The Disney Films*. New York: Crown, 1973.

"The Mark of Zorro." *Life*, Aug. 18, 1958, pp. 69–75.

"Meet Davy Crockett." *Look*, July 26, 1955, p. 36.

"Mr. Crockett is Dead Shot as Salesman." *New York Times*, June 1, 1955, p. 38, col. 1.

"Random Notes from Washington: Hero Stands in for Davy Crockett." *New York Times*, June 20, 1955, p. 12, col. 3.

Reston, James. "Even Davy Crockett Can't Do Everything." *New York Times*, May 22, 1955, Sec. 4, p. 8, col. 5.

Rourke, Constance. Letter to the Editor. *Saturday Review*, July 30, 1955, p. 23.

Schickel, Richard. *The Disney Version*. New York: Avon, 1968.

"Taxridden Hoppy to Unsaddle Enterprises." *Business Week*, Jan. 19, 1952, p. 151.

"U.S. Again is Subdued by Davy." *Life*, Apr. 25, 1955, pp. 27–33.

Walt Disney Productions, Publicity Department. "Davy Crockett, King of the Wild Frontier." Production story (n.d.), [1954].

———. Publicity office memos nos. 22871, 22874, 22875, 22876; (no dates) concerning the rerelease (about 1972–73) of the Davy Crockett film series for television.

"Where Are You, Davy, When We Need You?" (interview with Fess Parker by Cobey Black). *Honolulu Advertiser*, Oct. 28, 1975, Sec. B-I.

White, Peter. "Ex-King of the Wild Frontier." *New York Times Magazine*, Dec. 11, 1955, p. 27.

"The Wild Frontier." *Time*, May 23, 1955, pp. 90–92.

"A Wonderful World: Growing Impact of the Disney Art." *Newsweek*, Apr. 18, 1955, p. 60.

Wright, John P. "In Defense of Davy." In Letters to the Editor, *Harper's*, 211 (Sept. 1955), 4.

8. Davy Crockett Songs

MINSTRELS TO DISNEY

Charles K. Wolfe

.

In 1934 Constance Rourke wrote that songs about Davy Crockett "appeared in many news sheets of the day, in 'albums,' 'galaxies,' and other similar compilations," and that "minstrel songs of the eighteen thirties and forties contained allusions to Crockett, and occasional stanzas of these or of other songs about him may still be heard in the South."[1] Though she did not go into any detail on the popular, ephemeral songs, feeling that they only reflected the commercialization of Crockett's name, Rourke did identify one of the more enduring elements of the Crockett legend: the songs that became a part of folk tradition. Just as people told tales about Crockett's exploits, so did they sing songs, and the songs reflect, in a complex and at times indirect way, the folk values that attached themselves to Crockett. During the 150 years since Crockett's fame peaked, a number of popular songwriters have either written songs about him or mentioned him in songs; most of the songs quickly dropped out of sight and were never heard from again. A few, however, have endured to become significant examples of popular culture and folklore; these range from a minstrel song that became popular shortly after Crockett's death to a popular motion-picture theme song that became an anthem for a generation in the 1950s.

References to American vernacular music permeate the various writings by and about Crockett. Crockett was knowledgable about old-time fiddling, buck dancing, and backwoods dances, and was himself known as a fiddler;[2] indeed, a museum in Texas still has what is purported to be Davy Crockett's fiddle. In his autobiographical writings Crockett describes visiting a minstrel show in Philadelphia, where he saw "Jim Crow"—probably Thomas D. Rice's "Jump Jim Crow," the first blackface act to win widespread fame. "The fiddling was pretty good," Crockett admitted. "I do not think, however, from all I saw, that the people enjoyed themselves better than we do at a country frolic, where we dance til daylight, and pay off the score by giving one in our turn."³ In a more formal sense, Crockett saw the appearance during his lifetime of various published instrumental compositions, including "'Go Ahead:' A March Dedicated to Colonel Crockett" (see page 161), and "Colonel Crockett: A Virginia Reel" (1839), a fiddle tune by George P. Knauff that remained in fiddle repertoires until the 20th century (see page 162). Crockett might well have seen some of the vocal songs about him that were later included in an 1846 volume, *The National Songster*.⁵ Crockett's name itself appeared on two editions of a words-only songbook that came out in 1837 and 1846; this was *Crockett's Free-and-Easy Songbook*, described in the 1837 edition as being "a new collection of the most popular stage songs" as well as "Favorite dinner and parlor songs," and in the 1846 edition as containing "comic, sentimental, amatory, sporting, African, Scotch, Irish, Western and Texian [*sic*] national, military, naval and anacreontic."⁶

Whether or not Crockett had much to do with these songsters is uncertain, but what is clear is that by 1846, ten years after the Alamo, one Crockett song was emerging as a favorite with audiences. This was a song produced by an anonymous writer for the then-flourishing minstrel-show tradition, a lively mixture of dancing, banjo tunes, and "Negro melodies" performed by white entertainers in black-face. Earlier students of the minstrel show thought that most of the material was derived from popular culture of the day, but more recent scholars have suggested that much of the early minstrel material, such as that of Thomas D. Rice, drew from authentic folk traditions. From black tradition, the minstrels borrowed Afro-American songs, dances, and work chants; from Anglo-American tradition, they drew heavily on the tall tales and legends of the frontiersmen and southwestern humor. "In the best tradition of Mike Fink, black-faced riverboatmen sang, danced, and fought their ways up and down rivers as far apart as the Susquehanna and the Mississippi," writes minstrel historian Robert C. Toll. "And as blackface roarers, rivaling the likes of Davy Crockett, minstrel characters trumpeted their own boasts."⁷ Certain of these "blackface roarers" became favorite stereotype characters who appeared in numerous skits and shows; one was called Old Zip Coon, and another was Pompey Smash. By 1850 a song involving Pompey Smash and Davy Crockett had emerged

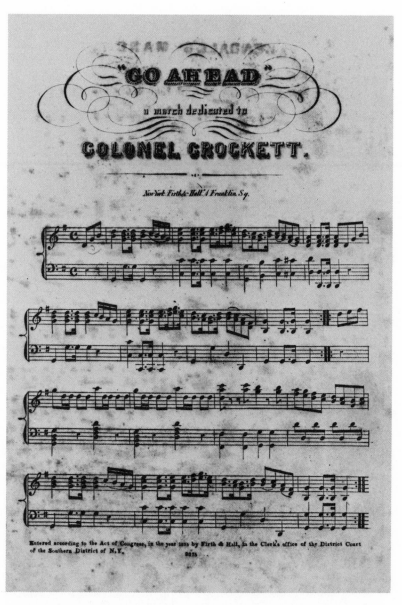

"Go Ahead! a march dedicated to Colonel Crockett," also known as "The Crockett Victory March" (New York: Firth & Hall, 1835). (Lilly Library, Indiana University, Bloomington, Indiana.)

Author's transcription of "Colonel Crockett: A Virginia Reel," by George P. Knauff
(published in Baltimore in 1839 by George Willig, Jr.)

as a minstrel standard of sorts and was being reprinted in a number
of the songbooks of the day. The song was called "Pompey Smash"
and was an odd mixture of Crockett legend and history with minstrel convention; it was, however, to become the most important
of all the Crockett music.

"Pompey Smash" appeared for one of the first times in a book
modestly entitled *The Negro Singer's Own Book; Containing Every
Negro Song That Has Ever Been Sung or Printed*, a thick collection
of minstrel song texts published in Philadelphia in 1846. It shortly
afterwards appeared in *Lloyd's Ethiopian Song Book* (London, 1847),
Elton's Illustrated Song Book (n.d.), *De Susannah and Thick Lip Songster*
(New York, 1850), and others. The original 1846 text contains the
following version.

POMPEY SMASH

The Everlastin and Unkonkerable Skreamer

As I sing to folk now dat I tink is disarnin,
Il'l tell you what I cum from and whar I got my larnin,
I'm hot from ole Wurginny, whar you fine all de great men,
An I'm Pompey Smash, one de principal statesmen,
I'm sekun bess to none, on dis side ob de sun,
And by de laud, I weigh widout my head half a ton,
Dis wurl's made ob mud and de Mississippi river,
De sun's a ball ob fox-fire, as you diskiver,
De moon's made ob cheese, and allus keeps a flyin
De wurl stands still, while de sun keeps a guyin,
And de stars are ladies eyes dat round de wurl flies,
To gib us a little lite when de moon don't rise.

Now I've splain'd dese tings in a logigraphic manner,
I gib you a little touch of ole Wurginny grammar
Dey say fotch and toat insted ob bring an carry
An dat what dey call grammar, by de laud Harry
And de Yankees all gues, but de french speak de bess,
For dey say *we mosheer,* when dey go to say yes.

Dare's anudder poor dam proud Suskehanner nigger
About as big as me, or maby little bigger,
De ole Zip Coon, is what de folks call him,
An if I eber catch him, I tend for to maul him,
Kase such trash as he, shan't take de libertee,
To wauk about de street, an scandalize me.

Now I'll tell you 'bout a fite I had wid Davy Crockett
Dat haff hoss, haff kune, an haff sky rocket,
I met him one day as I go out a gunnin,
I ax him whar he guine, an he say he guine a kunein,
Den I ax him whar he gun, an he say he got nun,
Den I say, Davy, how you guine to hunt widout one.

Den says he, Pompey Smash, just cum along ob Davy
An I'll dam soon show you how to grin a koon crazy
Well, I follow on arter, till Davy seed a squirrel,
Settin on a pine log, eatin sheep sorrel,
Den he stop rite still, and he gin for me to feel,
Says he, Pompey Smash, let me brace agin your heel.

I stuck out my heel, an I brace up de sinner,
An den Davy gun to grin hard for his dinner,
But de kritter didn't move—nor didn't seem to mine him,
But seem to keep a eatin, an neber look behind him.
At lass, Davy sed, he ralely must be ded,
For I seed de bark fly all 'bout de kritter's hed.

Den we boph started up, de truth to diskiver,
An may de debil roast ole Pompey Smash's liber,
If it wa'nt a great not, 'bout as big as a punkin,
Saz I, kurnel Davy, does you call dis skunkin.
                  Heah! heah!! heah!!!
Den sez he, you black kaff, now I tell you doan laff,
If you do I'll pin your ears back, an bite you in haff.

I throde down my gun, an I drop my amynishin,
Sez I, kurnel Davy, I'll cool you ambishun,
He back boph his years, an puff like a steemer,
Sez he, Pompey Smash, I'm a Tennessee skreemer,
Den we boph lock horn, an I tink my breph gone,
I was neber hng [*sic*, hug] so close, since de day I was born.

We fought haff a day, an den we greed to stop it,
For I was badly whipt, an so was Davy Crockett,
When we look for our heds, gosh we found 'em boph missen,
For he'd bit off mine, an I'd swallow'd hissen.
Den boph did agree for to leff de oder be,
For I was rather hard for him, an so was he for me.

Now, spose you all member de grate star shower,
Dey fall as tick as hail for mose seben hour,
When I see de stars a rainin, den I tink it all ober,
So I went an got drunk just to keep a little sober
When I wake from my sleep, I out de window peep,
An I see de stars lyin on de groun nee deep.

Dis star storm shows dat dar's someting bad a bruin,
An shows dat de niggers am on de brink of ruin,
For ebery single star, as it kum down a whizzen,
Says, Pompey Smash, here you see de fects ob abullishun,
We were kick'd from de sky, kase we tried to nullify
De laws ob de white folks, an so we hab to die.
Lord, I member bery well, how massa used to skin me,
When we lib down in de state ob ole Wurginny,

He take me in de barn, and he gib me such a scorin,
An I guess ole Pompey all de time kept a roarin;
For he cut, an he slash, on de back ob Billy Smash,
An I taut I'd clear myself, so I from de barn dash.

Den, sez he to big Sam, now do you run and kotch him,
An mine, you dam nigger, do you to de barn fotch him,
Big Sam started out, but he soon did diskiver,
Dat ole Pompey Smash had tumble in de river,
Bekase, I tell you what, I feel so tarnal hot,
Dat I tink my back a fire, if I didn't I be drot.

Den tinks I Pompey Smash, you'd better skull ahead,
Kase if massa kotches you, you'd raly better be dead.
So I gib a long dive, an I leff Sam behind me,
An he went an tole massa dat he couldn't find me,
Kase you all mus know, dat I don't dive slow,
For I dove eleben miles fore I eber gib a blow.

When I rise from de water, I look aroun perticular,
I look furs ahead, and den, slan-tep-dick-ler,
But laud, I feel bad when I seed an ally-gater.
Kase I didn't hab nothin' not a single sweet tater.
Den I feel a little skeard, so I neber sed a word,
For ebery tooph he had was like a broad sword.

But you all mus noe dat I'm quick pon de trigger,
An not to praise myself, I'm a dam smart nigger;
So an idy struck my mind, by the holy St. Peter,
To get upon his back and ride the tarnal kretur,
So I jump rite a straddle ob de dam ruff saddle,
De varmint gin to roar, an den gin to paddle.

Den I gin to feel about for a safe place to stick him,
But the kretur took a hint dat I guine for to trick him,
Den by de holy Golly, sez he, I tink you orter
Gib me haff a chance, out here in de water,
But, sez I, my good fellow, I want your hide an taller
So take em both togeder and dey'll fotch a silver doller.

Den I roll up my sleebe, an untye my kollar,
I took out my knife, an I whet it on a dollar;
When he hear de chink rattle, den he noe what I arter,
So he slip ftom 'tween my legs an he leff me in de water,

But I kotch him by de tail, an down de riber sail,
An we leff a streak behind us like a crooked fence rail.

We keep gwyne ahead till we got to New Orleans,
When I found myself dare I knew what was beans,
   up to de show shop, an dare begun to sing.
Golly! you ought heard how de house did ring,
I'm exceedin popular, an very much like,
Cause Turner & Fisher hab me in stereotype.

The narrator of this song, Pompey Smash, seems to be a black counterpart to Davy Crockett—a violent, bragging, "unknonkerable Skreamer" who at once sets himself up as a rival to the other great black minstrel braggart, Zip Coon. The overall song includes some twenty actual stanzas (stanzas one and two are combined in the original text, above), of which only six deal directly with Davy Crockett; indeed, Pompey's fight with Crockett is only one of several anecdotes given to show Pompey's prowess. After the fight with Crockett, the song moves into a discussion of "de grate star shower" and how it symbolizes the "facts" of abolition. The star shower was probably in reference to the 1834 visitation of Halley's comet, and the abolition issue was a major one in the 1840 elections; the fact that Pompey emphasizes his Virginia background may or may not refer to Nat Turner's 1831 rebellion. More relevant to Crockett lore is the next section, in which Pompey describes escaping from his master, being pursued by Big Sam, and diving into the river before he rides an alligator down to New Orleans. Although Pompey himself is the hero in the last stanzas, many of the details, including the deep dive, Big Sam, the escaped slave, and the taming of the alligator, are found in Crockett almanacs, especially those published by Turner and Fisher —the Philadelphia publishers also responsible for *The Negro Singer's Own Book* (ca. 1848).[8] Indeed, the last stanza of the song even includes a reference to Turner and Fisher getting Pompey in type. Of the section dealing directly with Crockett by name, the coon-grinning episode is well known through its appearance in *Sketches and Eccentricities*, while the fight between Davy and Pompey may have come from any number of almanac stories such as "A Scentoriferous Fight with a Nigger."[9]

The ultimate source of the song, though, is probably less important than its fate. "Pompey Smash" survived a number of songbook printings and minstrel show performances in the mid and late nineteenth century, and then, like a number of other minstrel favorites, went into oral tradition and began circulating as a folk song. In fact, virtually all of the collected folk versions of "Davy Crockett" can be traced back to "Pompey Smash," and the new research and collecting done since Constance Rourke made her 1934 statement has shown that her various "songs" about Crockett were probably variations of this one.

Unlike in England, very little folk-song collecting was done in America prior to the turn of the twentieth century, so it is impossible to tell just how early "Pompey Smash" began circulating orally. By the 1860s the minstrel shows were traveling out from their original home in the urban centers and exposing all sorts of people to their music,[10] and this doubtless helped spread their songs; at the same time, though, the black content of many shows began to decline. This decline, coupled with the fall from popular favor of the Crockett almanacs after 1856, suggests that "Pompey"'s survival during the decade after the Civil War depended on folk tradition.

What we do know is that among the very first songs collected in America by pioneer folklorists was "Pompey Smash," which folk informants were by now calling "Davy Crockett." The first published version was collected in Missouri by H.M. Belden in 1910, but a few years later another version—one learned by its singer about 1900—was recovered in Knott County, Kentucky, by Josiah Combs. The Combs text is thus the earliest folk version of "Pompey" and reflects some of the changes wrought by the folk imagination.

1   I knew a little boy whose name was Davy,
He wouldn't eat meat, but he did like the gravy;
And when he eat his bread, O then he went to bed,
He would double up his feet and put 'em under his head.

2   I met a man one day, he says, "Where are you going?"
I looked at him, says, "I'm going out a-cooning";
And he says, "Where's your gun?" Says I, "I hain't got none."
"Well, you can't kill a coon unless you had one."

3   Went on a piece further and there I saw a squirrel
Sitting on a pine log, eating sheep and sorrel;
And he says, "Black calf, you had better not laugh,
For if you do, I'll bite you two in half."

4   Throwed down my gun and all my ammunition,
    He'd bit off my tail and I'd swallowed his'n;
    (I says to Col. Davy, "I'll cool his ambition").
    When we both locked horns I thought my breath was gone,
    I was never squeezed so hard since the hour I was born.

5   We fit on a half a day, and then agreed to stop it,
    I was badly whipped, and so was Davy Crockett;
    And then we agreed to let each other be,
    I was hard enough for him, and so was he for me.[11]

Combs, who identified this as a "song of the Texas-Mexican [*sic*] war," collected it from a man named Wiley Parks, who ran a mill and was known in the community as "a mighty singer of ballads, descending from a mighty singing family."[12] The first stanza appears in no other folk versions, nor in "Pompey," and was probably a play-party song that was grafted onto the first of this one because of the reference to "Davy." The text is otherwise garbled by the omission of the central event, the grinning the bark off a tree and subsequent argument about it between the speaker and Crockett. Nonetheless, the text does set the tone for later texts in that it preserves of the "Pompey" song the Crockett fight incident to the exclusion of many of the other motifs.

A more complete text was recovered in 1917 by John Harrington Cox in Harrison County, West Virginia, and he published it in 1925 in his early collection *Folk-Songs of the South*. Cox was one of the first folklorists to note the song's connection to the minstrel stage and to compare traditional and minstrel texts.

1   Come all of you young men,
        Where you are yerning,
    I'll tell you where I come from,
        And where I got my learning.

2   My name is Pomy Smash,
        And my principle is a statement:
    Second best to none by the side of the sun,
        My life without my head would weigh half a ton.

3   He said he was going cooning,
        And said I'd go along;
    I asked him for his gun,
        And he said he hadn't none.

4 Said I, "Uncle Davy,
   How do you do without a gun?"

5 "Never do you mind,
   Just follow after Davy,
   And he'll pretty quick show you
   How to grin a coon crazy."

6 He grinned away a while,
   And he never 'peared to mind it;
   Eatin' away at sheep sorret,
   And never looked behind it.

7 And Uncle Davy said,
   "I think it must be dead;
   I saw the bark fly
   All around the thing's head."

8 We went to the tree,
   The matter to discover,
   Where the nations rose,
   Round Pomy Smash's liver.

9 There we saw a pine knot,
   As big as any squirrel
   A catin' sheep sorrel.

10 I laid down my gun
   And took off my am-minition;
   Said I, "uncle Davy,
   I'll cool your am-i-bition."

11 Then we locked arms,
   I thought my breath was gone;
   I never was squz so,
   Since the hour that I was born.

12 And then we did agree
   To let each other be,
   For I was too hard for him,
   And so was he for me.

13 And when we came to look,
   Both of our heads was missin';
   He'd bit off my head,
   An' I'd swallered his'n.

The Cox version can easily serve as a standard against which to measure other folk variants, but it was not the most widely printed version of the song. That honor goes to a version collected in Texas in 1927 by Julia Beazley, who recalled (in 1927): "Nearly a generation ago, before the advent of motor-cars and motor-boats, I heard some sailors on the Texas coast singing 'Davy Crockett.' They were old time sailor men, and the ruggedness of the meter of the song in nowise hampered their gusto in singing it."[13] This testimony places the song on the Texas coast about the turn of the century, but the actual version Beazley published came from a "Mrs. Melton" of Houston, who later recorded her song on a modern phonograph record (see Checklist B, below). This version is distinguished by the addition of the couplet:

> Oh, the world is made of mud out o' the Mississippi River,
> The sun's a ball of foxfire, as well you may discover,

another couplet borrowed directly from a stanza of the initial "Pompey Smash." The Beazley song was picked up by three popular folklore anthologies, including one by John and Alan Lomax, and emerged as the most widely circulated of the folk variants. (For a complete list of published folk variants, see Checklist A, below.)

All in all, this study has been able to trace and catalogue some twenty-two folk variants of "Pompey Smash" collected in the twentieth century. The variants were widespread and not all confined to the South; one was found in Vermont, another in Michigan, and one off the South Carolina coast. However, most of the variants (six) came from the Missouri-Arkansas Ozarks, with five coming from West Virginia, four from Kentucky, and three from Texas. Only a single version of the song has been found in the state most closely associated with Crockett, Tennessee. This geographical distribution, however, should be viewed cautiously; the prevalence of some versions of the songs may reflect more intense folk-song collecting in one region rather than a more widespread fondness for the song. The Ozarks and West Virginia, for instance, were relatively confined areas that were intensively "harvested" by folk-song hunters in the 1930s. Some of the twenty-two versions were collected with recording machines, others were transcribed. Checklist B, below, lists the known recorded versions of the song. Most of these recordings were what archivists call "instantaneous" recordings—i.e., recordings made for archival purposes and not generally circulated to the public or readily reproduced. They thus played little role in further disseminating the song to the American people. An exception, though, was a 1931 effort made for a commercial phonograph company.

During the 1920s a different sort of song hunter began to comb the South for old songs; he was not a folklorist or an academic, but a talent scout for the commercial phonograph record industry. Record companies were suddenly discovering vernacular music in the 1920s, and rushed into the backwoods to find "authentic" blues singers, fiddlers, and balladeers. A good many traditional songs and musicians were recorded this way, as commercial product rather than folklore, and their records, which were sold primarily in the South, served as major conduits for song dissemination. Others used radio as a medium to spread their songs, and, in some cases, to begin commercial careers that would eventually develop into modern country music. Among the 3,500-odd songs recorded during this early period (1923–35), however, there was only a single recording of the "Davy Crockett" song. As the first commercial recording of the song, and as the first documented instance of the song entering modern mass media, the effort deserves more than passing attention.

The "informant" in this case was Chubby Parker, a banjoist and songster who won fame playing on the radio—specifically on station WLS Chicago's "National Barn Dance," one of the country's first country-music radio shows. Details on Parker's life are sketchy, but he was apparently from Kentucky, and from his photos he appears to have been in his thirties in 1925; certainly by 1926 he was a star on the show and on records and was one of the nation's most popular banjo singers. His recorded repertoire included a number of odd folk songs that he might well have learned in his native Kentucky, and he is best remembered for his variant of an old Will Hays song called "The Little Old Sod Shanty on the Plains." Parker reportedly left WLS, and radio, in the late 1920s because he was upset with WLS's hiring of another folk song specialist, Bradley Kincaid. After 1932, Parker dropped out of sight, or at least out of the entertainment industry, and attempts to learn more about his fate have been fruitless.[14]

But just before he was swallowed up by the Great Depression, Parker traveled to New York on October 16, 1931, to do a final recording session. It was a marathon one, running to twenty songs—

almost as if Parker knew he was quitting and wanted to leave a last heritage. Accompanying himself on his banjo and harmonica, he recorded some of his rarest songs, including the only commercial recording of "Davy Crockett" prior to the 1950s. Given the three-minute restrictions of the old 78 r.p.m. disc, his text is remarkably full and coherent, starting with:

> Now I'll tell you about a coon hunt I took with Davy Crockett,
> He was half man, half hoss, and half sky-rocket,
> I met him one morning as I was gwine a-gunning,
> Says I, Colonel Davy, I hear you'se gwine cooning,
> But where is your gun? I ain't got none,
> Well how in the world do you expect to hunt without one?

Parker includes four more stanzas, describing the fight, but omitting the reference to biting off heads. The record was issued in the spring of 1932 on the Conqueror label, a label designed to be sold exclusively through the Sears catalogue; under the rubric of "Country Folk Songs," Sears sold Conquerors for twenty-three cents each, and mailed them all over the country. Had the depression not severely curtailed the sales of records, Parker's version of "Davy Crockett" might well have had a major impact on folk variants of the song. As it was, the disc probably sold fewer than 5,000 copies, and while it seems to have been the source for some folk versions, its overall impact is hard to assess.

Not all versions of "Davy Crockett," of course, contain the same elements or motifs, and while it would be impossible to reproduce all the texts of the different versions here, it is possible to get an overview of what motifs seem to have remained most popular. To this end, table 1 cross-references thirteen major texts with twenty-four selected incidents, phrases, or motifs from the song. It is curious that certain stanzas and motifs of the original "Pompey Smash" do not appear on the chart and have apparently not survived at all in folk tradition. These include:

1. reference to the "stars are ladies' eyes";
2. the stanza on grammar;
3. the "star shower" stanza;
4. the "abolition" references;
5. the New Orleans references.

Table 1 – Frequency of motifs in "Davy Crockett" texts

Text motif	published								unpublished				
	Combs (1900)	Cox (1917)	Scarborough (1925)	Beazley (1927)	Randolph A (1930)	Parker (1931)	Randolph B (1938)	Gunning (1965)	W. Va. C (1938)	W. Va. A (1939)	W. Va. B (1939)	W. Va. D (1940)	Hicks (1978)
1. "How I got my larnin"		x	x										x
2. "half man, half sky-rocket"					x	x	x			x	x		
3. "my name is Smash"			x										x
4. reference to speaker's blackness	x		x	x	x	x	x	x	x		x		x
5. reference to Pomp or Smash		x	x		x	x							x
6. "world is made of mud"				x									
7. going cooning/no gun	x	x		x	x	x	x	x	x	x	x	x	
8. as I walked out by light of moon		x		x									
9. "grin a coon crazy"		x		x	x	x	x	x	x	x	x	x	x
10. brace against heel				x		x	x		x		x	x	x
11. squirrel eating sheep sorrel	x	x		x	x	x	x			x	x	x	x
12. don't laugh, black calf	x			x	x	x	x	x	x		x	x	x
13. fight preparation/ammunition	x	x		x	x	x	x	x	x	x			
14. fight, squeezing	x	x		x	x	x	x	x	x	x			x
15. "I'm a Tennessee screamer"					x	x				x	x		x
16. bit in half/swallowed heads	x	x		x	x		x		x	x	x		x
17. little boy, name was Davy	x												
18. Big Sam													x
19. alligator									x				x
20. "mammy was a wildcat"									x	x	x		
21. "scandalize me"									x	x	x		
22. Big Billy drummer										x			
23. Jim Crow had a sister												x	
24. I can pick a banjo												x	

Three of these stanzas are topical or local, and presumably dropped out when their relevance declined; the stanza on grammar is a bit academic for folk tradition. The other elements of "Pompey" appear to have survived as shown above in table 1.

The table suggests that the coon-grinning episode is by far the most enduring of the various "Pompey" motifs. Almost all the folk versions (eleven of the thirteen) have references to Crockett going cooning with no gun, grinning until the bark flies, and seeing a squirrel eating "sheep sorrel," an eastern plant with pleasant-tasting leaves. Not quite as many (ten of the thirteen) have references to the "don't laugh / black calf" couplet, when Pompey laughs at Crockett's mistake, and to the actual fight and the squeezing. Nine of the thirteen versions describe the preparation for the fight (putting down ammunition), as well as the aftermath (bit in half, swallowed heads). In nine of the thirteen songs there is a distinct reference to Pompey's blackness. The second half of the "Pompey Smash" song (represented in table 1 by motifs 18–24) is not found at all in any of the published versions of "Davy Crockett." It survives only in fragmentary forms as part of four unpublished West Virginia versions from the late 1930s (see page 175) as well as in a Tennessee version collected as recently as 1978. Three of the West Virginia versions place garbled stanzas after the Crockett episode (as in the original "Pompey"), but the recently recorded version by Fentress County (Tennessee) singer Dee Hicks offers a coherent and detailed account of the Big Sam / Pompey escape story, although it is placed *before* the Crockett episode. The first five stanzas (of a total of nine) in the Hicks version are:

DAVY CROCKETT

1. Oh listen, Im a gonna tell you how my marster used to
     serve me,
   He would take me to the barn and give me all my
     schooling,
   He'd begin to cut and slash, on the back of Pompey Smash,
   Oh and when he wouldn't like from the barn he would dash,
   Anney-on.

2. Oh it's now Big Sam, we'll I'll go catch him,
   Back to the barn you infernal nigger fetch him,
   Big Sam looked around and there he did discover,
   Old Pompey gave a stumble and he fell into the river.
   Old Big Sam said, now you better be dead,
   For if marster gets a hold of you, he'll break your 'fernal head,
   Anney-on.

3. Then I div and I div and I left Sam behind me,
   And he went back and told his marster that he couldn't
     find me,

Oh I tell you of the fight, I had wi' Da - vy Croc-kett

aid I am half man, from sky rock-ett. I met him in the eve- ning, asked him

where he's go-ing, the Col - onel Da - vy says, "I'm a

go - in' out a- coon- in'" He asked him for a gun and he said he

ad none, Says I to Colo- nel Da - vy, "Can't you hunt wi'

out one?"

Transcription of first verse of "Zip Coon" as sung by Tom Whit, Mingo County, West Virginia (recorded by Louis Watson Chappell, 1940, West Virginia University Archives, disc 422). Original tune transcription by Rod Martin. (Courtesy WVU Archives and John A. Cuthbert.)

> Oh I want you to know that I didn't dive slow,
> For I div eleven miles before I brought a blow,
> Anney-on.

4. Oh, I popped up my head and looked so particular,
   First straight forwards and then slantidicular,
   I looked all around and I seen an alligator,
   And I never had a thing not as much a sweet potato
   But I felt a little scared, though I never said a word,
   Every tooth in his head looked like a broadsword,
   Anney-on.

5. I never went fur til I met Davy Crockett,
   Said, By gosh David, I can grin a coon crazy,
   Come and go along with me and we'll both go together,
   And I'll show you mighty quick how to tan a coon's leather,

Oh we hadn't went far til Davy did discover,
A Squirrel on a pine knot eating cheap sorrel,
And he began to feel, and he said, Pompey Smash let me
　　brace again your heel,
Anney-on.

For all its unusual character, the Hicks version is the only traced version of "Davy Crockett" collected so far in Tennessee.[15]

The oral variants of "Pompey Smash" formed a minor but vital part of the Crockett legendry. Just as oral tales of Crockett's exploits have been collected in Arkansas and Tennessee by folklorists, so have oral versions of his song.[16] And as folklore came into its own as a discipline in the 1950s, some of these genuine traditional tales began to find their way into print and even into mass media. But aside from Chubby Parker's 1931 recording, only one other commercial recording of "Davy Crockett" by a professional entertainer has been traced. This was a track on an album entitled *Ballads of the Civil War*, released in 1954 by Folkways Records of New York, a firm specializing in educational and folk recordings. *Ballads of the Civil War* (FH 5004) was obviously designed as the former; it came replete with a booklet of history and song background and emphasized educational aspects in its advertising. The version of "Davy Crockett" heard was the Beazley Texas variant, enriched by a spoken interlude of Crockett brag talk taken from other reprinted publications; it was performed by a Dallas attorney and song student named Hermes Nye. Though the album reached few of the people who were genuine traditional singers of the "Crockett" songs, it did reach into a number of classrooms, where puzzled teachers tried to figure out some way to shoehorn the song into their units on the Civil War.

Though Hermes Nye's 1954 recording of "Davy Crockett" was the first commercial one in twenty-three years, and though it was used in a number of schoolrooms across the country, neither he nor Folkways Records could have foreseen the cultural tidal wave that was about to sweep them up. The wave had its start inauspiciously enough in 1954, when veteran Hollywood producer Walt Disney became the first major movie head to make his peace with the new medium of television; that year saw the start of a new prime-time show called "Disneyland," which at first was a hodgepodge of old cartoons, nature films, and action shows, many taken from the Disney vaults.

Spurred by the instant success—both popular and critical—of the show, Disney decided to create some original programming for the series and in the winter of 1954/55 produced three one-hour episodes centering on the adventures of Davy Crockett. The series starred a then-unknown actor named Fess Parker paired with Hollywood veteran Buddy Ebsen, and the spectacular success of the shows amazed even Disney. Parents from Maine to Tennessee had to accustom themselves to the sight of their children wearing imitation coonskin caps and toting long plastic models of Old Betsy. No fool, Disney ordered up more hourly episodes and in May 1955 rushed into the theaters a ninety-minute feature, *Davy Crockett, King of the Wild Frontier*, that strung together three of the TV episodes—reversing the general trend of films premiering in movie houses and then moving to television. The success continued with the sequels "Davy Crockett and the Great Riverboat Race" and "Davy Crockett and the River Pirates," combined into a second feature film in 1956. For two full years Crockett mania again seized America.

One direct outgrowth of all this was to bring before the public an entirely new Davy Crockett song that bore no resemblance to the older ballad. The new one, called popularly "The Ballad of Davy Crockett," became the general theme song for all the Crockett shows as well as continuity music within the shows. The lyrics of the new song were crafted by Thomas Blackburn, the scriptwriter for the episodes that made up *Davy Crockett, King of the Wild Frontier*. Blackburn had had more experience as a Hollywood scriptwriter than as a songwriter; his film credits included a series of popular westerns such as *Colt 45* (1950), *Short Grass* (1951), *Raton Pass* (1951), *Cavalry Scout* (1951), and *Riding Shotgun* (1954). His words were set to music by George Bruns, a veteran and much-respected jazz trombonist who was then on the Disney staff. Though Bruns had played with some of the most important names in jazz, the Disney publicists liked to emphasize that he could play the trombone with his feet.

Though most people in the 1950s didn't realize it, the original "Ballad of Davy Crockett" ran about as long as the original "Pompey Smash"—a full twenty stanzas of six lines each. Indeed, the formal song title as represented on the sheet music published by Wonderland Music Company is: *The Ballad of Davy Crockett: His Early Life, Hunting Adventures, Services under General Jackson in the Creek War, Electioneering Speeches, Career in Congress, Triumphal Tour in the*

Northern States, and Services in the Texan War. Considering its importance to the popular culture about Crockett, the entire text deserves perusal:

THE BALLAD OF DAVY CROCKETT

1.

Born on a mountain top in Tennessee,
Greenest state in the Land of the Free,
Raised in the woods so's he knew ev'ry tree,
Kilt him a b'ar when he was only three.
Davy—Davy Crockett,
King of the wild frontier!

2.

Eighteen thirteen the Creeks uprose,
Addin' redskin arrows to the country's woes.
Now, Injun fightin' is somethin' he knows,
So he shoulders his rifle an' off he goes.
Davy—Davy Crockett,
The man who don't know fear!

3.

Off through the woods he's a marchin' along,
Makin' up yarns an' a singin' a song,
Itchin' fer fightin' an' rightin' a wrong,
He's ringy as a b'ar an' twict as strong.
Davy—Davy Crockett,
The buckskin buccaneer!

4.

Andy Jackson is our gen'ral's name,
His reg'lar soldiers we'll put to shame,
Them redskin varmints us Volunteers'll tame,
'Cause we got the guns with the sure-fire aim.
Davy—Davy Crockett,
The champion of us all!

5.

Headed back to war from the ol' home place,
But Red Stick was leadin' a merry chase,
Fightin' an' burnin' at a devil's pace
South to the swamps on the Florida Trace.

Davy—Davy Crockett,
Trackin' the redskins down!

6.

Fought single-handed through the Injun War
Till the Creeks was whipped an' peace was in store,
An' while he was handlin' this risky chore,
Made hisself a legend for evermore.
Davy—Davy Crockett,
King of the wild frontier!

7.

He give his word an' he give his hand
That his Injun friends could keep their land,
An' the rest of his life he took the stand
That justice was due every redskin band.
Davy—Davy Crockett,
Holdin' his promise dear!

8.

Home fer the winter with his family,
Happy as squirrels in the ol' gum tree,
Bein' the father he wanted to be,
Close to his boys as the pod an' the pea.
Davy—Davy Crockett,
Holdin' his young 'uns dear!

9.

But the ice went out an' the warm winds came
An' the meltin' snow showed tracks of game,
An' the flowers of Spring filled the woods with flame,
An' all of a sudden life got too tame.
Davy—Davy Crockett,
Headin' on West again!

10.

Off through the woods we're ridin' along,
Makin' up yarns an' singin' a song,
He's ringy as a b'ar an' twict as strong,
An' knows he's right 'cause he ain't often wrong.
Davy—Davy Crockett,
The man who don't know fear!

11.

Lookin' fer a place where the air smells clean,
Where the trees is tall an' the grass is green,
Where the fish is fat in an untouched stream,
An' the teemin' woods is a hunter's dream.
Davy—Davy Crockett,
Lookin' fer Paradise!

12.

Now he'd lost his love an' his grief was gall,
In his heart he wanted to leave it all,
An' lose himself in the forests tall,
But he answered instead his country's call.
Davy—Davy Crockett,
Beginnin' his campaign!

13.

Needin' his help they didn't vote blind,
They put in Davy 'cause he was their kind,
Sent up to Nashville the best they could find,
A fightin' spirit an' a thinkin' mind.
Davy—Davy Crockett,
Choice of the whole frontier!

14.

The votes were counted an' he won hands down,
So they sent him off to Washin'ton town
With his best dress suit still his buckskins brown,
A livin' legend of growin' renown.
Davy—Davy Crockett,
The Canebrake Congressman!

15.

He went off to Congress an' served a spell,
Fixin' up the Gover'ment an' laws as well,
Took over Washin'ton so we heered tell
An' patched up the crack in the Liberty Bell.
Davy—Davy Crockett,
Seein' his duty clear!

16.

Him an' his jokes travelled all through the land,
An' his speeches made him friends to beat the band,

His politickin' was their favorite brand
An' everyone wanted to shake his hand.
Davy—Davy Crockett,
Helpin' his legend grow!

17.

He knew when he spoke he sounded the knell
Of his hopes for White House an' fame as well,
But he spoke out strong so hist'ry books tell
An' patched up the crack in the Liberty Bell.
Davy—Davy Crockett,
Seein' his duty clear!

18.

When he come home his politickin' done,
The western march had just begun,
So he packed his gear an' his trusty gun,
An' lit out grinnin' to follow the sun.
Davy—Davy Crockett,
Leadin' the pioneer!

19.

(He) heard of Houston an' Austin an' so,
To the Texas plains he jest had to go,
Where Freedom was fightin' another foe,
An' they needed him at the Alamo.
Davy—Davy Crockett,
The man who don't know fear!

20.

(His) land is biggest an' his land is best,
From grassy plains to the mountain crest,
He's ahead of us all meetin' the test,
Followin' his legend into the West,
Davy—Davy Crockett,
King of the Wild frontier!

By the end of February 1955, even before the biggest part of the Crockett boom hit, singers were racing into the studios to do their versions of the catchy song. Within a few weeks, versions of the song had hit the *Billboard* charts—pop music's best trade barometer—in three categories: pop, country and western, and children's. Apparently the first pop singer to record the song was the man who in the end had the most popular single version of it: Bill Hayes. Hayes was an unlikely candidate for the honor; an Illinois native, he had had previous experience in light opera, and as a comic actor on the old "Ernie Kovacs" television show; in more recent years he has become known as a character actor on soap operas. Hayes recorded "The Ballad of Davy Crockett" for a new independent record label called Cadence—a rather small label that would later win fame as the company to make first recordings of national stars like the Everly Brothers and Andy Williams—and watched with amazement as the disc sold over two million copies in six months' time. For twenty weeks the Hayes version stayed on the best-seller charts, and for five weeks it was the number one hit in the United States, where it contended with the Four Aces' "Love Is a Many-Splendored Thing" and the Chordettes' "Mr. Sandman."[17] Though most of the song's popularity undoubtedly had to do with the Crockett films, part of it also came on the crest of a popular revival of folk music—or what passed for folk music in Eisenhower America. Tennessee Ernie Ford's Kentucky coal-mining song "Sixteen Tons" and Mitch Miller's "Yellow Rose of Texas" were also among the year's biggest hits, but so was a song that was to foreshadow an end to the charming, folksy movement—Bill Haley's "Rock Around the Clock."

Another aspect of the pop-record business in the mid-1950s was the prevalence of "cover" versions—hasty recordings of a pop song by Johnny-come-lately singers hoping to cut themselves in for a piece of the action. "The Ballad of Davy Crockett" attracted over twenty such cover versions by singers from every corner of American music: country/western singers Tennessee Ernie Ford, Mac Wiseman, Rusty Draper, The Sons of the Pioneers, Eddy Arnold, and Burl Ives; mainstream pop artists like Steve Allen, Vincent Lopez, Mitch Miller, Walter Schumann, and Fred Waring; and even jazz musicians like the Irvin Fields Trio and Paul Smith. Fess Parker, the star of the Disney films, made a recording himself of the piece for Columbia, one of the country's major labels, and saw it sell close to a million copies in just under a month. Indeed, most of the cover versions sold well, and in six months the combined "Crockett" record sales, from all versions, was close to 7,000,000—making it, according to discographer Joseph Murrells, "the fastest selling entity in the history of the disc industry."[18]

Very few of the popular versions of the song utilized all twenty verses; most, following Hayes's lead, chose to use only stanzas 1 (with its famous "Born on a mountain top" opening), 3 ("Off through the woods. . . ."), 15 (to Congress), 19 (to the Alamo), and 20 ("His land is biggest . . ."). (One of the few complete recordings of the song was done by an unlikely source, Fred Waring, who did a "complete" version running nine minutes, forty-one seconds (Decca DU 1011), but sequels to the first Disney film soon created even more stanzas beyond the "official" 1954 text seen above.) The nature of the five verses used tell us more about America in the 1950s than about Crockett's legendary status at the time. Only three incidents from Crockett's life are mentioned: killing a bear when three, going to Congress, and going to Texas; the rest of the five common verses are vague, patriotic platitudes that could be applied to any American hero. None of the surreal and violent southwestern humor of the "Pompey Smash" song survives in this version, and there is no evidence that either the composers or Disney were even aware of the earlier song. "The Ballad of Davy Crockett" is conspicuously lacking in the kind of gritty detail that so endeared the earlier folk ballad to generations of Americans, but is rather a superb reflection of the bland, innocuous Disneyized notion of American history that was so much in favor during the Eisenhower era. Indeed, when the song was performed at Disney theme parks, the only violent element in the abridgement of the song, the reference to Davy killing a bear when he was three, was changed to "tamed him a bear."

People not only rushed to record cover versions of the Blackburn-Bruns "Ballad" but were soon jumping on the Crockett bandwagon with a plethora of sequels and follow-up songs. Bill Hayes himself went into the studios for the small educational company Folkways Records to produce *The Real Story of Davy Crockett* (Folkways, FP 205, 1955), in which he did not sing but read from the text of the Citadel Press's popular 1955 edition of *Davy Crockett's Own Story*. Another type of authenticity was sought by famed cowboy singer (and writer of topical ballads) Red River Dave McEnery, who wrote and recorded, on August 30, 1955, an opus called "When Davy Crockett Met San Antonio Rose"; released on Decca, a major label, the recording label bore the notice: "Recorded with the original authentic Davy Crockett fiddle. Courtesy of the Witte Memorial Museum." The record does indeed include a thin, reedy fiddle playing the instrumental chorus. Much further afield were such recorded efforts as Irving Fields's "Davy Crockett Mambo" or veteran Hollywood actor Stepin Fetchit's "Davy Crockett Boogie." *Crockett* film stars Fess Parker and Buddy Ebsen tried their hand at writing with "Davy Crockett's Motto—Be Sure You're Right (Then Go Ahead)"; its refrain was:

> It's up to you,
> To do,
> What Davy Crockett said!

This song, as well as "Old Betsy," a George Bruns–Gil George collaboration that was also in the original Davy Crockett movie, was released by the dean of America's folk singers, Burl Ives, on a popular Decca recording.[19] Country singer Red Kirk's "Davy Crockett Blues" (Republic) zeroed in on the general nationwide Crockett fad as a whole:

> I got the Davy Crockett blues.
>
> I hate to go home anymore,
> Find the Alamo built around the door,
> The kids with questions by the score,
> I got the Davy Crockett blues.
>
> They go around wearing coonskin caps,
> Shootin' their guns and setting their traps,
> Got me afraid to take my nap,
> I got the Davy Crockett blues.
>
> © Murray Nash Associates, BMI. All rights reserved.

Offshoots of a different sort began to appear as the "Ballad of Davy Crockett" permeated the folk culture of the 1950s; these took the forms of parodies of the "Ballad," parodies born out of the song's infectious rhythm and easy rhyme scheme. Some of the first parodies to appear were commercial takeoffs by professional musical comedians. Two of the most popular were records relying on ethnic stereotypes: Lala Guerrero's "Pancho Lopez" (Real Records) and Mickey Katz's "David Crockett" (Capitol). Guerrero's version began:

> Born in Chihuahua in 1903,
> On a serape out under a tree,
> He was so fat he could almost not see.

Mickey Katz's Crockett, a fugitive from Manhattan's Lower East side, liked food of a different sort:

> Born in the wilds of Delancey Street,
> Home of gefilte fish and kosher meat.

Veteran song parodists Homer and Jethro (who, ironically, as Homer Haynes and Jethro Burns came from the northeastern Tennessee area that produced some of the genuine Crockett folk ballads) were making a good living in the 1950s with their lampoons of pop songs; they weighed in with "The Ballad of Davy Crewcut" (RCA Victor):

> Born in a taxicab in Tennessee,
> Slowest cab that you ever did see,
> Warmed up his bottle and he took him a nip,
> He didn't even leave the driver a tip.

The commercial parodies were surprisingly successful, and within a month or two had sold as many copies as many modest hits; the Guerrero and Katz versions quickly sold over 200,000 copies each, while the Homer and Jethro country version sold over 110,000 copies. The phenomenon was so odd that *Time* magazine did a major story on the parody versions of "Davy."[20]

The big brothers and sisters of the coonskin-cap set showed their scorn for Disney and Davy by generating a host of folk parodies that, in some ways, are more revealing than the commercial variants. Kids in Missouri sang a version called "Adolf Hitler," which began, "Born in a gutter in Germany." From Texas came reports of a version that began:

> Born on a tabletop in Joe's cafe,
> The dirtiest place in the U.S.A.,
> Killed his pa with TNT,
> Killed his ma with DDT.

Parodies are a staple in children's folklore, but most of the songs parodied are patriotic songs, religious songs, or seasonal favorites (such as "Jingle Bells"). Though no one has yet done any studies to explore the correlation between folk parody and pop songs, available collections suggest that it is rather rare for a relatively new song like the "Ballad" to make it into the folk process so soon. Indeed, Davy himself made it into other forms of children's folk parody in the late 1950s. In 1960 a Tennessee folklorist collected this version of "On Top of Old Smokey."

> On top of Old Smokey, all covered with snow,
> I saw Davy Crockett, kiss Marilyn Monroe.
>
> He asked if she loved him, and she said No,
> BANG, BANG, 'twas the end, of sweet Marilyn Monroe.[21]

Children were not alone in making parodies of this song, however; its melody was so catchy that it was borrowed by numerous grassroots civic organizations and clubs. Such songs were considered ephemeral documentation of the clubs' activities, and few of them have survived. A rare example is a text from an Eastern Star order in southwest Missouri, which begins:

> Served as an Officer in Eastern Star,
> Working for her Sisters, near and far,
> Always straight and honest, she,
> Worthy Matron came to be!
>
> Worthy, Worthy Matron,
> Fair and just was she![22]

(The Worthy Matron was an honorary post, an officer who presided at Eastern Star meetings.) By the 1960s, the various Crockett parodies began to decline in number, and to settle into the rich stratum of children's folk song and poetry and riddle, to surface occasionally in later years in the hands of children who had never seen the Disney films, or heard of the coonskin-cap craze, and who knew Crockett only as a vague name found in a schoolbook.

The two songs discussed here, though vastly different in content, style, and tone, do share some important qualities, and do reflect the distinctively American interplay between pop culture and folklore. Shortly after Crockett's death, pop culture produced the first important song about him, a song that soon passed into folk tradition, edited and structured by an elusive folk aesthetic and preserved for later generations. A little over a hundred years later, another Crockett song was produced by pop culture, and it too soon moved into a folk tradition, likewise changed and altered (via parody) by the people to better suit their needs. We know little about the circumstances behind the composing of the first pop version, but much about its eventual survival in tradition; we know much about the circumstances surrounding the later song, but cannot as yet gage the extent to which folk tradition has accepted it. Both cases, though, represent the mysterious transformation of hype into genuine legendry, and both represent the complex way in which America celebrates its heroes.[23]

NOTES

1. Constance Rourke, *Davy Crockett* (New York: Harcourt, 1934), 258.

2. For an account of these references placed in a fiddling context, see Charles Wolfe, "Davy Crockett's Dance and Old Hickory's Fandango," *The Devil's Box*, 16 (Sept. 1982), 34–41.

3. *Davy Crockett's Own Story, As Written By Himself* (New York: Citadel Press, 1955), 169.

4. "'Go Ahead:' A March Dedicated to Colonel Crockett" (New York: Firth and Hall, 1835).

5. See Rourke, *Davy Crockett*, 258.

6. The first edition appears as *Crockett's Free-and-Easy Song Book: A New Collection of the Most Popular Songs, as Given By the Best Vocalists of the Present Day; and also of Favorite Dinner and Parlour Songs* (Philadelphia and Pittsburgh: Kay and Company, 1837) and contains 128 pages; the second appears as *Crockett's Free-and-Easy Songbook: Comic, Sentimental, Amatory, Sporting, African, Scotch, Irish, Western and Texian National, Military, Naval and Anacreontic: A New Collection of the Most Popular Stage Songs, Together with Glees, Duets, Recitations, and Medleys* (Philadelphia: Kay and Troutman, and Pittsburgh: C.H. Kay, 1846) and contains 319 pages.

7. Robert C. Toll, *Blacking Up: The Minstrel Show in Nineteenth Century America* (New York: Oxford Univ. Press, 1974), 40–41.

8. Turner and Fisher had published at least seven Crockett almanacs prior to 1847, almanacs especially rich in tall tales. Richard Dorson drew heavily on them for his compilation, *Davy Crockett: American Comic Legend* (New York: Spiral Press for Rockland Editions, 1939). Possible sources for motifs in "Pompey Smash" appear in Dorson on pages 84, 112, and 131. Dorson retitles "A Scentoriferous Fight . . ." as "A Black Affair." See Richard M. Dorson, "The Sources of *Davy Crockett: American Comic Legend*," *Midwest Folklore*, 8 (Fall 1958), 145.

9. Dorson, *Davy Crockett*, 86–88.

10. Toll, *Blacking Up*, 184.

11. Julia Beazley, quoted from Josiah Combs, *Folk-Songs of the Southern United States*, ed. D.K. Wilgus (Austin: Univ. of Texas Press/American Folklore Society, 1967), 182.

12. Combs, *Folk-Songs*, 48–49.

13. Quoted in B.A. Botkin, ed. *The American People* (London: Pilot Press, 1946), 33.

14. For more on Parker and his circle, see Charles Wolfe, *Kentucky Country: Folk and Country Music of Kentucky* (Lexington: Univ. Press of Kentucky, 1982), 44–45.

15. I transcribed this Dee Hicks version from a field recording made of Hicks in 1978 by Bobby Fulcher; the recording has since been published in an album produced by The Tennessee Folklore Society, *Tennessee Folk Heritage: The Mountains* (TFS 103), 1982.

16. For example, noted Ozarks folklorist Vance Randolph actually associated an oral variant of "Pompey" with a group of oral Crockett legends found in the Ozarks in his *Ozark Mountain Folks* (New York: Vanguard, 1932), 133–41.

17. Hayes's recording first appeared on the *Billboard* best-seller charts on March 20, 1955; other cover versions of the song to make it on the charts included those by Fess Parker, Tennessee Ernie Ford, and The Voices of Walter Schumann. (Data drawn from *Billboard* magazine files.)

18. Joseph Murrells, *The Book of Golden Discs*, rev. ed. (London: Barrie and Jenkins, 1978), 74.

19. Fess Parker and Buddy Ebsen also recorded the two songs for Columbia (45 r.p.m. issue 40510).

20. "King Davy and Friends," *Time*, August 1, 1955, p. 30.

21. John E. Brewton, "Folk Rimes of Southern Children," *Tennessee Folklore Society Bulletin*, 26 (1960), 98.

22. Author's files.

23. The following individuals have been especially helpful in doing the research for this paper: John A. Cuthbert (West Virginia University), W.K. McNeil (Ozark Folk Center), Gordon McCann (Springfield, Missouri), Harlan Daniel (Memphis), Archie Green (San Francisco), Bob Pinson (Country Music Foundation), Ronnie Pugh (Country Music Foundation), Michael A. Lofaro (University of Tennessee), and especially Stephen Wade, of Washington, D.C., for his aid in working through the Library of Congress.

CHECKLIST A

Printed Twentieth-century Versions
of Traditional "Davy Crockett" Songs

1910   H.M. Belden, ed. *Song-Ballads and Other Popular Poetry*. Exact place and publisher not known, no. 59.

1925   Josiah H. Combs, ed. *Folk-songs du midi des Etats-Unis*. Paris: 1925; transla-
       tion reprinted as *Folk-Songs of the Southern United States*, ed. D.K. Wilgus.
       Austin: Univ. of Texas Press/American Folklore Society, 1967. Pp. 182–83.
1925   John H. Cox, ed. *Folk-Songs of the South*. Cambridge: Harvard Univ. Press.
       Pp. 494–500. No. 177.
1925   Dorothy Scarborough. *On the Trail of Negro Folk-Songs*. Cambridge: Har-
       vard Univ. Press. Pp. 177–78. (Possibly not a "Pompey Smash" variant.)
1927   Julia Beazley, "The Ballad of Davy Crockett," *Texas Folk-Lore Society Publica-
       tions* 6 (1927), 205–6. Reprinted in Alan and John Lomax, eds., *American
       Ballads and Folk Songs* (New York: McMillan, 1934), 251–53; in B.A. Bot-
       kin, ed., *A Treasury of American Folklore* (New York: Crown, 1944), 15–16,
       and (New York: Bantam, 1980); in B.A. Botkin, ed. *The American People*,
       (London: Pilot Press, 1946), 33; and in William Owens, *Texas Folk Songs*
       (Austin: Texas Folklore Society, 1950).
1932   Vance Randolph. *Ozark Mountain Folks*. New York: Vanguard. Pp. 138–39.
1949   Vance Randolph. *Ozark Folk Songs*. Vol. 3. Columbia: University of Mis-
       souri Press. 1949, 165–67; Reprint edition, 1980; abridged edition, ed. Norm
       Cohen, Urbana: Univ. of Illinois Press, 1982. Pp. 338–40.
1965   Archie Green. "Notes" for Sarah Ogan Gunning, *Girl of Constant Sorrow*.
       (Folk Legacy LP record FSA-26). Sharon, Conn.: Folk Legacy, 1965. Pp.
       23–24.

CHECKLIST B[1]

Commercial(*) and Noncommercial Recordings,
of "Davy Crockett/Pompey Smash" Songs.

1931 * "Davey Crockett." Sung by Chubby Parker, with harmonica and banjo acc.
       New York, Conqueror Records No. 7895.
1936   "Pompey Smash." Sung by David Rice, Springfield, Mo. (recorded by Sid-
       ney Robertson). Library of Congress No. 3208 B1 and B2.
1937   "Davy Crockett." Sung by Mrs. Minnie Floyd, Murrells Inlet, S.C. (recorded
       by John A. Lomax). Library of Congress No. 1046 B1.
1938   "Davy Crockett." Sung by Lester Wells, Traverse City, Mich. (recorded by
       Alan Lomax). Library of Congress No. 2305 B1.
1938   "Davy Crockett." Sung by Mrs. Pormola Eddy, Daybrook, Monongalia
       County, W.V. (recorded by Louis Watson Chappell). WVU Archive disc
       362.
1939   "Davy Crockett." Sung by Worthy Perkins. Wirt County, W.V. (recorded
       by Louis Watson Chappell). WVU Archives disc 160.
1939   "Davy Crockett." Spoken by Finley Adams, Dunham, Ky. (recorded by Her-
       bert Halpert). Library of Congress No. 2772 B2.

[1]Note: All dates given are original recording dates.

1939　"Davy Crockett." Sung by Elmer Barton, Quebec, Vt. (recorded by Alan Lomax and Helen Hartness Flanders). Library of Congress No. 3694 B1.

1939　"Old Zippy Coon." Sung by Lafe Cogar, Calhoun County, W.V. (recorded by Louis Watson Chappell). WVU Archives disc 222.

1940　"Zip Coon." Sung by Tom Whit, Mingo County, W.V. (recorded by Louis Watson Chappell). WVU Archives disc 422.

1941　"Davy Crockett." Sung by Pearl Brewer, Ozarks (exact location unknown) (recorded by Vance Randolph). Library of Congress No. 12036 B23.

1941　"Davy Crockett." Sung by Mrs. Will Redden, Ozarks (exact location unknown) (recorded by Vance Randolph). Library of Congress No. 13131 B3.

1954 *　"Davy Crockett." Sung by Hermes Nye with guitar acc., Dallas, Tex. Folkways Records No. FH 5004 (*Ballads of the Civil War*).

ca. 1964 *　"Ballad of Davy Crockett." Sung by Mrs. Melton, Central Tex. Candid Records no. 8026 (*A Treasury of Field Recordings*).

1965 *　"Davy Crockett." Sung by Sarah Ogan Gunning, southeastern Ky. Folkways Records No. FSA-26 (*Girl of Constant Sorrow*).

1978 *　"Davy Crockett." Sung by Dee Hicks, Fentress County, Tenn. TFS Records No. TFS 103 (*Tennessee Folk Heritage: The Mountains*).

Contributors

CATHERINE L. ALBANESE is Professor of Religion at Wright State University in Dayton, Ohio. Her books include *America: Religions and Religion* (Belmont, California: Wadsworth, 1981), *Corresponding Motion: Transcendental Religion and the New America* (Philadelphia: Temple University Press, 1977), and *Sons of the Fathers: The Civil Religion of the American Revolution* (Philadelphia: Temple University Press, 1976).

RICHARD BOYD HAUCK is Abe Levin Professor of English at the University of West Florida. A specialist in American humor and tall tales, he is the author of *Crockett: A Bio-Bibliography* (Westport, Conn.: Greenwood Press, 1982) and *A Cheerful Nihilism: Confidence and "The Absurd" in American Humorous Fiction* (Bloomington: Indiana University Press, 1971).

MARGARET J. KING, a freelance writer living in Philadelphia, is on the staff of Lippincott Publishers and the Philadelphia City Paper. She is the author of "The Davy Crockett Craze: A Case Study in Popular Culture" (Ph.D. diss., University of Hawaii, 1976), and is presently editing *The Disney Effect: Walt Disney Films in American Life*.

MICHAEL A. LOFARO, Associate Professor of English at the University of Tennessee, is in the process of completing *Boone and Crockett: The Role of the Frontier Culture Hero in American Thought, 1784–1980*, a project begun under the auspices of a fellowship to the National Humanities Center (1980–81). He is the author of *The Life and Adventures of Daniel Boone* (Lexington: University Press of Kentucky, 1978).

JOHN SEELYE is Graduate Research Professor of American Literature at the University of Florida. He is presently completing work on the second volume of a critical trilogy which began with *Prophetic Waters: The River in Early American Life and Literature* (New York: Oxford University Press, 1977). Other major works include *Mark Twain in the Movies: A Meditation*

191

with Pictures (New York: Viking Press, 1977), *The True Adventures of Huckleberry Finn, As Told by John Seelye* (Evanston, Ill.: Northwestern University Press, 1970), and *Melville: The Ironic Diagram* (Evanston, Ill.: Northwestern University Press, 1970).

CHARLES K. WOLFE, Professor of English at Middle Tennessee State University, is the author of many works on traditional and popular music. Among his books are *Everybody's Grandpa: Fifty Years Behind the Mike* (by Louis M. "Grandpa" Jones with Charles K. Wolfe, Knoxville: University of Tennessee Press, 1984), *Kentucky Country: Folk and Country Music of Kentucky* (Lexington: University Press of Kentucky, 1982), *Tom Ashley, Sam McGee, Bukka White: Tennessee Traditional Singers* (co-author, Knoxville: University of Tennessee Press, 1980), *Tennessee Strings: The Story of Country Music in Tennessee* (Knoxville: University of Tennessee Press, 1977), and *Grand Ole Opry: The Early Years* (London: Old Time Music Press, 1975).

Index

Davy Crockett: The Man, the Legend, and the Legacy, 1786–1986 has been set into type on a Compugraphic digital phototypesetter in eleven point Goudy Old Style with two points of spacing between the lines. Goudy Old Style was also selected for display. The book was designed by Jim Billingsley, composed by Metricomp, Inc., printed offset by Thomson-Shore, Inc., and bound by John H. Dekker & Sons. The acid-free paper on which the book is printed is designed for an effective life of at least three hundred years.

The University of Tennessee Press : Knoxville